WHAT READERS SAY A

"An enjoyable read that blends humo
narrative. Brace yourself for laughter,
the book down!" — **Alicja and Gary Moates,** *Co. Armagh*

"This book confirms that the author is the spiritual and cultural guide par excellence. Sincerity, humility and wisdom flow from his pen." — **Monsignor Bryan McCanny,** *Diocese of Derry*

"A very personal account, using true stories to weave the natural/supernatural elements of the Christian life. The simplicity of style is disarming. Recommended to all pilgrims journeying to the Father's House." — **Fr Sebastian M Jones,** *Cardiff Oratory*

"More than a collection of delightful tales, this book addresses in layman's language concepts central to Faith: the sacrificial nature of the Mass, the priesthood, the inerrancy of Scripture, suffering. A most enjoyable read, it teaches and inspires without preaching."
— **Dr Oswaldo Castro**, *Maryland, USA*

"Captivating. Rooted in God being a co-partner in all that we do, even if we are unaware of it, while drawing our attention to significant faith matters in a completely accessible way."
— **Josephine Furey,** *Belfast*

"This book doesn't just recount the many adventures experienced over the years. Catholic teachings are explained and developed in great detail. A thoroughly good read, informative and entertaining."
— **Jim Walsh,** *Co. Meath*

"Not just a travelogue but a journey through Christianity."
— **Maria Flanagan,** *Co. Antrim*

"Kieran's knowledge of Christian history and art is reflected on every page. A compelling read." — **Marie O'Leary,** *Dublin*

"An engaging, informative and, at times, challenging book, sprinkled with a wry, self-deprecating humour."
— **Damien White,** *Co. Offaly*

REVIEWS OF THE FIRST VOLUME IN THIS SERIES

"Captivating. Amid the humorous tales of human frailty, the author reveals moving glimpses of the extraordinary graces of pilgrimage, signs of divine favour poured upon those who undertake these journeys of love."
— ***Elizabeth Lev***, *Professor of Art History, Rome*

"I am delighted that K. Troy has set down in writing some of his vast experiences of guiding pilgrims. This entertaining volume gives a flavour of them and illustrates that they are times of great happiness and satisfaction."
— ***Cardinal Seán Brady***, *Archdiocese of Armagh*

"It's the wry humour and great humility of the author that holds this book gloriously together. I laughed out loud many times, and told the stories to others who laughed just as hard."
— ***Sally Read***, Author, *Night's Bright Darkness: A Modern Conversion Story*

"K. Troy is a much-loved tour guide in Rome. He enchants pilgrims with stories from the past along with his knowledgeable reflections on dogmas, rituals, and relics."
— ***Bishop Brendan Leahy***, *Diocese of Limerick*

"A unique and insightful perspective. Kieran communicates his love and regard for the treasury of Christian faith— visible and invisible."
— ***Archbishop Kieran O'Reilly***, *Archdiocese of Cashel and Emly*

"All of the author's adventures – for all the funniness that he brings to them – are infused with a sense that there is no place on earth where God's glory may not be seen."
— ***Eleanor Hammond,*** *Catholic Herald*

"What sets Troy's book apart is that it is told as if we, the readers, are on a coach bus traveling along for an adventure. He tells the stories of people and places with history, humour, and heart, all in small bite-sized, easy-to-read chapters."
— ***Christopher Siuzdak***, *Homiletic & Pastoral Review*

K. Troy

I See His Blood Upon The Rose

*More Tales from an
Irish Tour Guide in Rome*

LAURETUM

Cover art by Paula Troy Doherty
(after Fra Angelico, *Noli Me Tangere,* San Marco, Florence)

ISBN-979-8-3336836-7-0
©2024 Lauretum
All rights reserved

To my mother, Dympna Troy

ADORO TE DEVOTE (extract)

Godhead here in hiding
whom I do adore
Masked by these bare shadows,
shape and nothing more.
See, Lord, at thy service
low lies here a heart
Lost, all lost in wonder
at the God thou art.

Seeing, touching, tasting
are in thee deceived;
How says trusty hearing?
That shall be believed;
What God's Son has told me,
take for truth I do;
Truth himself speaks truly
or there's nothing true.

Like what tender tales
tell of the Pelican,
Bathe me, Jesus Lord,
in what thy bosom ran;
Blood that but one drop of
has the power to win
All the world forgiveness
of its world of sin.

- **St Thomas Aquinas** (translated by G M Hopkins)

Contents

Prologue	*Ave Maria*	*1*
Chapter One	*Instrument of Blessing*	*11*
Chapter Two	*According to Your Word*	*30*
Chapter Three	*Et Incarnatus Est*	*58*
Chapter Four	*The Bones of St Peter*	*97*
Chapter Five	*Higher Love*	*144*
Chapter Six	*Sown in Virginal Ground*	*182*
Chapter Seven	*Grace and Nature*	*214*
Chapter Eight	*Chastised by Love*	*260*
Chapter Nine	*The Blood and the Rose*	*291*

Prologue
Ave Maria

It was the early days of November 2019. A parish choir from Ashbourne had just spent four days in Rome and Assisi. They had sung in St Peter's, St Mary Major, the basilica of St Francis and other places. Even though the weather in Rome in early November is usually dry and sunny, the conditions these four days had not been pleasant at all. Bad weather can test the mettle of any group. If people can appreciate the wonders of Rome through the rain it is not a bad sign. Ashbourne choir had made the best of every moment, despite the inclement weather.

We were due to fly out of Rome that night and were having a final dinner by Lake Albano, just below the town of Castelgandolfo. It was the largest restaurant on the lake and there were separate areas reserved for different groups on a busy Sunday. Our fifty-strong group was placed in an internal room, not far from a large table around which were seated about twenty Italians.

The waiting staff knew Laura and me well. They were aware that our groups were generally on the way to the airport and wanted hot food and fast service. After serving the first course, the waitress responsible for our tables, Anita, realised that this gathering was a little younger in profile than some of our previous groups.

"What sort of group do you have with you today?" she asked.

"It's a parish choir," I replied. "And they're very good. They sang at St Peter's a few days ago."

The waitress clasped her hands together. "I love choral singing! Can you ask them to sing for us?"

"There are people on the other tables, Anita, though," I said. "Maybe we might disturb them?"

"I don't think that would be a problem," Anita replied, furrowing her brow. "Go on, ask the choir to sing!"

I went over a little reluctantly to the choir director, Giovanna.

"Um, Giovanna, the waitress here asked if the choir would sing a song of some sort for her, but you're all probably tired singing, right? It's been a hectic few days. Maybe we should just leave it?"

"It's no problem, we can sing something," Giovanna replied cheerfully.

"Are you sure?" I said in a worried voice. "You're in the middle of your food. We don't want anyone choking, or getting indigestion. I don't think Anita would mind if we politely decline."

"Kieran, honestly, we love singing. It would be a pleasure. Maybe we could do it between courses?"

I told Anita the "good news" and slunk back to my table, which was set slightly apart from the group. Our coach driver, Salvatore, was tucking in to an enormous portion of seafood pasta. Salvatore had a prominent Roman nose and sported ample sideburns like a rock star from the nineteen seventies. He always wore beautiful shirts with high collars, the top few buttons open to reveal a gold chain nestling upon his hairy chest. If your average Irishman tried this particular look, it probably wouldn't come off too well, but Salvatore just oozed Italian style and charisma. He had been our driver on many occasions and I had great respect for his opinion.

"Salvatore," I said earnestly, "the waitress has asked our choir to sing her a song. Do you see that group of Italians sitting over there alongside our group? How do you think they'd react to a group breaking into song right beside them when they're in the middle of their dinner?"

The driver and I were sitting at a table for two. I had my back to the area where our group and the party of Italians were sitting. Salvatore lifted his chin and looked over my shoulder, studying the situation carefully. "Not a good idea," he said after a while, shaking his head. "Those tables are too close together. Meal times are sacred for us Italians, you really ought to know that by now. That family have probably paid a high price for their menu and the last thing they need is for some loud group to disturb them."

I could see him squinting his eyes as he studied the Italian table more carefully. "And look at the way they're dressed," he said. "That is no ordinary family group. It's either some really special occasion, or some really wealthy group. They could be aristocrats, or diplomats, or . . ."

"Or what?" I asked worriedly.

Salvatore's voice reduced down to a husky whisper. "*Mafia*," he said, darting a glance over his shoulder in case anyone might be near enough to hear. "Italians like to dress well for Sunday dinner, but these people seem to be dressed a little too well, a little too well by half. Look at those suits the men are wearing! When the *men* are dressed that good, it can only mean one thing." Salvatore winked, tapped his nose and gave me a knowing look. No-one had ever explained to me what the wink and nose-tapping gesture meant, but it seemed safe to assume that it was some sort of Italian code referring to the mafia.

Salvatore was waving his fork at me now as he chewed on his food. "But, anyway, it doesn't really matter who they are. You know what people value above all when they go out for dinner?"

"What do they value above all?" I asked in a slightly panicky voice. "Good food?"

The driver leaned forward over the table and looked into my eyes with a grave expression. "*Peace*," he said sombrely. "Peace and quiet."

"I'd love some peace and quiet myself, Salvatore!" I said miserably. "Instead, I always find myself in the middle of some embarrassing mess! Maybe if I just sit here for the rest of the meal, Anita might just forget the whole thing. Yes, I think that's what I'll do, sit here and play dumb!"

Salvatore hadn't finished giving me advice, however. "What you have to work on," he said, still brandishing his fork at me between mouthfuls, "is maintaining the good relationship you have with the management here."

"What do you mean?" I asked.

"Angelo and Massimiliano have been very good to you and Laura over the years, isn't that true?" He was referring to the father and son team who owned the restaurant. "Remember last year on the feast of Corpus Christi you were desperately looking for a restaurant for a last-minute dinner and every single place was booked out on account of the fact that so many First Communions groups had booked that day?"

"I remember, I remember," I replied, looking over towards the cash desk on the other side of the room where both Angelo and Massimiliano were standing at that very moment.

"No other restaurant would give you a slot, but here they did you a favour and fitted a large group for you in between their other clients. I was very impressed with the way you managed to get that group sorted. They seem to have a bit of a soft spot for you, in fact. Didn't you tell me also that they have been giving you more or less the same rock-bottom price for the last five or six years?"

"Yes, Salvatore. It's true, they've been good to us," I said dejectedly.

"And the quality of the food they give you doesn't reflect the paltry sum you pay for it. You don't want to jeopardize that relationship by having one of your groups standing up and spoiling the dinner of some very special clients of Angelo and Massimiliano, now do you?"

"They're just going to sing a little song, Salvatore! How disruptive can it be?"

"A little song! I've been with your Irish choirs before, don't forget, and I know what they're like! Once they've had a glass of wine or two, there's no such thing as a little song! They'll sing at least four, each one more raucous than the first! Then they'll start dancing! We'll have to drag them out of here in the end. Haven't you seen the amount of wine Anita has been carrying to their table!"

"Relax, Salvatore!" I said with a hollow laugh. "With a bit of luck Anita will forget the whole thing. Let's just lie low here and hope that dessert is served very soon."

"Oh-oh," said Salvatore, turning suddenly down towards his plate. "Trouble coming." Before resuming eating, he made a motion with his eyes to indicate that someone was approaching from behind. It was Anita.

"The group has all finished their second course now. Just the dessert left to serve! Maybe this would be a good time to sing that song for us?"

I looked officiously at my watch. "Gosh Anita, is that the time! We need to get to the airport this evening, you know, and we don't want to be late. There's always traffic on the ring road. Maybe we should just serve the dessert right away and then we'll get going? We'll do that song for you another time. What do you say?"

"Oh, but it will take about ten minutes before the chefs have the dessert on the plates! Plenty of time to sing! Come on, let's do it!"

I stood up lethargically. Salvatore glanced at me, rolled his eyes towards heaven, and then returned to his food.

"Anita, maybe I should explain to the group on the table beside us what is happening. Just out of courtesy. What do you think?"

"Certainly, go on ahead."

I felt a little awkward as I approached the table where the group was seated. As Salvatore had said, Italians can be quite formal in their eating habits and I couldn't help noticing that they were right in the middle of one of their courses. As I got closer, however, I noticed for the first time that one of the women was holding a tiny baby dressed in white who seemed to be asleep. "Oh," I thought to myself. "This must be a baptism celebration, that makes everything simpler! If I tell them we want to dedicate the song to the baby, then they can hardly object to us singing - Italians love children even more than they love food. We'll sing for the baby, problem solved!"

I caught the eye of one of the men sitting at the table and said, "Excuse me, are you celebrating a baptism today?"

"No," the man replied, "It's Carlo's retirement dinner." He closed one eye and pointed his fork over to another man sitting on the opposite side of the table.

"That's him. He doesn't look very old, but he's already retiring and we're celebrating it!"

Then followed some banter from a couple of young guys at the table about how few people actually work in Italy, yet everyone celebrates when they don't have to work anymore. I laughed politely, but the wind had been taken out of my sails. It would have been a bit more natural to dedicate a song to a baby that had just been baptized. It didn't seem quite as natural to dedicate a song out of the blue to a stranger who was retiring – especially a guy who looked like he really ought to stay working for a *few* more years at least. However, there was little option but to proceed. I addressed Carlo directly, but everyone at the table was sitting up straight and listening to me now. "Our choir would like to dedicate you a song. I thought it was a baptism, in which case we would have dedicated the song to the baby, but instead we dedicate it to you."

At this point, Giovanna and her husband Ephrem were already getting the choir into formation between the tables. The Italians all stood up and gathered around with their smartphones. I was mortified to see that they were leaving their food half-finished on the plates. They were eating fish, and it was going to be cold by the time they got back to it. "This song better be something good!" I said to myself. I looked back over towards Salvatore and saw that he was standing up and gobbling down the last of his dish in a most undignified manner. The gold medallion was dangling dangerously close to the plate. He was evidently going to make himself scarce before anyone associated him with an embarrassing disruption of dinner. Most worryingly of all, Massimiliano had left his position at the cash register and was now standing motionless in no-man's land a few metres away from us, watching proceedings with a serious expression.

Giovanna made her characteristic four-toned hum to give all the various sections of the choir their proper notes. I had no idea what they intended singing, but was relieved when they began the beautiful *Ave Maria* by Jacob Arcadelt that they had sung in front of the *Salus Populi Romani* icon in St Mary Major a couple of days previously. This was the icon that St Pius V had taken in procession around Rome when he had initiated his rosary crusade prior to the great sea battle of Lepanto. As they sang, I noticed through the window that Salvatore was beating a retreat towards the coach worthy of the Turkish fleet.

When the choir had finished and received a round of applause, Carlo, the man who was retiring, came over to me. He had tears in his eyes and seemed quite emotional. "We are members of a Neo-Catechumenal community," he said, referring to a Catholic group founded in Spain that is very active in many Italian parishes. "For us the most important thing is prayer. We began this dinner by saying the *Ave Maria* together, and then a choir that we had never met before spontaneously dedicates a sung *Ave Maria* to us!"

Carlo was visibly moved. He asked me to record on his phone a description of the song that we had just dedicated to him and his family. This recording was for his son who was unwell and unable to be present. After exchanging phone numbers, I went back to the table and took my place for the rest of the meal. Across the room, I saw that Massimiliano had returned to the cash desk and was conversing happily with one of his customers. Through the large windows at the end of the restaurant, Salvatore could be seen already sitting in the safety of the bus, though none of his dire warnings had materialised.

Our choir was also back in their seats, chatting away to each other about the things that had happened in Rome over the past few days, apparently oblivious to the effect their singing had had on Carlo. As far as they were concerned, they had only sung another *Ave Maria*, one of many they had performed during the trip. This would have seemed no big deal for them, but it was something special for Carlo because of the circumstances in which it had happened. He and his family had placed his retirement in the hands of Mary by saying the *Ave Maria*, and then, just a few minutes later, a beautiful, polyphonic *Ave Maria* was sung to them by a group of complete strangers. I didn't know the first thing about Carlo, but as I looked over at him now on the other side of the room, who could doubt that the Lord had arranged things today so that this would happen? Whoever Carlo was, whatever he had done, our group had just been used by God for him as an instrument of blessing.

Chapter One
Instrument of Blessing

"As mariners are guided into port by the shining of a star, so Christians are guided to heaven by Mary."
St Thomas Aquinas

It was mid-afternoon and there was a little matter to attend to before meeting the group at the hotel. Being a Tuesday, that is when you queue up dutifully outside the bronze door in the colonnade of St Peter's to pick up the tickets for the weekly papal audience on Wednesday. Upon arriving there, I found scores of people in line, each one clinging to the letter they had received upon application for the tickets. The Swiss guards standing at the great bronze door were motioning people forward one at a time. Each person would ascend the steps and then enter the little office on the right to discover their fate. Of course, one's "fate" in this office is nearly always the same, for the vast majority of tickets are of the standard type, admitting you only to the main sections of the square, far from the hallowed spot where the pope would be sitting.

When I was given our envelope, however, it was clear immediately that it was something special because it contained a single slip of paper, not the usual wad of individual standard tickets. I was already opening it unabashedly as I descended the stairs in front of the

Swiss guards and saw to my delight the precious words, *"prima fila"* – front row – written large across the top.

The group we were working with had asked us to organise an event for them that evening at a pub in the centre of Rome. After speeches had been made in the establishment on Via Nazionale, I sat at the bar with the group leader, Jerry, and proudly took out our front row ticket for the next day's audience. It was rare for me to have a ticket of this sort and I was relishing the moment. Jerry asked me to leave the ticket on the bar while he photographed it. Members of the group gathered round and murmured sentiments of admiration that I had managed to obtain such a prized ticket. Esteem tended to be very fleeting in my profession and I generally lapped up whatever morsels came my way.

"Kieran, you obviously have powerful connections to be able to get us into the front row with Pope Francis."

"Well," I said, in the most modest tone that I could muster, "after all these years in the business you *do* get to know a little of how the wheels of power operate." The sad truth was that I had no friends at all in the Vatican, neither high up nor low down, and not too many friends anywhere else either, but no-one needed to know that right now. The only reason we had the front row ticket was because Laura had written a good letter in impeccable Italian and got the local bishop to sign it. This didn't seem like a good time, however, to deflect the good vibes onto anyone else, least of all my wife, so I went on, "Of course, I wouldn't be asking for front-row tickets for *every* group, just the more special ones like yourselves."

"I suppose you and Pope Francis must be nearly on first-name terms by now!" The person who said this had a twinkle in their eye, but other people in the group were looking on reverentially as if there could be some truth in it.

"Not exactly first-name terms," I replied humbly. "But I've been at so many of these audiences that he really ought to recognize me at this point." As I said this, I couldn't help recalling that, on the one occasion I had gotten near enough to Pope Francis to be included in an official photo, an overly-zealous security man promptly rugby-tackled me off the front steps of St Peter's Basilica. He thought I looked suspicious for some reason.

After another hour of backslapping and being offered drinks, with toasts being raised to "Kieran's friends in high places," I wandered off home and turned in early so as to be ready for an early start the next morning. At 7.30am, I was back at the hotel. Upon counting the group on the coach outside the entrance, I discovered that there was one missing. Before dashing inside to find the wayward pilgrim, I turned to our driver.

"Aurelio, I'm leaving my backpack here on the dashboard. Keep an eye on it while I find this person." I said this in my most stern voice as I knew from previous experience that items often went missing from the front of coaches while groups were being loaded. Inside, I found one of the pilgrims slouched in the breakfast room having his umpteenth cup of tea. A minute or two later I had steered him onto the coach and then mounted the steps myself. To my alarm, I saw that my backpack was missing.

"Aurelio, where's my backpack? Did you leave it somewhere for safety?"

Aurelio opened his eyes wide, his mouth even wider and then swore profusely. When he had recovered his composure, he told me what had happened. Just after I had gone inside, a man appeared on the street at the driver's window and asked for directions to St Mary Major Basilica, which Aurelio obligingly gave. The man seemed to have trouble understanding and asked for certain things to be repeated. Evidently, while this diversion was occurring, the man's partner in crime had stepped onto the coach from the other side and taken my backpack. No-one seated in the front rows had noticed anything.

I went inside and told the hotel staff what had happened. Their security footage did not extend to the area occupied by the coach. Nothing else could be done, so I boarded the bus in a daze and told Aurelio to head for St Peter's. Normally, on the way to an audience I would try to get the group prepared by giving a little bit of history of the Petrine ministry - the fact that there have been two hundred and sixty something successors of St Peter, that, for the first three centuries, many of them suffered martyrdom, and other information mostly relating to the way Peter was executed and the memory of his burial place conserved by the early church – but I was shaken by the theft. There was a lot of stuff in my backpack, but the most critical item was the front row ticket for the papal audience. We had been in the situation once before where a group leader had managed to procure a good ticket, but couldn't find it as we approached security. After much rummaging in pockets to no avail, we appealed to the official guarding the front section. Surely there was a ledger somewhere of the seating arrangements with our presence registered on it? But the official firmly shook his head. The only way into that section was with a physical ticket, and he dispatched us politely to the back of the audience.

I recalled this as we drove to St Peter's and felt despondent. It was a rarity to be granted such a good ticket and here we were without it. Our chances of sitting in the front row had vanished with the missing backpack. Grudgingly, I took to the microphone. It was better to face the music now before we arrived at St Peter's Square.

"Excuse me everyone. I'm sorry to say that my backpack has just been stolen." There was a sympathetic groan from the group. I went on. "The most important thing in it was our ticket for the papal audience. You might have heard that we had been given quite a good spot. Now, the officials tend to be very fussy and may want to see a physical ticket, so we're not sure if they will allow us up to the front. When we get to the square, we'll talk to them and do our best to get through. Your patience and understanding is very much appreciated."

I put down the microphone and bit my lip. In reality, our prospects were much bleaker than the picture I had just painted.

"We'll be grand," I could hear someone saying a few rows back. "Kieran has friends in high places and they'll get us up to the front. He just needs to make that call."

"This could work out even better for us now," someone else was saying in a cheerful tone. "Kieran just has to phone one of his contacts in the corridors of power and they'll whisk us right up to the front, maybe even onto the podium with Pope Francis himself!"

When I heard these upbeat comments, my heart sank even further. And it reminded me that not only did Kieran have zero contacts in the corridors of power, he didn't even have a phone at that point - it was in the stolen backpack.

We disembarked in the Janiculum coach park beside the Vatican and spent the next forty minutes getting through the metal detectors into St Peter's Square. I did what our stolen ticket had instructed us to do - approach the front section from the left side, under the great statue of St Peter holding the keys of the Kingdom of Heaven. I left the group standing in the aisle between the sections and went with our group leader, Jerry, to the Swiss guard at the top of the square.

"I was robbed this morning at the hotel," I said. "Our front row ticket was in the backpack."

The guard looked at me suspiciously. "I can't let you forward without a ticket, but leave the group here and you go and speak to that man." He pointed at a small, elegantly dressed official in the usual attire for the staff of the papal household, a white frilly shirt under a grey suit with tails.

Jerry and I approached the man and explained the situation. He was soft-spoken and extremely gracious, but shook his head sympathetically. "I am very sorry," he said. "We need to see the ticket in order to let the group pass."

In an effort to garner some sympathy, I told the official how, of all the things that had been in my backpack, the only one that mattered to our group was that ticket. He looked back at me with a genuine expression of benevolence, but he was still shaking his head. Then Jerry spoke up. "Would a photo of the ticket suffice?" he asked. "I took this yesterday evening." Jerry took out his phone and opened the photo that he had taken in the pub. The man peered at it and then suddenly smiled broadly.

"Well, it's not normal protocol, but we can accept it in these circumstances! You've already had enough to deal with, having been robbed. Go and bring your group!"

A few minutes later we were all ensconced in the front row, just a few feet from where Pope Francis would soon be sitting. The group was in high spirits and not a few of them still seemed to think that we were only there because of my vast network of contacts. In reality, without Jerry's photo, we would all have been standing at the back.

As we waited, the official from the papal household came over to speak to me. *"Mi dispiace davvero per quello che è successo oggi a lei"* ("I am truly sorry for what happened to you today"). He seemed to be a man of great compassion and I felt touched by his concern.

The very next Wednesday, we had another group at the papal audience. This time my pocket was bulging with the usual wad of standard tickets. As we entered the square, I asked the Swiss guard at the entrance to the section furthest from Pope Francis if our group could go in.

"Sorry," he said. "We're filling the other sections first and then this one back here last of all."

"We need to get away quickly when it's over," I said in my most earnest voice. "Is it ok if we go in here?"

The guard relented and allowed us in. I had been using this strategy regularly the past while with some success. If you're going to have standard tickets, then you might as well sit at the very back and make a quick exit before thousands of people start exiting the square. We would be half-way through lunch before those hungry critters in the front row finally got out of the place.

On this particular Wednesday, once the group was seated, I admonished them severely: when Pope Francis gave the final blessing, we would make a beeline straight for the exit, no photos, no messing, no delays. Then we reclined in our backrow seats waiting for the ceremony to begin. A slight drizzle of rain was falling but nothing too unpleasant. After a while, a lady in our group, who had been leaning over the barrier on the side, called me over. She was talking to a young couple in the corridor.

"Kieran, this young couple was married a few days ago. They had a front row ticket, but they left it back at their hotel. The Swiss guard wouldn't let them go forward. Is there anything you can do?"

"Do your wedding rings have the date of the wedding on them?" I asked.

"Yes," said the girl with a puzzled expression. "Could that help?"

"I think so," I replied. "A few years ago, newly married couples didn't even need a ticket to get into the front section. They just had to show a marriage cert or wedding rings with a recent date on them. A few things have changed around here, but that should still work."

The lady from our group tuned to me with a pleading expression. "Kieran, can you go with them? You have the lingo and maybe you'll be able to explain things better."

We were in the back-most section of the square, to the left behind the obelisk. If we went directly to the front row on our side, we might very well meet the official who was so kind to me in that section the previous week, and he would have no option but to conclude that I was a complete charlatan. I know what *I* would think if the same guy approached me two weeks running claiming that a front row ticket had gone missing. It struck me that if he hadn't been so kind to me, it wouldn't have mattered, but he had been extremely gracious and I didn't want to look like a shameless fraudster. So we crossed over to the right and approached the great statue of St Paul holding the sword. I explained the situation to one of the two Swiss guards standing there and we offered to show him the couple's wedding rings.

"Stay here just a moment," the guard said. "I need to get an official from the papal household."

A moment later, to my absolute horror, I saw him returning with the very same official that we had met the previous week. It was dropping rain slightly and before they reached us I quickly pulled up my hood. With two hands, I drew the hood tightly around my face so that just my eyes were peeping out.

"Can I assist you?" he asked in his kindly voice, looking at each of the three of us in turn. The couple looked at me and I began to explain the situation about the missing front row ticket, trying to alter my voice so that I wouldn't be recognized. I could see the couple looking at each other in bewilderment at the sudden change in my comportment, but, as before, the gracious official was effusing empathy.

"Will the date on their rings suffice to get them into the front section?" I asked in the huskiest voice I could muster, my eyes bulging out from the hood. It was a case of ET meets Darth Vader.

The official glanced up at the sky, probably to check if weather prospects were really as bleak as I seemed to be expecting, given how well cloaked I was. Suddenly, he removed his glasses and peered under my hood more intently. "I'm sorry," he said, "but don't I know you?

Aren't you the person who was robbed just before the papal audience last week?"

The game was up. "Yes, that was me," I said, pulling down the hood. "Just doing my good deed for the day. I don't even know these people actually, so I'll let you sort it out." With that, mortified, I turned around and fled to the safety of the backmost section, and there I have remained for every papal audience to this day.

It was only the theft of a backpack, one of thousands that happen in Rome every year, but for the next five years my perspective on that robbery changed a number of times. For that first hour or so after it happened, it seemed that the only thing that mattered was the front-row ticket. Once Jerry's photo turned up, however, the physical ticket ceased to have any importance whatsoever. Later that day, the most critical items stolen seemed to be my credit cards. I called Laura with Aurelio's phone shortly after the robbery and she cancelled them, discovering from the bank that someone had already tried to use them without success multiple times. Then, a day or two later, the fact that my driver's licence was in the backpack seemed to be the most disastrous thing, as Laura's parents needed me to do a few errands with the car. It would take a month to get the licence reissued. For the rest of that year, however, it felt like the loss of my phone was most consequential. The contacts on it had not been backed up and couldn't be retrieved. There were hundreds of vital numbers that could only be got out on the road - boatsmen and taxi drivers, sacristans and restaurants, eccentric locals with keys to places that weren't open to the public, like the chapel in the corner of the ruined castle where Thomas Aquinas was born. Some of those contacts were lost forever.

The robbery happened on April 3rd 2019 but it would be well into 2024 before I realised that the most important thing stolen that day wasn't a ticket, nor a bank card, nor a driver's licence, nor a phone. It was something else entirely. Before travelling to Rome that week, Laura had bought me a copy of St Louis de Montfort's "Secret of the Rosary". It was in my backpack that morning, as I had resolved to read it while we awaited the arrival of Pope Francis. We were already praying the rosary daily as a family, and we knew there was something vital about it, but that book would have enabled me to see its significance more clearly, and a few years earlier. When the theft happened, however, of all the things that had been taken that morning, I hadn't given the book a second thought.

During our pilgrimages, I had been recounting for years the story of the feast of Our Lady of the Rosary, and how the Christian forces, entrusting themselves to the rosary, had saved Europe from Turkish domination against all the odds on October 7th 1571. The Turkish sultan had vowed to desecrate the tomb of St Peter and to turn Europe into an Islamic state. The Ottoman military was in the ascendancy and had a formidable fleet. Pope Pius V had seen the writing on the wall and knew that only the power of heaven could save Christendom. A rosary crusade was organised and the churches of Rome were left open night and day to facilitate prayer. The ancient *Salus Populi Romani* icon of Mother and Child was taken in procession in the streets. The sailors on the Christian fleet were each given a rosary before the battle. The Eucharist was celebrated on the ships and each sailor received absolution and communion.

In those days, the direction of the wind was vital for a sea battle. As a numerically inferior Christian fleet went out into combat, the wind was against them, but it swung one hundred and eighty degrees just before engagement. Virtually all the Turkish fleet was sunk or captured. The Christian fleet suffered much more modest losses. Even the leaders on the Turkish side admitted afterwards that God had favoured their enemy.

I may have told and retold this story, but to appreciate the power of the rosary I still could have done with the book by Louis de Montfort, a book stolen by a man whose nefarious plan involved asking directions to St Mary Major - what irony! The *Salus Populi Romani* icon is conserved there to this day and Pope Francis visits it each time he is about to make a foreign visit. Pope St Pius V, the man who organised the rosary crusade, is buried in the basilica. St Mary Major, in fact, is the place most associated with the origins of the feast of Our Lady of the Rosary, but the thief had used the basilica to steal the treasure contained in my backpack, the book on the rosary. As Revelation tells us, the forces of evil wage war on the woman and her son. The demonic knows how precious each soul is to God and it does what it can to impede grace destined even for the most commonplace of people. Recently, I have come round to thinking that maybe the theft of my bag that day was all about depriving me of the most precious treasure it contained.

It takes me ages to cotton on to things. I am always the last to get a joke, and sometimes very detailed explanations (and even diagrams) are needed. It took a long process of crystallisation before I became interiorly convinced of the importance of the rosary. Over the years, we took a number of groups to Fatima to coincide with October 13th, anniversary of the miracle of the sun. Our Lady had promised the children she would reveal her name in October and perform a miracle. On that day in 1917, she revealed that she was Our Lady of the Rosary and then she performed a miracle that was witnessed by seventy thousand people, the most public supernatural occurrence in history. I began to realize that the revelation of her name and the magnitude of the miracle are not unrelated: the immensity of that wonder is meant to impress on us the importance of the rosary.

In other places too, we began to hear of the power of the rosary. Visiting the cradle of the Dominican order in Toulouse, we heard how Our Lady made fifteen promises to St Dominic for those who recite the rosary faithfully. These include the overcoming of personal vice, the special protection of Our Lady during life, and the assurance of not dying without the sacraments.

Of the many testimonies we heard, one of the most dramatic was from a priest called Fr Paul Ruge. On August 6, 1945, the first atomic bomb was dropped on Hiroshima. The bomb exploded half a mile from the Jesuit Church of Our Lady's Assumption. More than one hundred thousand people were killed instantly and thousands more died later from the effects of radiation. However, the church building and eight Jesuit priests stationed there survived. On the morning of the bomb, Fr Hubert Schiffer had just finished Mass, went into the rectory and sat down at the breakfast table. He had just begun to eat when there was a bright flash of light and he was hurled through the air. The next thing he remembered, he opened his eyes and he was lying on the ground. He looked around and saw that the buildings in all directions had been levelled. As far as he could tell, there was nothing physically wrong with him. After the war, army doctors and scientists explained to him that his body would begin to deteriorate because of the radiation. To the doctors' amazement, Father Schiffer and the other priests developed no ill-effects from the bomb. When asked to account for their remarkable preservation from harm, he said: "We believe that we survived because we were living the message of Fatima. We lived and prayed the rosary daily in that home." In Nagasaki, St. Maximilian Kolbe's Franciscan Friary was also unharmed. The brothers there also prayed the daily rosary and they too had no effects from the bomb. Father Hubert Schiffer died in 1982, thirty-seven years after that fateful day. He gave his account of the atomic bomb at the Eucharistic Congress in Philadelphia in 1976. At the time, all eight members of the Jesuit community from Hiroshima were still alive.

We heard of a Canadian squadron with dozens of crew members that was based in England from 1940 until 1945. The squadron leader was a man called Stan Fulton, a Catholic. Every night, he would kneel on the floor of their sleeping quarters and pray the rosary. Gradually, other members of the squadron began to join him each evening in prayer. Soon, they were all answering the Hail Marys and Our Fathers, Catholics and non-Catholics alike. Before they began a series of night raids from England over Germany, Fulton gave each of them a rosary beads. He assured them that if they kept the beads with them and recited the prayers, Our Lady would bring them all back safe. They recited countless rosaries in the skies. When they returned to Canada in 1945, theirs was the only squadron that had not lost a plane or a single life. Each man was fully convinced that Our Lady had taken care of them and they continued to pray the rosary, even those of them who were not Catholic.

On October 8, 1871, the Great Peshtigo Fire broke out in Wisconsin, burning over a million acres. Near the town of Green Bay, Adele Brise and others gathered to pray the rosary inside the chapel at the shrine of Our Lady of Champion. They prayed the rosary throughout the night, asking Our Lady's protection. Eventually the flames subsided and the group went out to survey the scene. They discovered that the fire had stopped right at the shrine's boundary. Everything beyond the fence was utterly incinerated, but nothing inside the grounds of the shrine had been harmed. The fire had claimed the lives of over two thousand people. It remains the deadliest wildfire in history.

By 2024, having heard of many occurrences of this sort and even experienced some ourselves, we had become more aware as a family of the importance of this prayer. On the one hand, we could see how meditation on the mysteries changed people interiorly. They were being drawn into the biblical events by which we are saved. On the other hand, it was clear that heaven was bestowing providential blessings on those who recited the rosary faithfully.

At the same time, the culture in Ireland, as with the West in general, seemed to be in an ever more rapid spiral of decline. Whole categories of people could now legally be discarded. Everything was being done, of course, for reasons of "compassion", but what was once the sacred prerogative of God had now become the whim of Caesar. There were constant reports of the damage been done to teenage children by unlimited access to social media. The numbers of young people reporting depression, mental illness and self-harm was ever-increasing. We didn't need to hear the statistics to know that the incidence of suicide had reached epidemic proportions. The victims included people of all ages, former teachers of ours, neighbours, school friends, relatives and acquaintances.

When our problems are, at root, spiritual, any focus on purely physical or social remedies will have limited success. Society's desperate plight results from its rejection of the fatherhood of God, the very thing that Adam and Eve rejected in the garden when they chose to rely on themselves at the serpent's instigation. All of our problems, our discord, our addictions, our despair, result from the effort to construct our existence upon material things, our possessions and our projects, our fixations and our compulsions. Cut off from our creator, our lives are ultimately fruitless and meaningless. What we really lack is entrustment to the fatherhood of God, an entrustment that we can learn by imbibing the spiritual milk offered to us by Our Lady.

Just as Mary once gave human life to the Son of God in her womb, now she gives spiritual life to her children who attach themselves to her. We can do so above all in the rosary. In this remarkable prayer, we are drawn into the mysteries of the life of Jesus by repeating the words of the Angel Gabriel, uttered at the very moment that Jesus was about to join himself to humanity - to each one of us - in the flesh. "Hail full of grace, the Lord is with thee."

It took me five years to realise what had truly been stolen from me, but the Lord has helped me in other ways to discover that the rosary is a vital component of what Ireland needs for its renewal. During centuries of persecution, with no possibility of attending Mass, the Irish were faithful to the rosary in a way that few other nations have been. In the prosperity of a few decades, we have abandoned the rosary and our society is now in a state of degeneration that few politicians wish to speak about openly – rampant consumerism, frivolity, antisocial behaviour, family discord.

Those suffering from depression, addictions and compulsions can receive solace by praying the rosary. Meditating on these mysteries, we anchor ourselves in the transcendent, in that which has ultimate meaning and lasting power. We are no longer purely at the mercy of material forces. Our Lady has promised that the discipline of saying the rosary will bear abundant fruit. She is someone who keeps her word, so it can be repeated with absolute assurance that the daily recitation of the rosary is what Ireland needs now to resolve its ailments. The rosary is the instrument by which we can bring the blessings of heaven upon our country. Every time we pray it, we are effectively placing ourselves before heaven's messenger, Gabriel, and opening our hearts to his annunciation of our salvation. Only one reply is possible: *"Be it done onto me according to your word."*

Chapter Two
According to Your Word

"God provides the wind, Man must raise the sail."
St Augustine

We had long been booking flights with a particular airline but this year they were making our lives particularly difficult. The carrier had declared war on travel agents like ourselves and wanted passengers to book with them directly. To modify the details of a booking - change names, add luggage, and a whole host of other things - a complicated and time-consuming procedure was now necessary.

"Kieran!" I was glued to my phone and barely registered the man calling my name, for Laura had sent me a message recounting the latest series of hoops that the airline had made her jump through just to change the name on a ticket.

"Kieran!" Seamus had raised his voice. "Can you ask the guy in the shop if they can deliver to Ireland? He doesn't understand what I'm saying!"

We were standing outside a religious goods shop in the ancient town of Monte Sant' Angelo in the south of Italy. St Michael the archangel had appeared here on a number of occasions from the fourth century onwards. The cave of the apparitions became for a while one of the most frequented pilgrim destinations in Europe, visited by sovereigns and luminaries, including saints like Francis of Assisi and Gerard Majella.

The item in question that the man wanted delivered to Ireland was a big and heavy statue of Padre Pio. The owner of the shop shook his head when I asked.

"We don't ship these statues. Too heavy. Too easy to break. But I can pack it up well in bubble wrap if you want to bring it yourself and check it onto the plane?" The shopkeeper gave me a toothy grin, but he didn't seem to have much faith in his own suggestion.

I passed the news on to Seamus. It was evident that he was in a quandary. The statue was incredibly good value for its size, but it was clear that he would be charged exorbitant luggage fees by the airline if we checked it in at Rome airport.

"It's such a great price," Seamus was looking pensive, shifting his weight from one foot to the other. "Maybe it fell off a truck or something? I'll never get a bargain like this again."

I was feeling a bit guilty because I had been impatient and even a little rude with Seamus over something very trivial a day or so previously in the hotel restaurant. Perhaps it was this feeling of guilt that prompted me to want to help. Or maybe it was a desire to put one over on the airline that had been making our job so difficult these past few months. Whatever the reason, I said on impulse to Seamus, "Don't worry, I'll look after this. You go ahead and buy the statue and I'll make sure it gets to Dublin."

"But the airline will charge you a fortune!"

"Not necessarily," I replied breezily. "It's just a matter of getting it on board as hand luggage."

"*Hand* luggage!" Seamus looked the statue up and down, his eyes opening wide, and then looked back at me, incredulous.

Ten minutes later, I was already regretting my rash offer as I lugged the statue towards the coach park. When we arrived back at the hotel, to save me dragging it upstairs to my room, I asked the staff if I could leave it behind reception until our departure the following morning.

The next day we arose early as the journey time to Rome airport would be more than five hours, with plenty of potential delays along the way. The luggage loaded, the keys returned to reception and the pilgrims counted, I gave the driver the go-ahead to start the coach and leave. At just that moment, the receptionist stumbled out of the entrance to the hotel, weighed down by the statue – I had almost forgotten it! Slightly red-faced, I repossessed the package and hauled it onto the coach, strapping it into one of the empty seats near the front.

Padre Pio sat there for the next five or six hours as we followed the Adriatic coast northwards and then turned inland to cross the spectacular Apennine mountains. During our frequent breaks for coffee and lunch and then more coffee, there was plenty of good-natured banter about the holy occupant in row three of the bus.

Upon arrival in Fiumicino airport in Rome, I directed the group towards the check-in desks while I hung back slightly, not wishing to draw attention to my bulky item of "hand luggage". Once the first person had checked in, I asked them to look after the statue – keeping a healthy distance from the check-in area so that airline staff would not notice anything - while I helped everyone else with their suitcases. A quarter of an hour or so later we were all done, so I recuperated my unwieldly item of merchandise and headed for the security checkpoint.

The staff at security were not interested in the size or weight of what I was carrying, but they were very curious to know what was in the enormous package. "It's a statue," I told the girl as she looked perplexedly at the item that I was heaving onto the table. It wouldn't fit in the usual security baskets and had to be placed directly on the conveyor belt. I looked on with concern as it approached the x-ray machine, sighing with relief as it just about fitted through the opening and eventually emerged on the other side. Another member of staff in this area was looking at the package curiously as I walked through.

"It's Padre Pio," I said to him.

"Who did you say?" he replied with a blank look.

"It's a statue of Padre Pio," I repeated, but all I heard in response was a grunt. Maybe the saintly friar was not as well known and loved in these parts as I imagined.

So far so good, but the real test was yet to come – boarding the aircraft with a package that was vastly larger and heavier than standard hand-luggage.

It was still over an hour until boarding, so I carried the statue in stages towards the gate and got a coffee or two along the way. Huffing and puffing, I arrived down at gate E1 to discover that most of our group was already there and that boarding had already commenced.

My first task was to get rid of my own backpack since I would be making an appeal to the airline staff that this statue was my one and only piece of carry-on luggage. Earlier I had noticed that one of our married couples had only one piece of hand luggage between them, so I asked the husband, Michael, if he wouldn't mind taking my bag just for boarding. He could return it to me once we were on the plane. Then I placed myself in the line for the gate, standing the statue on the floor behind me as we shuffled along in the hope that the staff wouldn't notice it coming.

To my dismay, I noticed the stewardess ahead of me challenging one of the passengers about the size of his luggage. She had scanned his boarding pass as normal, but then, as he walked by her to board the plane, she observed that he was wheeling behind him a larger-than-permitted trolley. It didn't take her long to get his credit card and charge him for the privilege. Then she took the microphone and made a general announcement: "Passengers, please be advised that bulky items of hand luggage will not be allowed on board. You must check them in and pay the appropriate fee."

My heart sank. This cheap statue of Padre Pio would no longer be cheap once we paid the luggage fees. And the penalty would be even higher because it was being paid at the gate! Why had I been my usual cheapskate self, instead of just biting the bullet and forking out the necessary costs in advance?

At that moment, a little old lady from our group hobbled over and whispered in my ear. "Don't worry, I'm praying to Padre Pio that you'll be able to get the statue on the plane."

"Thanks, my dear," I wanted to say. "But the problem is not getting him onto the plane, it's getting him on without having to *pay*. This airline would take an elephant on board if we paid them enough. I'm just trying to smuggle a big statue of Padre Pio on for free, and I'm not sure if we should be praying about *that*."

The queue continued to move along towards the gate. There were two stewards, a man on the left and a woman on the right. Towards whom should I go, I wondered? As I shuffled along, the statue was still standing upright behind me, my hands extending behind my back to drag it along in the hope that it would not be spotted. In truth, this unconventional method of porterage was probably drawing every eye in the airport towards the suspicious-looking package. The key moment, I knew, would be just after the steward scanned my boarding card and I walked by them towards the plane. At that point, the statue needed to be shielded from view in some way or other, but how could I manage that?

My turn came. The man on the left seemed to have a benevolent aura about him. He might well be sympathetic towards a holy statue, I felt, whereas the stewardess on the right exuded a sort of razor-sharp air of efficiency. It was hard to see her turning a blind eye while an enormous object of pious devotion was being smuggled on board. I kept my head down and veered left.

The steward was looking intently at his screen as I drew level with him. Just at that moment, a lady in our group - who was about to show her boarding pass to the stewardess on the right - called over to me. "Look, Kieran, there's a backpack over there on the seat. Someone has left it behind. Maybe it belongs to one of ours?" She was pointing to a bag on a row of seats near where she was queuing.

In the same moment, the steward turned to me and asked for my boarding card. This seemed like a heaven-given opportunity that no self-respecting devotee of Padre Pio could let pass. As he scanned my card, I said loudly. "Look, there's a backpack over there on the seat. Should we see who left it behind and maybe I could carry it for them on board?"

"Oh, no, thank you, that's our responsibility," the steward replied with a smile, handing me back my boarding pass. "I'll check it out." Then he turned his back to me, left his post and headed towards the seat with the bag. Hardly believing my luck, I spun around and, with a momentary surge of superhuman strength, picked up the statue as if it were made of paper and slipped through the entrance towards the plane.

The staff on board glared at me as I tried to squeeze the statue into the overhead compartment, occupying a space that would normally have held the luggage of three or four people, but there was nothing they could do about it at this point as their colleagues at the gate were the ones responsible for screening the onboard luggage. As virtually everyone's bags at the back of the plane were being rearranged to accommodate the statue, I caught the eye of the little old lady who had been praying to Padre Pio and she gave me a double thumbs up. There were cheers and salutations all round as the group got wind of the news that the saintly friar had made it into the cabin with us.

Three hours or so later, when Seamus arrived down at the luggage belt in Dublin airport, I was already waiting there triumphantly with the statue of Padre Pio nestling on a trolley.

The triumphant feeling was short-lived, however, and was replaced by a sense of perplexity. How could those prayers have helped in this case? Padre Pio was famous for his no-nonsense approach to people. He had no time for petitioners who were wallowing in their own self-interest. And my behaviour that day was well and truly rooted in my ego. Getting the statue back to Ireland was never an insurmountable obstacle. It just had to be paid for, and I didn't want to part with cash for this airline that had made our lives so difficult. And yet the discovery of the abandoned backpack at precisely that moment was just like an answer to a prayer. It was this timely turn of events that allowed me to sneak the statue onto the aircraft. Could a saint in heaven be assisting me with something so trivial and at the same time so duplicitous? It was hardly an occasion for a theological crisis, but it was still puzzling. Padre Pio had been accused of being involved with the Italian mafia while he was still living. Now that he was in heaven, had he nothing better to do than help the Irish mafia in smuggling holy contraband?

This perplexity about the dynamics of prayer, in truth, was not such a new feeling for me. It was a constant challenge to understand why some prayers were heard and others weren't. A few years previously, I had been in Rome with a choir from the north of Ireland. It can happen with choirs that some of the members care little for the faith. Their main interest is in singing, and being part of a good church choir gives them ample opportunity. The phenomenon of church choirs doing "tours" of Masses in Italy has become a bit of a problem in recent years, in fact. Prestigious churches in Tuscany, such as the Duomo of Florence, have become reluctant to allow visiting choirs to sing at Sunday Masses. Some foreign choirs treat the Mass as if it were a concert opportunity with a captive audience guaranteed. Congregations and priests are held hostage while the choirs indulge themselves with never-ending performances. True, the singing is often polyphonic and high quality, but the problem is that some choirs just don't know when to stop.

The choir from the north of Ireland was not of this sort. It was mostly composed of people who practiced their faith regularly, as far as I could tell, and the choir mistress knew that her task was to enhance the liturgy, not dominate it. A few members of the choir, however, seemed disinterested during our visits to the holy places. One of the men, Aidan, told me on the very first afternoon in Rome that he was "churched out". He had been in three churches already that day and couldn't face another.

"By the way, I'm a bit of a scientist," he said, "I've been running an empirical study on religion for years now and the results are in."

"Oh?" I replied. "And what are they?" I felt sure I wasn't going to like the answer.

Aidan gave a wheezy laugh. "It's all a heap of nonsense!"

"How do you figure that?" I asked.

"Well, my method is very simple, but it's purely empirical. I have enough data now to conclude that the Catholic faith is a load of superstition." He lowered his voice and looked around furtively. "Don't tell Father Andy I said that or he'll kick me out of the choir!"

"So how can you say that it's all superstition?" I queried, finding it hard not to sound defensive.

"It's a simple case of cause and effect, or should I say *lack* of effect. If you went to a doctor time after time with different ailments and the doctor failed to cure any of them, then you'd conclude that the doctor wasn't fit to be called a doctor. If people continually took a particular medicine for an illness but none of them ever got any better, then you can infer that the 'medicine' is not in fact medicine at all."

Aidan was looking at me as if trying to gauge my reaction. I said, "Go on."

"Well, I have been with this choir for nearly ten years now. Every time we go into a church, we have members praying and lighting candles for this or that person. They're asking God for help for relatives with addictions and illnesses. I don't know how many times I have heard people being prayed for with cancer or some other desperate condition, but I don't remember hearing even once of someone being healed. So, it's high time we drew the empirical conclusion. We've gone to the spiritual doctor and taken the spiritual medicine countless times, but none of it is effective. Therefore, the doctor and the medicine are not real. You know, I sometimes think that these candle shrines in churches are a bit like the slot machines down at the local casino. Your chances of winning are just about as slim. Every now and then you get lucky, but you can kiss goodbye to most of the money you put in."

"Hold on a minute, Aidan, surely there are plenty of healings that can't be explained," I objected.

"Sure, sure," he said, waving his hand dismissively, "but have you ever met one personally?"

I racked my brain for a moment. "Um, yes, I have come across a few, but they're not coming to mind right now."

"A few doesn't damage my empirical case anyway," Aidan replied. "Even placebos have success, but what I'm talking about here is backed up by the overwhelming numbers. Most prayers are not answered, as far as I can see. Therefore, the man to whom the prayers are directed has a shaky case for existence."

Aidan had a very satisfied look on his face as if his point was unassailable. As it turned out, that would be the only conversation we would have for the entire trip. He was absent for everything afterwards except for the singing engagements. As one of the better tenors, he was very involved in the performances and was always discussing this or that musical point with some other member of the choir. There was no chance to talk to him and our paths didn't cross again.

Long after he had returned to Ireland though, I was still carrying on a conversation in my mind with Aidan. He may not have collected rigorous data, but what he was saying seemed to fit the evidence. When Catholics went to sanctuaries and altars to make their petitions, wasn't it similar to what practitioners of primitive religions did when they asked their gods for favourable weather or deliverance from danger? If we considered the prayers of primitive religions to be so much mumbo-jumbo with zero efficacy, then who could blame Aidan for inferring that our prayers were mere gibberish from their apparent lack of efficacy?

Some obvious responses to Aidan came quickly to mind, but none seemed very satisfactory. I could reply that the Lord is hearing our prayers and is actually responding to them in his own way and in his own time, but his ways and his times are not ours. St James offers another sort of response in his letter when he writes: *"You do not have, because you do not ask. You ask and do not receive, because you ask wrongly"* (James, 4, 2-3). It seemed unlikely, though, that I could convince

Aidan that all those prayers he had witnessed were fruitless because they were offered in the wrong way. I knew many instances myself of people praying sincerely for worthy causes – young mothers with cancer, children with life-limiting conditions, families whose members suffered from addictions. No doubt the prayers were offered with some element of self-interest inherent in them, but did this explain their apparent lack of efficacy? How could I respond to Aidan's conclusion that all such prayers were mere babble before a non-existent god?

At just this time, Laura was reading the biography of a Peruvian saint called Martin de Porres, who had died in the 1600s. Every evening for a week or two, Laura would recount to me the latest remarkable series of events that she had read about earlier that day. The number of documented prodigies associated with Martin were stunning: instantaneous cures, miraculous knowledge, levitations, passing through locked doors to help the sick, and bilocation, among many others.

Was it because he was a saint that this man's life displayed such supernatural qualities? His incredible humility and utter attachment to God made his prayers effective in a way that the prayers of ordinary people were not? The contrast between Martin de Porres and the picture Aidan painted of the average Christian was striking: on the one side, almost everything Martin did bore miraculous fruit; on the other side, continual petitions of ordinary people seemed to evince little supernatural effect.

If I was perturbed by Aidan's critique of the faith, however, I was soon to encounter a much more sophisticated challenge to the apparent inefficacy of Catholic prayers - this time from a protestant perspective. Laura's sister, Cristina, lived in Texas and we were paying her family a visit during the school holidays. The first leg of our flight was from Dublin to Atlanta. The plane had eight seats in each row, four together at the centre and two seats on either side of the aisles. Laura and the three kids had the four seats at the centre and I was in one of the pair across the aisle. Shortly after we had boarded, a well-dressed gentleman excused himself and took the seat at the window beside me. The man had a reserved air about him and was soon reading a small, leather-bound book and scribbling every now and then in a slim notepad. This suited me fine. I wanted to add the finishing touches to a book outlining a new theory of matter and light, and this journey would give me the perfect opportunity (by the way, the book has been since published and everyone who has read it considers it to be a work of brilliance. I'm hoping to find a second reader soon).

For the next few hours, I sat there with my laptop open in front of me. Every time I looked up, it was impossible not to notice that everyone in sight was hooked up to the inflight entertainment system. From my vantage point, there was an entire sea of screens showing everything from James Bond to Spiderman to Harry Potter. The only person who wasn't coupled to his screen, as far as I could see, was the man seated next to me. As time went on, and the man continued to read and scribble in his notebook, I started to become curious, but not curious enough to want to start a conversation. When you are just a mathematical calculation or two from scientific immortality, you don't want to get waylaid by prittle-prattle with a stranger. However, when the man left his book for a moment on the tray in front of him and rummaged for something in his bag, I took the opportunity to turn my head and have a good look at what he was reading, even though I was already pretty sure what it would be. It was a well-worn King James Bible. Someone who is taking a stand against the fleeting entertainment offered by this world – as this man clearly was doing – is very likely going to turn out to be Christian.

There was only an hour left in our flight and I folded up my computer with a sigh. Out of an entire planeload of three hundred people in the thrall of virtual reality, the Lord puts me beside the one person reading the Bible. Scientific immortality would have to be relinquished, perhaps forever, as it was clear now that I had little option but to speak to this man.

"Nice to see someone reading the Bible," I muttered, not sure how to break the ice.

The man looked over at me with a start, clearly not expecting a conversation to start after so many hours of silence. "Oh, yes, quite," he replied, in a slightly posh English accent. And with these words began a conversation that has continued intermittently to this day, more than ten years later. Ben, for that is what his name turned out to be, was a retired airline pilot. I would discover much later that, on the day we met, he was on his way back home to Virginia after attending the funeral of his first wife in London. A year or so afterwards, Ben would fly back to Ireland and stay in our house, patiently enduring my tour of the monastic ruins in the Irish midlands. It would emerge unexpectedly at some point that he and I were born on the same day, twenty-five years apart, a coincidence that confirmed in my mind at least that our meeting was providential. In 2024, he and I were due to share a room in the Holy Land on a pilgrimage with a group from Kilkenny. I was looking forward to hearing his perspective on the biblical sites, but the war in Gaza put an end to that trip. Throughout these ten years, we have never stopped for long from discussing the faith, sometimes to the point of almost falling out.

Ben's challenge to the Catholic way was very different to that offered by Aidan. Aidan was a sceptic about the existence of God, but Ben's faith in the God of the Bible was absolute. He saw everything - the trials of his past, the sometimes-turbulent events of the present - from the standpoint of someone whose life was in the hands of a loving God. Like Aidan, though, he was sceptical about the Catholic way of approaching God, the forms of prayer, the liturgy, devotion to the saints. As I got to know Ben better, I discovered that he was quite radical in this respect. For him, worship of God was something that must take place in the individual heart. Even church buildings were superfluous. Ben, in fact, would have viewed much of the Catholic way of interacting with God as an obstacle to true worship. He advocated the dissolution of everything that could hinder the personal relationship with the Lord on a heart-to-heart level. Even to call oneself "Christian" was an illegitimate presumption.

The radical nature of the personal relationship with the Lord being advocated was impressive, but I still felt an obligation to defend the Catholic way, and sometimes insistently so. Over these years, Ben and I have exchanged nearly eight hundred emails. At times my tone has been often belligerent, but Ben has never been anything less than a gentleman, polite in manner and humble to a fault.

The first few emails concerned the question of the nature of the Church. In simple terms, Ben thought that an institutional Church was not willed by God, a position that seemed to me easy to rebuff. I invited Ben to look around at the multiplicity of interpretations of the Bible when one does not accept the authority of the Church. Jehovah's Witnesses, Mormons, Seventh Day Adventists and countless others hold to radically divergent interpretations of Scripture. Within Protestantism itself there is a dizzying array of conflicting opinions on fundamental matters, both doctrinal and moral. All of this, I argued, shows us that an authoritative interpretation of the Bible is necessary for the transmission of the faith. The Lord would not have abandoned us to fend for ourselves without establishing such an authority.

In his replies, however, Ben made clear that he did not believe that such an authority was essential. He felt that the Holy Spirit would guide the individual's heart to understand Scripture sufficiently and follow the Lord faithfully. Even if two people's views on God were different in certain respects, this was not a major problem. What mattered was sincere attachment to God in the heart. Indeed, Ben held that such a personal adherence to God's word was the only way to live as a disciple of Jesus. Following prescriptions or interpretations handed down to us from above would destroy the personal character of our interaction with the Lord. In vain I tried to argue that the quality of our relationship with God necessitated having right ideas about him, and this required a Church with the authority to make pronouncements about who Jesus is. The Mormons share our Bible, yet their conception of Jesus was completely incompatible with ours. How was a right relationship in the heart even possible if we have a wayward understanding of Jesus' identity?

Ben felt, though, that history substantiated his claim that Jesus did not intend to found a Church. The great flowering of the Spirit that we read about in the Acts of the Apostles seemed to come to a sudden halt once the Church took on the more institutionalised form that it still has today. As with Aidan, this line of reasoning had an empirical form. According to Aidan, the way Catholics approach God bears little fruit, therefore the existence of the Catholic God is problematic. What Ben was saying was that the Catholic Church showed few signs of the fruits of the Spirit, therefore this institutional body and all of its trappings was problematic.

If this argument against the Church was empirical then, I felt, the response should also be empirical. Some of my emails detailed how the Church has, in fact, borne immense fruits of the Spirit in every age. One long letter described the life story of Don Bosco, the miracles, the dreams, the healings and also the human transformation of industrial cities in Italy by the educational efforts of the Salesians. Another detailed the life of Mother Teresa.

It is probably fair to say that Ben was not particularly moved by any of these examples. Though he never said it exactly in these words, I think his point would have been more or less as follows: if the Catholic Church was really instituted by Christ, then the fruits of the Spirit should be much more generally manifest than they actually are, not just in the lives of these saints, few and far between as they actually are. Those manifestations were very evident in the very early Church, as we read in the Acts of the Apostles: why are they so much less evident ever since?

The emails between Ben and me eventually became less theological and more uncontroversial. Often, we seemed to be going in circles, arriving right back at the very same points that had been made earlier. Now, though we still talk about faith issues, we have reached a sort of polite impasse. Yet, you could say that after all these years I am still debating with Ben in my mind regarding the question of the fruitfulness of the Church.

It is a question that frequently arises involuntarily during parish pilgrimages to Rome. Often, the people who come on pilgrimage are the prominent Catholics in the parish, the daily Mass goers, readers and Eucharistic ministers. It is not unknown, though, that the pilgrim who behaves the worst during the trip turns out to be one of these very ones who is receiving the Eucharist daily. Where are the benefits and fruits of daily reception of the sacrament? Is it enough to say that it is all hidden and will only be manifested in eternity?

We had a pilgrimage to Rome from the parish of Newtownards and Comber in County Down led by Fathers Martin and Eugene O'Hagan, two well-known tenors who had been singing as part of a trio for fifty years. Given the importance of music for the O'Hagan brothers, we wanted to include a visit to the basilica of St Cecilia, an early Roman martyr and patroness of music. This ancient church with mosaics from the early ninth-century is in the Trastevere area of the city. When the saint's tomb was opened during renovations in 1599, her body was found to be incorrupt, causing a sensation in Rome. The sculptor, Stefano Maderno, made a statue of the saint in the position in which she was found, and this statue still lies at the foot of the altar above her tomb.

In the apse above the statue, we viewed the striking mosaics depicting Christ, Peter, Paul, Cecilia and others, noting that the square halo around the head of Pope Paschal indicated that he was still alive in the 800s when this work was created. Then we descended underneath into the archaeological level and down to the crypt. After a beautiful rendition of a hymn from the brothers close to the mortal remains of the patroness of music, we emerged onto the street again and continued our walk into the heart of Trastevere. A dinner had been organised for the group, but we were a little early, so I suggested to Fr Martin that we make a quick visit to Santa Maria in Trastevere, one of the oldest churches in the city, with part of it dating back to the 200s.

"We can look at the mosaics of the great Pietro Cavallini while we're there, including the Visitation." I said. This was a reference to the cycle of mosaics dating from the late 1200s on the life of Mary in the apse of the church. Fr Martin's church on the Comber side of his parish was dedicated to the Visitation and I knew that he was interested in this theme whenever we encountered religious art.

Fr Martin readily agreed, but when we got into the basilica of Santa Maria in Trastevere, I was embarrassed to discover that the Visitation was not one of the episodes chosen by Cavallini for his decoration of the apse. There were depictions of the Annunciation, the Nativity and virtually every other major event in Mary's life, but no Visitation. To help hide my blushes, I took the group outside and we looked up at the twelfth-century mosaic on the upper façade. Despite the age of this scene, its colours are still vibrant. The Virgin Mary is depicted in the centre, feeding the child Jesus. Five women flank Mary on either side. The common interpretation is that they represent the Wise and

Foolish Virgins from the parable in Matthew's Gospel. The problem is that there seem to be only two foolish virgins in the scene, as only two have let their oil run out.

As I described the mosaic to the group, I recalled again my discussion with Ben. In the parable, the virgins are challenged to store oil in their lamps so that they are ready to enter the banquet when the Bridegroom eventually appears. If we are to be in communion with the Bridegroom – Christ - then it is clear from the parable that we need to have already stored up something that will make that encounter fruitful. Is that what was missing in so much of the Church? We have little oil in the sense that we do not cultivate our relationship with Christ on a daily basis, but when someone in the family gets sick, or some other crisis emerges, then we make our way to sanctuaries and candle shrines to make our petitions. Like the foolish virgins we say, "Lord, lord, open to us." But the Bridegroom replies, "Truly I tell you, I do not know you" (Matthew 25, 11-12).

Sitting in the trattoria for the next hour, I felt that this was the response I could give both Aidan and Ben, but it was the most un-protestant of answers. The protestant-Catholic divide is often cast in terms of faith alone versus faith *and* works. The parable of the oil lamps indicates that our lives are not fruitful by faith alone, but only through actively conforming them to Jesus. Sometimes, there can be a tendency to think that getting an answer to prayer is all about having faith, where "faith" is understood as believing unfalteringly that God will do what we asked. "Have faith!" people are always saying,

"God will answer." But what is really required to make our prayer effective is something that needed to be there *before* the prayer was ever made, the storing of oil in our lamps, a radical relationship with God, a relationship that involves consigning ourselves over to him in both faith and works.

Next morning, we had Mass in the basilica of San Clemente, one of the most fascinating churches of Rome. Until the 1800s, it was generally believed that the church was a twelfth-century reconstruction of the original fourth-century basilica mentioned in the historical records. In the 1800s, the Irish prior, Fr Mullooly, discovered that the more ancient basilica was actually still extant underneath the present church. Further excavations revealed a Roman first-century road and a place of pagan cult at a still deeper level.

Fathers Eugene and Martin had studied at the Irish college nearby and remain the last pair of brothers to have been students there. During his student days, Fr Martin developed a deep interest in the San Clemente archaeological excavations. Given this connection to the basilica, it seemed a good place to commemorate the fact that the O'Hagans had been singing publicly (with Fr David Delargy) for fifty years. The Irish Ambassador to the Holy See, Frances Collins, attended and addressed the group afterwards.

As Mass was celebrated, we had as a backdrop the stunning twelfth-century apse mosaic. It was just a couple of days after Easter. Some of the parishioners from Newtownards had commented to me how Fr

Martin had sung the full ancient version of the Exultet in the light of a candle during the Easter Vigil a few nights previously. As we gazed at the mosaic behind the celebrants, it occurred to me that this was the Exultet in pictorial form, a song to the life of Easter. Out of the cross a swirling vine is growing which embraces every aspect of life. The vine produces five groups of five spirals to the left of the cross and five groups of five to the right, fifty spirals in total, recalling the fifty days between Easter and Pentecost when the sacrifice on the cross reaches full fruition in the explosion of the Holy Spirit at Pentecost. "O happy fault, O necessary sin of Adam, which gained for us so great a Redeemer!" Underneath the mosaic an original inscription in Latin reads: "We have likened the Church of Christ to this vine; the Law made it wither but the Cross made it bloom."

The debate with Ben came back to mind. The manifestation of the Spirit at Pentecost had become for him a sort of counter-sign to the institutional church. The Church does not manifest the Spirit, he alleged: therefore, it is not of Christ. Yet, Jesus had anticipated this very question when he described himself as the vine and specified what was required if we were to be fruitful branches.

"Abide in me, as I abide in you. Just as a branch cannot bear fruit by itself unless it abides in the vine, so you cannot bear fruit unless you abide in me. I am the vine, you are the branches. Whoever abides in me, and I

in him, will bear much fruit. Apart from me you can do nothing" (John 15, 4-5).

Abiding in Jesus entails being attached to him radically, living for him, keeping his commandments, obeying the teaching of his Church, serving others. If we abide in him in this all-pervasive way, then he will abide in us. Our lives will be fruitful and our prayers will be heard.

Aidan had seen in the lack of Catholic fruitfulness a proof for the non-existence of God. Ben had seen in it a proof for the non-divine nature of the institutional Church. But, in truth, this lack of fruits is sometimes an indication of something else - the lack of personal adherence of many Catholics to the Lord. As Chesterton remarked, "The Christian ideal has not been tried and found wanting. It has been found difficult; and left untried." Whenever we are in grave need, we fly to God for assistance, but do we adhere to his teaching?

Once this penny had dropped for me before the mosaic in San Clemente, I began to hear the same point being made all over Scripture, starting with the opening verses of the very first psalm. *"Blessed is the man who walks not in the counsel of the wicked, nor stands in the way of sinners, nor sits in the seat of scoffers; but his delight is in the law of the Lord, and on his law he meditates day and night. He is like a tree planted by streams of water that yields its fruit in its season, and its leaf does not wither. In all that he does, he prospers"* (Psalm 1, 1-3). If we are poor in spirit, pure of heart, merciful to others, peacemakers, then we will be blessed. It seems a tautology to say that, by living the beatitudes, our lives will become blessed, but the sad truth is that many of us have a cafeteria attitude to the teachings of Christ yet wonder why he doesn't hear our prayers when we are in need.

That is only one aspect of the story, however. It is not the case that leading a saintly life will surely lead to supernatural experiences and spiritual consolations. Mother Teresa was one of the great saints of modern times but lived through a long period of spiritual aridity. A fundamental element of the faith is the call to trust in the Lord even when he seems completely absent or even non-existent. St Peter tells us that *"you may for a short time have to bear being plagued by all sorts of trials; so that, when Jesus Christ is revealed, your faith will have been tested and proved like gold"* (1 Pet 1,7). Abraham continued to trust and obey although the promise God made to him seemed to be falling apart. Mother Teresa held firm through fifty years of spiritual darkness. Indeed, the very lack of supernatural consolations made her sanctity all the more heroic, but Aidan would not have appreciated that. He was looking for signs of holiness of a different sort altogether.

Sitting in San Clemente, looking at the vine swirling out of the cross of Christ, it occurred to me that Aidan had been looking askance at the apparent absence of God in the lives of praying Catholics. I recalled what our children had been taught when preparing for their own encounter with Pentecost at Confirmation. In Galatians, St Paul lists the fruits of the Spirit as love, joy, peace, patience, kindness, goodness, faithfulness, gentleness and self-control. Like the aspects of life encircled by the fifty spirals in the image before me, these fruits are very much of an everyday nature. Unless you have the eyes of faith, you could miss them altogether. Mother Teresa's life was replete with these everyday fruits. She was famously serene, joyful and boundlessly compassionate, but her many critics still denounced her as a fraud. That is not even to mention the immense fruits still being manifested in the order she founded. Dozens of hospitals, orphanages and homes for the sick have transformed the lives of countless people. In a way that no-one else has done, she raised humanity's awareness on a global level of the immeasurable dignity of the poor.

None of these considerations would have any effect on Ben. For him, debate is futile regarding the rights or wrongs of this creed or that. Our focus should only be on our adhesion to Christ in our heart, not on our doctrinal orthodoxy nor moral rectitude. As I left San Clemente and had a last look at that fruitful vine, I could feel the irony. I had never met a person like Ben who was so radically attached to the word of God. He is a true protestant after all. If a Catholic with Ben's personal adhesion to the Lord approached the treasure house of grace that is to be found in the sacraments of the Catholic Church, then what abundant fruits would result!

It is quite a simple story, yet true. God created us for himself, but - as the story of Genesis expresses - we rejected his fatherhood and chose instead to exalt ourselves by becoming the be-all and end-all of our own existence. Cut off from the source of life, our lives are ultimately meaningless and fruitless, even if for a brief time we receive the passing adulation of others for our transitory achievements. A branch that has broken itself off from the tree has no hope of producing fruit, but God himself takes on our flesh and roots himself in our nature. By his righteousness, Jesus undoes our unrighteousness and grafts us back onto the source of life which is God. He does the work, but asks our cooperation. We must abide in him, just as he has chosen to abide in our race forever by the taking on of our flesh.

Chapter Three
Et Incarnatus Est

"For the Son of God became man so that we might become god."

St. Athanasius

During the Second World War, an intrepid Irishman named Hugh O'Flaherty was working as an official in the Vatican's Holy Office. When the Nazis occupied the city in September 1943, he put together a formidable organisation that would come to be known as the Rome Escape Line. This network would assist thousands of escaped Allied prisoners of war and countless civilians, including numerous Jews. There were many heroic individuals operating the network - foremost among them a British soldier, Major Sam Derry, and a Maltese widow named Henrietta Chevalier - but Monsignor O'Flaherty was the very heartbeat of the organisation and the Nazis wanted him arrested at virtually any cost.

One of the stories regarding the German efforts to apprehend the Monsignor had become the stuff of legend – his dramatic escape from the Pamphilj Palace in central Rome while surrounded by the Gestapo. In 2012, while organising the first trip to Rome for the O'Flaherty Memorial Society, the question was raised whether this particular story was fact or fiction. Its sensational nature led many people to dismiss it as part of the lore that had grown up around the Monsignor.

That same year, Pope Benedict XVI finally completed the third volume in his *Jesus of Nazareth* trilogy. The work was something profoundly personal, the fruit of a lifetime search for the truth about Christ. The trilogy was also driven by a particular conviction: that the person of Jesus must be salvaged from the wreckage created by biblical scholarship during the twentieth century. The traditional understanding of the identity of Christ as the Son of God, miracle-worker and healer had been left in tatters by the "historical-critical" school, an umbrella of methodologies that had gained ever greater traction as the century progressed. These scholars claimed that there was a marked distinction between the Jesus of history and the Christ of faith. Pope Benedict, by contrast, was convinced that the testimonies of the Gospels were historically reliable.

An important premise of modern scholarship is that the Gospels are not biographies in the modern sense of the term. A modern biography generally aims to give a fairly comprehensive account of a person's life and seeks to present the facts as accurately as possible. The Gospels, by contrast, focused only on the latter part of Jesus' life and their overriding goal - according to scholars - was to inspire faith in the person of Christ and his message. Each of the four was written from a different perspective and for a different audience. Many scholars believed that the Evangelists - as with ancient biographers in general - were willing to "colour" the facts about Jesus in order to edify or motivate their particular audience. Virtually everyone agreed that the Gospels rested on a historical foundation, but, as the twentieth century wore on, there were growing doubts about where history ended and theological embellishment began.

A characteristic of this scholarship, beginning in the eighteenth century with Ernest Renan and Adolf von Harnack, and continuing into the twentieth century with people like Albert Schweitzer, was a general scepticism regarding the miracle stories in the Gospels. The thinking was as follows: since ancient biographies tended to embroider the facts for motivational purposes, the stories about the miraculous powers of Jesus were very likely to be embellishments, intended to inspire a particular response of faith. In order to return to the historical Jesus, these scholars felt that the miracle stories had to be reinterpreted or discarded. The feeding of the five thousand, according to this approach, could well have grown from a story about the way Christ nourishes his people with his word. If we *really* want to retain the belief that the crowd ended up being physically fed, then the miraculous element in the story must be reinterpreted in natural terms, such as the people taking out from their pockets the food that they had brought with them and sharing it with those who had none. The "miracle" was not in the supernatural transformation of five loaves and two fishes, but the moral transformation of the people in response to Jesus' message.

Benedict XVI's trilogy praised the positive contributions of the historical-critical method, but also pointed out its limitations. He was concerned at the scepticism it had fostered with regard to the historical basis of the Gospel narrative. In eliminating everything that it considered ahistorical from the story of Jesus, it had reduced him to a figure who was so banal that it would be impossible to understand how he could have changed the course of history in the first place. It is only when we read the Gospels in faith, accepting their testimony for what it is, that the world-changing activities of the apostles - onto their eventual martyrdoms - makes any sense.

In the wake of the publication of the work, there was a storm of criticism from biblical scholars, some of whom, incidentally, did not even profess faith in Christ in the first place. Ratzinger, these voices asserted, paid lip-service to the historical-critical method, following its rules only whenever they suited his theological preconceptions. At the end of the day, they alleged, his interpretation of the Gospel narratives was little different to the traditional interpretations of the early Church Fathers.

In 2012, when we were asked to organise the trip for the O'Flaherty Memorial society, I had already read the first two volumes of the trilogy. It never occurred to me that the O'Flaherty trip would help me appreciate better the content of Benedict's books, but help me it did, in a peculiar kind of way.

It was a cold day in the late spring of that year and I was filling our stove with wood.

"There's an email here from a princess," Laura called to me from the office.

"Oh, that must be Princess Pamphilj," I called back. "What does she say?"

"She has invited you and the O'Flaherty group to her palace for a reception of some sort."

"Did she say that we can see the coal cellar?"

"The coal cellar! No, she didn't mention it! Whatever are you talking about?"

Princess Gesine Pamphilj was the granddaughter of Filippo Andrea Doria Pamphilj, a hero of the struggle against fascism in Italy before and during the Second World War. Prince Filippo was one of the main benefactors of the Rome Escape Line. In order to hide and feed large numbers of refugees in German-occupied Rome, O'Flaherty needed a steady supply of money, and, for a time, Prince Filippo was his most generous supporter.

The story of O'Flaherty was later made into a film starring Gregory Peck. One of the most memorable scenes from the film took place at the Pamphilj residence on Via del Corso, Palazzo Doria. Kappler, head of the Gestapo in Rome and the self-proclaimed archenemy of O'Flaherty, had long suspected that the Irishman was receiving funding from the Prince. With the aid of information extracted from prisoners under torture, Kappler knew all about the Rome Escape Line, and he had given orders that O'Flaherty be arrested on sight. When he got a tip-off that the Irishman was inside the Pamphilj residence, he ordered the Gestapo to encircle the building, then drove directly to Via del Corso. He wanted to be there in person when O'Flaherty was finally caught.

From a window inside the building, the Prince's secretary had spotted the cordon of German soldiers outside. He notified the Prince, who looked out to see Kappler himself alighting from his car. "The game's up," Prince Filippo said quietly to O'Flaherty. "I don't believe there is any point in resisting this time. The Germans are everywhere!"

"No!" replied the Monsignor. "They're not going to catch me here with you! I'll find a way out. Goodbye and God bless you!"

He quickly ran down the stairs to where some of the palace servants were huddled nervously on the ground floor. The Gestapo were banging heavily on the door. "Don't open for a few minutes!" O'Flaherty called over to them in a hushed tone, as he scurried away down the hall. He spotted a narrow stairs leading down to a cellar. Unable to think of anything else to do, he disappeared down the steps. Below, in the poor light, he was surprised to hear a loud rumbling noise ahead. Then he realised that the winter coal supply was being delivered to the palace at that very moment! The Monsignor scrambled up the hill of coal to the patch of daylight coming in through the trapdoor which led to the courtyard of the palace. He could see the coal truck and, beyond it, about twenty SS troops lining up across the yard. There were some empty coal sacks in arms' reach. He grabbed one and slid back down to the cellar. Into the bag went his cassock and hat. O'Flaherty had begun rubbing some coal dust on his hair, face and shirt, when he heard one of the German officers giving an order in heavily-accented Italian. "You workmen! Empty the sacks you're holding and get out of here! You can finish the delivery later!"

The Monsignor peeked out again to see one of the coalmen carry his sack of coal to the trapdoor. Just before its contents were emptied in on top of him, O'Flaherty called out, "Hold on a moment! I'm a priest, wanted by the Gestapo!"

The coalman came down into the cellar and O'Flaherty told him his plan. The Monsignor would leave the courtyard with the coal truck whilst the coalman lay low in the cellar for a while. Once O'Flaherty had escaped, the coalman could come out of the cellar, catch up with his truck, and finish the coal delivery later on.

The Irishman then climbed up to the courtyard with the sack containing his clothes over his shoulder. He walked boldly towards the lines of SS men standing between him and the exit. The SS officer who had ordered the coalmen to leave gestured to the soldiers, and they made a gap for him to pass, probably not wishing to have their immaculate uniforms dirtied by contact with this scruffy looking coalman. Once O'Flaherty had left the building and emerged into the street, he made his way to a nearby church where he was given refuge by the sacristan. Later, O'Flaherty discovered that the furious Kappler had spent over two hours searching every inch of the Pamphilj Palace.

This was the story that had been passed down and found its way into the 1983 film on O'Flaherty, ***The Scarlet and the Black***. But was there any historical basis to it? For the 2012 trip to Rome, we had the job of organising an itinerary that would take in sites associated with O'Flaherty's life in the city. For me, the coalman event summed up his resourcefulness and courageous spirit, the "never say die" attitude he displayed even when the situation seemed hopeless. This prompted me to write to the Princess to ask if we could have permission to see the coal cellar. When you write to someone to ask if you can visit her house, you wouldn't normally specify that you only want to see the cellar. In the case of the Pamphilj palace, in particular, it would seem a pity not to see the rest of the building. The palace is home to one of Rome's best private art galleries, including the finest portrait in the entire city – that of Pope Innocent X Pamphilj by Velázquez. But we had a busy programme squeezed into four days in Rome and time was at a premium. In any case, I felt that the more minimalist our request, the more likely it would be granted. All we wanted was a glimpse of the cellar so that we could relive this unique story in our imagination.

Nearly every group has its disagreeable members, and they can be the bane of the courier's life, especially a courier who is often tripping along hopefully from one day to the next, hoping no one will ask him any hard questions. The devil's advocate in this particular group was a lady called Alexandra.

"So we're going to trek half way across town just to see a coal cellar!" she said as we boarded the coach at the Irish Embassy on October 12th 2012. "Of all the things we could see in Rome, you want to take us into some dungeon where no one has been in fifty years!"

I had been waxing lyrical about the visit to the coal cellar for some days now, but I was a bit unsure about the visit and didn't want to engage with Alexandra.

"Come on now, everybody! Let's load up! Time to go!" I said, rubbing my hands. I felt that everyone would appreciate the visit once we got into that beautiful palace and tried to envisage the events that unfolded there in the winter of 1943.

When we got to Palazzo Doria, however, everything turned out differently to what I had imagined. Princess Gesine gave us a warmer welcome than expected with a champagne reception upstairs in her private rooms. We were afforded free access to the art gallery and our group admired the masterpieces by Caravaggio, Raphael, Guido Reni, Claude Lorrain, Titian and, of course, the magnificent portrait by Velázquez. Speeches were made and the group was made to feel very welcome. But suddenly we were already late for our coach appointment and it was time to go. Lunch was booked at Lake Albano, nearly an hour's drive away, below the town of Castelgandolfo. From there we would head directly to Rome airport and back to Dublin.

"I thought we were supposed to see the coal cellar in the palace this morning?" Alexandra remarked later that day as I passed her table during lunch at the lake. "You've been talking about the coalman incident since we arrived! A couple of nights ago you made us all eat some pasta dish with a funny name as a salute to the Monsignor, as if pasta had anything to do with O'Flaherty and his work!"

"Alexandra, *pasta alla carbonara* literally means 'coalman's pasta,'" I replied with forced cheeriness. "It's a Roman specialty and that restaurant in Campo dei Fiori is renowned for its version of the dish. It was just a fun way of marking that event in the Monsignor's life. I thought you would enjoy it!"

"Well, how come we didn't see this famous coal cellar today? We go to the palace to see the cellar and we end up seeing everything else except the cellar! Paintings by Lorraine this and Claudia that - maybe the cellar doesn't exist at all! If you ask me, that whole coalman saga was just a fairy story made up after the war! Why keep a legend going just to make that old fool O'Flaherty look good?"

"Of course the cellar exists, Alexandra!" I said, pretending to laugh. "Every palace in Rome has a cellar. The Princess had gone out of her way to be kind to us. I didn't feel like pushing my luck in demanding to be taken down to the basement. In any case, we were under pressure for time."

"It's very strange that we didn't see it, that's all I'm saying." Alexandra was waving her fork at me with one hand and brandishing her wine glass with the other. Then her eyes narrowed and she glared at me intently. "I have a feeling you and the Princess are keeping something from us, and my feelings are usually right!"

I gave another phony laugh and started to slink away in the direction of the next table. "Pardon me, Alexandra," I said, as breezily as I could muster. "Must help out with the menu over here."

I couldn't argue with Alexandra because she actually had a point. We had indeed kept something from the group. You see, the Princess had mentioned in an email a few weeks previously that she was convinced that the coalman incident never happened. It was too late then to change the group's programme, so I had asked her if we could see the coal cellar of the palace anyway. Later we could try to ascertain the historical facts, but I felt that there was little value in expressing doubts about the event while the group was present at the palace. It was the typical tour operator's response. Let's complete the itinerary on the brochure, at all costs. The show must go on, even if the facts have to be bended to suit.

Before we had gone to the palace that morning, we had a reception with the Irish Ambassador in the striking residence at Villa Spada on the Janiculum Hill. Here, there were more speeches and everything was delayed by the fact that an Italian film crew showed up, hoping to interview various members of the group for a documentary that they were making. We were later than scheduled leaving the embassy and our journey to the Pamphilj Palace was made in great haste. Then the

Princess gave us a more elaborate reception than we had expected. To cap it all, an English war-hero, Harry Shindler, ninety-one year old veteran of the campaign that had liberated Italy, showed up and made a speech in recognition of O'Flaherty. As time wore on, I was conscious that we hadn't yet seen the cellar, but I was hesitant to mention it to the Princess because of the content of her email a few weeks previously. When I realized that it was already late, I simply announced to the group that it was time to leave the palace and head for Castelgandolfo.

As I shook Princess Gesine's hand at the exit, however, I couldn't let the issue go unmentioned.

"Princess, do you mind if I write to you about the coalman incident? I'd like to hear the reasons why you think it couldn't have happened."

"It's very simple," she said. "My grandfather had already left the palace to go into exile *before* the German occupation of Rome. We know this for a fact, down to the date he went into exile. So he couldn't have been still here at the time that O'Flaherty was being pursued around Rome by Kappler."

"Oh?" I replied, taken aback. "That's strange. I had always heard that your grandfather was one of the greatest benefactors of O'Flaherty's network. Is it possible that he returned to the palace after an initial period of exile?"

"Maybe it is possible," said the Princess slowly. Then she shrugged her shoulders. "Write when you get back to Ireland and we'll see if we can sort the question out!"

A couple of hours later, as we finished our lunch on Lake Albano, I had to admit to myself that Alexandra was right. We hadn't seen the cellar, not so much because of the hectic nature of the schedule, but because of the question mark that was standing ominously above O'Flaherty's alleged escape. If that question mark hadn't been there, we wouldn't have allowed the group to leave the building without seeing the cellar, no matter how late we were for lunch.

After lunch, we drove up to the village of Castelgandolfo above the lake. There we had over an hour to visit the town and admire the views. Then the moment came to leave for the airport. Many of our group were sitting out in front of the cafes in the town square.

"Time to head for the coach!" I announced. "Down the hill, turn right down the steps through the underpass and into the carpark! The coach will be on its way in five minutes!"

"Can't we have just a few more minutes, Kieran?" someone called plaintively.

"Sorry!" I replied. "We really need to go right away!"

There was the grating of chairs as people stood up and got their things together. I went inside the bar to see if any of our group was inside. The barman saluted me in a friendly manner. I didn't know his first name but our groups had been regular visitors here for well over ten years at this point, especially in the days that Popes John Paul II and Benedict used to hold events in the courtyard of the Papal residence. Once, this barman had told me the story of how he used to bring a particular ice cream (chestnut flavour) to John Paul in the palace above during the hot summer months.

"A quick cappuccino before you go?" he asked, well aware that this was my preferred beverage.

"Oh, that's nice of you, but I better not," I replied, looking longingly at the drink that he was handing at that moment to another customer, the dark veins of coffee rising into the smooth white foam of the milk. "Oh, what the heck, go on! I'll have a quick one, thank you!"

Less than a minute later I had the cappuccino cup up to my mouth and I could feel the foam forming a creamy moustache on my upper lip. To this day, my wife still has to wipe my mouth like a baby whenever we are leaving a café. Just at that moment Alexandra walked in to the bar.

"There you are! I went behind the church to have one last view of the lake and I just knew it was you that I spotted in here! The cheek! Standing there drinking coffee when you wouldn't even let me finish my glass of wine!"

I removed the cup quickly from my lips and almost spurted coffee all over her. "Alexandra! Oh no, it's not like that! I can get down that hill in less than two minutes and hop on the bus. But the group moves slowly, you see. It was time to get everyone moving. I'll easily catch up."

"I can get down the hill just as quickly as you and 'hop' on the bus! And I must have waited a good fifteen minutes for that glass of wine to be served. And here you are, cool as you like, still drinking coffee! The nerve of it!"

I sighed and put down my cup. I had been caught in the act and there was no point arguing. "Come on, let's get down to the coach." All craving for coffee had vanished. "I'll tell you what, Alexandra. The next O'Flaherty trip we do, we'll have that glass of wine together, and it's on me."

"And we better see the famous cellar next time!" she retorted. "If it exists at all!"

In late November, our trips for the year were finished and we were back at the office in Ireland. It was traditionally the quietest time of the year for us and there was time to read the recently-published third volume of Benedict's trilogy. The issue of biblical interpretation had become a bit of an issue for me. As a Catholic, I knew that there were two extremes to be avoided when reading Scripture: fundamentalism and liberalism. For example, in the Book of Judges, Sampson is described as killing one thousand men with the jawbone of a donkey. A fundamentalist reading of Scripture would assert that this description must be literally true, however historically implausible it might sound. Liberal readings of Scripture, on the other hand, tended to question the historical reliability of *any* narrative that contained elements that were deemed implausible from a scientific or historical point of view. Such elements included angelic appearances, healings, walking on water or foresight of future events.

It was clear that neither the fundamentalist approach nor the liberal approach was correct, but what criteria should be used to get at the historical facts beneath any given description of events? We had protestant friends who took the Bible literally. For them, if Genesis described the creation of the world in six days, then that meant that the world was created in literally six days. Being Catholic, I had no problem accepting that texts like these from the Old Testament had a deeper significance than their literal meaning. The issue of interpretation became more critical, however, when we turned to the Gospels. When Jesus is described as healing lepers, the blind and the deaf, are the Evangelists really describing events that originally had a spiritual meaning rather than a physical one? In other words, was the healing of a leper really a way of saying that he purified someone's heart? Was the cure of the deaf and blind really an opening of people's ears and eyes to the truth? The problem is, if *some* of Scripture is to be read in a spiritual or non-literal sense, how do we know where to draw the line?

From reading Pope Benedict's books, it was clear that he too was concerned about where this line would eventually be drawn. The historical-critical methodology tended to assume that the supernatural elements of the Gospel narrative (the healings, walking on water, the transfiguration) were additions designed to foster faith in his divinity. Stripped of these miraculous elements, Christ could be made to take on the appearance of an anti-Roman revolutionary or a moral preacher. As

Benedict pointed out, however, these reconstructions of the "real" Christ made him staggeringly banal and were probably more representative of their authors and their ideals than of the historical Jesus.

As I was reading Benedict's book, a nagging question recurred in my mind: were the Evangelists really willing to *alter* details in Jesus' life in order to further their theological purposes? For example, some very prominent biblical scholars were arguing that the accounts of the birth of Christ in Luke and Matthew were not simply different but irreconcilable. Luke had his particular purposes, and Matthew had his, which led them to shape the stories according to their own interests. Perhaps what was most disconcerting for me was that the same scholars did not seem at all bothered about this alleged manipulation of facts. What really mattered, they declared, were the spiritual truths that the Gospels wished to present.

When I mentioned to a friend that I was troubled by this attitude on the part of biblical scholars, he wondered aloud if my real problem was some sort of underlying insecurity. He had no problem with the claim that the Gospel writers moulded the facts to suit their narrative because, when all was said and done, he believed that what the narrative was pointing to was essentially accurate. "It doesn't matter if Jesus never walked on water during his earthly life!" he said. "He is risen now and could walk on water if he wanted to! That is all we need to believe! If the Evangelists included a little bit of 'mythology' here and there in their accounts, what's the problem? They were pointing to higher truths."

This conversation did nothing to help ease my "insecurity." It didn't seem right to claim that details were misrepresented by the Evangelists for higher purposes, even if I could accept that there are higher truths than factual ones. Was it too much to expect of the Evangelists that they should do their best to stick to the truth when they tell the story of the God of truth?

At the same time, there were much more mundane issues that had to be dealt with in the office. As we entered December, Laura was becoming very busy taking bookings for the following year and I had begun arranging the itineraries. As well as that, I knew that sooner or later we would be involved in the organisation of another O'Flaherty trip to Rome and therefore we would have to confront the question of the truth of the coalman story. We could hardly include a visit to the cellar if we thought the entire event was a fabrication, could we?

To get some advice, I phoned Father Pat Horgan in Kerry. Father Pat was on the committee of the O'Flaherty Memorial Society and was a rock of common sense. He had come on a parish pilgrimage to Italy with us many years previously and it was thanks to him that the O'Flaherty Society used us to organise their trips to Rome.

I explained to him Princess Gesine's doubts about the historical basis of the famous escape. "We've already been to the palace," I said to Father Pat. "Maybe for the next trip we should just do something different and avoid the whole coalman controversy?"

"If the incident really didn't happen, then you would be right to avoid it," he replied. "There are enough genuine events from the Monsignor's life that show us his heroic character. We don't need myths to tell his story."

The reference to "myths" reminded me of the debate about the Gospels. After a moment's hesitation, I mentioned to Father Pat that I had been grappling with the question of whether the Evangelists had included mythical elements in order to emphasize higher truths.

"This kind of discussion has been going on for decades now," Father Pat said with a sigh. "Everything is being rewritten by those who reject the traditional narratives about history and religion. It seems to me though that the biblical revisionists lack *faith* in Jesus. If he really was the Son of God, completely free from sin, full of virtue, in intimate relationship with the Father, then his life would already have been remarkable in certain ways, even if hidden. The Evangelists wouldn't have needed to make up their own stories in order to paint a particular image of Jesus. The truth would have been enough by itself."

Father Pat paused before going on. "You know, the old Latin Creed said it very starkly: *'et incarnatus est'* – *he became flesh*. If a biblical scholar doesn't really believe that Jesus is God, then he will obviously treat miracle stories and prophecies with suspicion."

It was a relief to hear someone affirm the reliability of the Gospels. But before finishing the call, I brought the topic of conversation back to O'Flaherty and remarked that maybe our next trip should not include the Pamphilj Palace.

"Oh, no, that's not what I meant." Father Pat replied in his usual quiet tone. "If the story weren't true, then it should be avoided. But, given what we know of the Monsignor, it *could* very well be true, and in that case a visit to the cellar would be great for the group. Maybe you could reconsider the evidence? And if you manage to prove it really happened, then you'll strike a blow against those pesky revisionists who doubt every traditional narrative!"

That was encouragement enough for me. The same day, I wrote to Princess Gesine to take up once again our debate. She had two reasons, it turned out, for believing that the coalman story was fictional. The first she had mentioned before and it seemed the most decisive. The Germans occupied Rome in September 1943, and the coalman incident was supposed to have happened soon afterwards during the oncoming winter. But her grandfather, according to the historical records, had already been exiled from Rome more than three years earlier. The order to go into exile came from Mussolini on August 13th 1940. Prince Filippo had long resisted fascism and had refused to fly the swastika above his palace, located right at the centre of the city, when Hitler visited Rome in 1938. His forced departure from Rome was only a matter of time. In 1939 he endangered his own position further by courageously writing a forthright letter to the king demanding that Italy not enter into a war pact with the Nazis.

The second reason Gesine had for doubting the coalman story was more personal. The film, ***The Scarlet and the Black***, had been released in the 1980s and she watched it with her mother, Orietta. When the coalman scene ended, she recalls her mother remarking, "It didn't happen that way." Orietta spoke rarely about wartime events and didn't elaborate further, but Gesine had taken this comment as a negative appraisal of the entire factuality of the incident. In an email to us she said that she believed the coalman story to be a fictional elaboration of other events that happened at the palace which did not involve O'Flaherty, including a search by the authorities for her grandfather that occurred during the war. On that occasion Prince Filippo had escaped by hiding in a secret room. Gesine wondered aloud in her email if the makers of the film had used a bit of poetic licence for dramatic purposes.

This was where my scant knowledge of the English language material on O'Flaherty's life came in handy. I was aware that the coalman story had been recounted in J.P. Gallagher's original book, ***The Scarlet and the Black***, and this surely preceded the film by many years. I consulted my copy to find that it had been originally published in 1967. But where did Gallagher get his information? In the preface of the book, he states that O'Flaherty himself refused to speak about his wartime exploits, so the author had to rely on interviews with people who knew the Kerryman in the different periods of his life.

Among the works that Gallagher consulted was Major Sam Derry's book, ***The Rome Escape Line***, published in 1960 when O'Flaherty was still alive. Derry had been given refuge in O'Flaherty's room in the Teutonic College during his early days in Rome. He and the Monsignor ran the Escape Line together and trusted each other implicitly. If the coalman incident were true, then Sam Derry would have known of it and, surely, would not have omitted it from his book, but it was out of print for many years.

I had just read the email from the Princess and wanted to reply to her efficiently, presenting her with as many facts as could be mustered about the coalman story predating the release of the film. But how would I get my hands on a copy of Sam Derry's book? With a thrill I discovered that there was an old version that could be read online in full.

A passage in the preface by the author was highly revealing: "This book was written unbeknown to Monsignor Hugh O'Flaherty, C.B.E., one of the finest men it has been my privilege ever to meet. Had it not been for this gallant gentleman, there would have been no Rome Escape Organisation. I sincerely trust that nothing I have written will cause him any pain or embarrassment."

It was clear from this that Sam Derry was not in the business of perpetuating myths about the Irishman. O'Flaherty was still alive at the time of publication and

Derry didn't want to say anything that might cause the Monsignor embarrassment. If he *did* go on to mention the coalman incident, then surely it was grounded in historical fact.

The first half of the book made gripping reading. It chronicled the adventures of Sam Derry as an escaped prisoner of war who was eventually secreted into the Vatican hidden under a pile of cabbages and asked to coordinate the work of the Escape Line. On the very first evening, Derry had dinner with D'Arcy Osborne, the British Minister to the Holy See. During that meal, Osborne told Derry the full story of O'Flaherty's organisation up to that moment in time. This included the fact that Prince Filippo Pamphilj was helping with the funding of the organisation and that O'Flaherty had made his escape out of the palace on one occasion dressed as a coalman while the building was surrounded by the SS.

There it was! Recounted to Sam Derry by none less that Sir Francis D'Arcy Osborne, British Minister to the Vatican. And the details of the story reveal that Osborne was telling it only a few weeks after it had happened. Derry does not give precise dates in his book for his arrival in Rome, but from his references to the sequence of events prior to his arrival in the eternal city, it must have been around mid-November 1943. The coalman incident is likely to have happened in late October or early November, the natural period for the delivery of the winter coal supply in Rome. To this day, mid-November is the traditional date for the first lighting of central heating systems in Rome's apartment blocks. Therefore, it seems likely that when D'Arcy Osborne recounted the coalman story to Sam Derry on his first night in Rome in November of 1943, it had only just happened in the preceding weeks.

The big question remained: if the Princess was correct in her belief that Prince Filippo was exiled from his palace in August of 1940, then how could O'Flaherty have met him there in 1943? Back at the office in Ireland we had few resources as far as the history of the war in Rome was concerned. However, I found the answer in an online Italian biographical dictionary (***Dizionario Biografico degli Italiani***). This work specifies that the Prince was exiled to Tuscany in August of 1940, but, following an appeal by the Vatican, he was permitted to return to the palace fourteen months later. Sometime in late 1943, he fled the palace again and went into hiding in the Trastevere district of the city.

In the meantime, completely independently, we received an email from Princess Gesine, who had been checking the family archives to see if her grandparents had come back to Palazzo Doria after their exile in Tuscany and before the end of the war. She confirmed that she had found documentary evidence that her grandparents and her mother DID live in Palazzo Doria after returning to Rome from exile in Arezzo! She was not sure of the exact date when they were forced to go into hiding again, but it was certainly after the German occupation of Rome in September 1943. So there was a period between September and November of that year when the prince was in his palace. This meant, she realised now, that the coalman story could well have happened.

We couldn't have asked for more. Now we had reliable testimony (Derry and Osborne) as well as opportunity (the fact that the Prince was indeed living in the palace in late 1943 at the time of the German occupation). There was just one last thing that needed to be checked: was coal used to heat the palace in those years? If coal was not used, then the entire story could not be true to begin with.

"Can you check to see if coal was used to heat Palazzo Doria during the war years?" we asked the Princess by email. The following day she replied to say that coal was indeed used to heat the building and that it was stored in the cellar. We no longer had any reason to doubt the historical character of the coalman story! Princess Gesine added that she was delighted to be able to help clarify the issue.

We still wondered why Orietta had commented to Gesine, "It didn't happen that way," after having watched the film version. Maybe there were elements of the scene in the film that were at odds with reality? It would be a full two years before we would be in a position to answer that question better.

Coming up to that Christmas of 2012, the historical reliability of the coalman incident seemed to be finally established. For our next O'Flaherty trip to Rome, we could place a visit to the cellar at the top of the agenda without scruples. It was personally pleasing to have the matter settled. It is natural to want your heroes to succeed when all the odds are against them. Sometimes, though, I recalled my conversation with Father Pat and realised that my bigger grievance was not with those who denied the reliability of the O'Flaherty story; rather, I had a bone to pick with those who took a revisionist view on the traditional narrative concerning Christ. And my concern that scholars were undermining the truth of the Gospels was not going to be alleviated anytime soon.

Discussions with our protestant friends did not help the matter. For them, the issue was starkly simple: the Bible is inspired by God and every word must be taken as truth in the literal sense. But if this uncomplicated principle brought them solace, for me it did no good at all. Sampson could hardly have killed one thousand men in the manner described in the Book of Judges. Noah could not have taken representatives of every animal species onto his ark. The world manifestly was not made in six days, even though the Lord could have done so if he wished.

Our discussions would go something like this. I would say that biblical scholarship indicates that a significant portion of the Old Testament was written down during the Babylonian Exile of the sixth century B.C. and later. This means that the texts often describe happenings that occurred many centuries previously. Thus, they are not written by eye-witnesses and are so far removed from the events that they are liable to be filled with historical inaccuracies. The truths contained in the books, however, are deeper than historical truths. For example, a description in the Book of Kings of an event from King David's life may not have the factual details exactly right, but they still depict King David – his faithfulness to the Lord, his courage, his faults, his repentance - in a truthful manner. It is also likely that exaggeration was considered by the biblical writers to be an acceptable technique for emphasizing a spiritual point.

The response from our protestant friends would always take the same form. If Scripture is indeed divinely inspired, then the Holy Spirit would see to it that the texts are free from factual errors. They felt that to cast any aspersions on the historical accuracy of the Bible was an act of irreverence towards these sacred texts. In addition, they pointed out the danger of expressing scepticism about the factual underpinning of any part of Scripture. If you begin to doubt the veracity of some biblical stories, where do you stop? I had to admit that I shared some of these concerns. Surely, though, the historical accuracy of the Genesis creation account (for example) is a different question to the accuracy of the Gospels regarding the life of Jesus?

The new pilgrimage season began and the election of Pope Francis raised the profile of the eternal city once again. In August 2013, we had a parish group in Rome on pilgrimage. One of the Masses was in St Peter's basilica at the altar of St Jerome, the great Doctor of the Church who had translated the Bible into Latin in the fourth century. On account of the fact that we were at the altar of the Church's greatest biblical scholar, the priest's homily was on a biblical theme - the historical reliability of the Gospel accounts of the life of Jesus. I groaned inwardly as the homily took a predictable direction: scholarship - the priest was saying - indicates that the Gospels are not simply historical narratives written by eyewitnesses; rather, they have a different literary form altogether; they were written by particular communities with particular interests; the way they cast the stories about Jesus reflected those interests; if we wish to benefit from reading the Gospels, then we need to get in touch with their original moral, religious or pedagogic intentions, and not be too hung up on worrying about the historical basis of the accounts. The priest then gave the example of the resurrection narratives: whether or not these narratives were ever intended to refer to historical facts is to miss the main point, which is a deeper spiritual reality – the new life without sin. As a way of illustrating his point, the priest mentioned that the chronology of the passion in the synoptic Gospels (Matthew, Mark and Luke) contradicts the chronology in John. The synoptic authors wanted to emphasize that the Last Supper Meal on Holy Thursday coincided with the Passover, whilst John was more preoccupied with showing that the death of Jesus on Good Friday coincided with the slaughter of the lambs at the Temple for the *coming* Passover. Both chronologies cannot be right: the Passover was *either* Friday or Saturday. This proved, he asserted, that the Evangelists had no problem moulding the "facts" to suit their own purposes.

As we trudged out of St Peter's basilica - the shrine to the rock of our faith – I felt that what I had just listened to, no matter how well-intentioned, undermined the faith because it undercut the historical credibility of the Gospels. I recalled the warnings expressed by our protestant friends. If we allow that some important details in Scripture are pious fictions intended to motivate a particular response, then how can we be sure that *any* of the narratives in the New Testament are true? Did Jesus heal the sick? Did he multiply the loaves and fishes? Did the Holy Spirit really take on the appearance of tongues of fire, or is this description just a way of referring to the burning zeal that consumed the Apostles?

When the pilgrimage was over, I took down the second volume of Pope Benedict's book and looked again at his explanation of the discrepancies in the chronology of the passion accounts. For the Jews, the Passover feast begins when the sun sets the previous evening. The meal then is eaten shortly afterwards. In the chronology of Matthew, Mark and Luke, the Passover is described as falling on Friday, which meant that the ritual meal was eaten after the sun had set on Thursday. In the night between Thursday and Friday, Jesus is arrested. On Friday morning he is condemned by Pilate and dies on the cross that afternoon at the ninth hour (3pm by our reckoning).

John's Gospel agrees that the Last Supper occurred on Thursday evening, that Jesus was arrested afterwards, condemned the following morning, and then died on Friday afternoon. In all of these details, John concurs with the synoptic Gospels. However, there is a major discrepancy. For John, the Passover falls on *Saturday*, not Friday. The Last Supper consumed with the apostles on Thursday evening is *not* a normal Passover meal. When Jesus dies on Friday afternoon, the timing of his death coincides with the killing of the sacrificial lambs at the Temple in readiness for *that* evening's meal.

Pope Benedict pointed out that many scholars have seen in this neat "coincidence" the theological motivation for why John's account differs to the other Gospels. John wished to emphasize that Jesus is the new Passover lamb, so he modified the chronology of the feast, claiming that the Passover fell on Saturday, thus making Jesus' death on Friday coincide with the sacrifice of the lambs at the Temple in readiness for the upcoming feast.

As I read, I had that familiar sinking feeling with regard to biblical scholarship. Are we really to believe that an Evangelist would introduce a pious fiction – that the lambs at the Temple were sacrificed at the exact same hour as Jesus' death – in order to make a theological point? Happily, after pointing out that this is the opinion of many scholars, the pope then gave a true masterclass in how to approach difficulties such as these. Even if scholars are inclined to be suspicious of John's theological interests, Benedict showed that his account of the passion is actually the most historically convincing of all the Gospels.

According to the synoptics (Matthew, Mark and Luke), the Jewish religious leaders spent Thursday night and Friday morning engaged in activities that were absolutely forbidden for them on the Passover (a Jewish trial for blasphemy, a Roman court proceedings, etc.). Given the obsession of the pharisees with religious minutiae – which is well-attested in both biblical and non-biblical literature - all of this is extremely improbable, to say the least. John's chronology, by contrast, does not suffer from this incongruity because for him the Passover hasn't begun yet. In addition, he includes the very plausible detail that the chief priests refused to enter Pilate's building on Friday morning because it would make them ritually impure for the Passover meal that *still* had to be eaten after sundown that evening.

If we accept, then, that John has the correct chronology (the Passover beginning on *Friday* evening after dark), how do we reconcile the fact that the synoptic Gospels describe the Last Supper meal on *Thursday* as a Passover meal? After mentioning various attempts to resolve this discrepancy, Benedict summarized the best solution he had so far found. Jesus knew that he was about to die and that the meal on Thursday would be his final one with the disciples before his death. Indeed, the Last Supper discourses from *all* four Gospels make it clear that Jesus knew that this meal would be his last. Thus, he would not be around to eat the Passover on Friday because he was about to *become* the Passover lamb himself on that day. So, he invited his disciples to share this last meal with him, a meal with a unique significance in which he refers to the bread and cup as his body and blood given in sacrifice for them. This Last Supper meal, then, becomes what will soon be called the "Passover of the Lord." It did not coincide exactly with the Jewish eating of the Passover meal, but, as Pope Benedict pointed out, the distinctive element in this meal was that it brought the ancient meaning of the Passover to its fullest realisation.

I had read this passage the year before without paying much heed to it, but it now seemed like a good remedy for the sceptical homily I had heard in St Peter's a couple of days previously. Some scholars looked on the Gospel writers as being more interested in making theological points than in recounting the historical facts. Discrepancies between the Gospels lead people to scepticism as to their historical underpinning. Are we really to believe that John would willingly introduce a fairly dramatic disagreement with the synoptic Gospels in order to make a theological point – that Jesus died at the same time as the Temple lambs – a point that he *would have known* was actually a pious fiction? Would John have willingly contradicted the synoptics in order to pursue his own theological agenda?

The solution presented by Pope Benedict was much more convincing. John sticks to his chronology because he is truthful and that is *how things actually happened*. He has not made history subservient to theology but has simply presented history and theology together. In fact, only his chronology makes possible the very proceedings that are chronicled in the synoptics (the trials during Thursday night and Friday morning). Does this mean that the other three Evangelists deliberately misrepresented the Last Supper meal as being on the Passover? No, there is no need to assume that the writers of the synoptics are deliberately manipulating the facts. It is possible that in the decades after the resurrection and before the eventual writing of the synoptic Gospels, there may have been some dimming of the memory that the Thursday meal actually occurred a day ahead of the Jewish Passover. After all, the meal that Jesus ate with his disciples on Thursday was quickly understood by the early Church to be the "Passover of the Lord." This meal, even if it was not exactly on the day of the Jewish feast, was perceived clearly to be the bringing to completion of the Passover. Thus, the early Church became accustomed right from the start of considering the Last Supper as the genuine Passover, for that is what it was. It is easy to see then how the synoptic writers could have presented it as such.

I was struck by the contrast between Benedict's approach to Scripture and that advocated by these biblical scholars. When the scholars see a discrepancy between different accounts, they come to a sceptical conclusion: one of the accounts *must* be non-factual and *deliberately* so because of vested theological interests. Benedict, by contrast, trusts the honesty of the Evangelists and tries to discern how sincere writers seeking to abide by the truth could have come up with divergent accounts. The result is a natural and harmonious interpretation of Scripture which does not undermine its historical content. On the contrary, the historical essence beneath the narrative – in this case the providential coincidence that Christ died along with the sacrificial lambs – comes more clearly into relief.

When I discussed this with Laura, we got onto the wider subject of biblical interpretation and she made a telling point. The fact that *some* books of the Bible are lacking in historical accuracy is not a reason for doubting the historical accuracy of the Gospels. Many of the Old Testament books were not written by eye-witnesses to their events but centuries later. The precise details of those stories are often not crucial to their spiritual relevance. The author of the work is going to get some of the details wrong, possibly because decades of oral transmission altered or exaggerated the account, as, for example, in the story of Sampson killing one thousand men. This imprecision is not a reason for dismissing the spiritual value of the Book of Judges. We still trust that the author has been faithful to the truth that he has received and we believe him to be divinely inspired. The Gospels, by contrast, were written by *eyewitnesses*, or as a result of the testimony of eyewitnesses. We trust that the Evangelists did their best to be faithful to the truth, within the limits that confronted them. Of course, they still had the freedom to select, arrange and present the stories in a particular light, as evidenced by Matthew's concern to show that Christ is the fulfilment of the Old Testament prophecies, or Luke's concern with highlighting the central role of women and the importance of prayer. But to claim that the Evangelists modified or invented "facts" in order to further their own higher motives is a very grave charge indeed. It undermines the historical credibility of the Gospels and consequently damages the central claim of the Christian faith - that the Son of God became incarnate at a particular time and place and sacrificed himself for us.

In the first week of November 2014, the O'Flaherty Memorial Society in Killarney made another visit to Rome. By this time, I was no longer duly preoccupied by the machinations of biblical scholarship. For me, Benedict's balanced response had provided a lasting antidote. We once again contacted Princess Gesine to ask if we could visit the coal cellar. She replied with the same gracious welcome as always. We could visit the palace and see the cellar, but she herself would be out of Rome with her children on account of the mid-term school break. A member of her personal staff would assist us in organising the visit.

In our correspondence with this member of staff, we specified that we only wished to visit the cellar, and that Laura and I would call to the palace ahead of the group in order to see the spot ourselves. In August, we had some free time and made an appointment to see the cellar and give the place the once over.

We made our way down Via del Corso and into the main entrance of the Doria Pamphilj Gallery. When the ticket man phoned upstairs to say we had arrived, however, he was instructed to give us free admission to the art gallery because the staff member was busy at that moment. She would find us later in the gallery and take us directly to the cellar. Of course, Laura was delighted to be given the chance to visit this wonderful art gallery, including the famous painting by Velasquez, for she had not been with the group on the previous visit, but for me it evoked the frustrating situation of two years ago when we saw the gallery but failed to see the cellar.

After forty-five minutes in the gallery, I was getting edgy and approached a member of staff to remind them that we were still there waiting to be met. A further twenty minutes passed and then we were told to go back down to the ticket office where the staff member was waiting for us.

"Thank you for meeting us!" I said cheerily as I shook her hand.

The lady had a concerned look on her face. "I am sorry that you have had to wait so long," she said. "But I cannot take you to the cellar today. Some unexpected items of business have turned up today and I do not have time to accompany you."

"Oh? But we just need to see the cellar - even the entrance to it - and then we'll go," I replied. "If you point us towards it then we could probably even find it ourselves."

"I am sorry" the lady replied, shaking her head. "It is in a courtyard that is not open to the public, but there is no need to be concerned. When you come with the group, we will have someone here to take you."

As we exited the gallery, I exclaimed to Laura, "I don't believe we are EVER going to see it! O'Flaherty's difficulties in getting out of that cellar are nothing to our difficulties getting in!"

Three months later, on November 3rd, I led the O'Flaherty group with some trepidation down Via del Corso. My nemesis, Alexandra, had declined to travel with the group. When we spoke on the phone, she said that she had "seen more than enough last time."

When you are with a group of this sort in Rome, it is hard not to feel every yard of cobblestone with them. The Italian capital is an inhospitable place for private coaches. We were obliged to disembark at the nearest official dropping-off point behind Teatro Marcello and walk into Piazza Venezia, crossing chaotic traffic on no less than three occasions, then down a narrow sidewalk to the Pamphilj Palace, about eight hundred metres in total, not a huge distance, but significant for those members of the group who were elderly or who had mobility issues. And to do this not knowing if we were going to see anything at all or not! Maybe we would have to turn on our heels and return to the coach if the right member of staff was not available to take us in?

Once again, the man in the ticket office told us to wait, but within a minute a member of staff, who introduced himself as Mario, appeared from inside to greet us. With a wide smile, Mario told us that he had worked for the Doria Pamphilj family for fifty-three years. Then he asked, "*Volete vedere la cantina da dove è scappato il prete irlandese?*" ("Do you want to see the basement from where the Irish priest made his escape?")

After all the obstacles before arriving at this moment, I was stunned by the matter-of-fact nature of Mario's statement. It was as if he and the other staff of the palace had been privy all along to facts that we outsiders had been labouring strenuously to clarify.

"Si!" I answered enthusiastically. He took us through a barrier into a much larger internal courtyard. Here we could see the windows of the cellar covered with a strong metal mesh. Concrete steps underneath a metal grille led down to the basement. So here it was! Mario described the event to us as if he were present there himself. "The Irish priest came up these steps and over to this entrance which leads directly into the piazza in front of the Collegio Romano, where Galileo studied and taught. The Germans were lined up there, but he just walked through them alongside the coal truck and out."

It struck me how different this courtyard was to one depicted in the film with Gregory Peck. In the film, the courtyard was much smaller and located immediately off the street. The entrance to the coal cellar in the film, in fact, stood just inside the main entrance to the palace. But the real coal cellar is much further away from the principal entrance to the palace and much less accessible from outside. This made perfect sense. The exit from the cellar as depicted in the film seemed too obvious as an escape route. If it had been as close to the main entrance as the film suggests, then the Germans would have put a proper guard on it long before

O'Flaherty had made his way down there. Orietta may have been referring to this when she said, "It didn't happen that way."

The group was given ample time by Mario to explore the courtyard. I asked Father Pat Horgan to pose with me for a photo in front of the entrance to the cellar. As things turned out, it would be his last trip with the O'Flaherty Society. In May 2016, the group would travel once again to Rome. The ever-enthusiastic Father Pat would be among the first people to book on the trip, but he cancelled later because of illness. Sadly, he died a few days after the group returned to Ireland. He had a profound appreciation for the O'Flaherty story and did much to preserve the memory of his fellow Kerryman.

By this point, we were both standing in the middle of the courtyard and looking at other members of the group peering down the steps into the basement. Father Pat gave a chuckle and said, "No wonder they say people from Kerry are a little strange!"

"Oh? Why do you say that?"

"Here we are looking down into a coal cellar that no-one has paid attention to in years!"

"Well, you *could* describe it that way," I replied, feeling a little bit touchy. After all, this business of the coal cellar had been a bee in my bonnet for quite some time now.

"While the inhabitants of Kerry are gazing down here," Father Pat went on, "the rest of the visitors to this city are over in the Vatican looking down at St Peter's bones!"

Chapter Four
The Bones of St Peter

"We can't get too excited about the to-do in Rome occasioned by the Pope's announcement ... We make no bones about the fact that we are perverse enough - or Protestant enough - to believe that no bones, not even a saint's, are sacred. If there is a connection between bone veneration and the gospel, we have yet to find it."
<u>**The Christian Century**</u>, 10 July 1968

We had a typical morning's itinerary planned for the eastern side of Rome's historic centre. The coach would drop us at the end of Via Merulana, the tree-lined thoroughfare connecting the Cathedral of Rome (St John Lateran) to the most important Marian church in the city (St Mary Major). From here, we would cross the road and visit the ancient church of Santa Prassede - its unobtrusive side door almost unnoticeable down a short alleyway - then celebrate Mass in St Mary Major, before boarding the coach again and visiting the relics of the Passion of Christ in the Basilica of the Holy Cross in Jerusalem a little over a mile away.

The group had only arrived the previous night and there wasn't much opportunity to get to know them. We had eaten a light dinner in a restaurant in Fiumicino village not far from the airport and then driven to the hotel close to the Vatican. Check-in had been so quick and efficient that I had managed to save myself a taxi fare and caught the last metro home. This morning, I arrived at the hotel while the group was having breakfast and parked myself with a cappuccino and croissant in front of the tired-looking spiritual director of the group, a priest in his early sixties.

For me, the first morning with a group was always the hardest. I would feel weighed down with bashfulness, an introvert doing an extrovert's job, reluctant to try to get to know an entire group of fifty people again. It was guaranteed that among them there would be one or two difficult people to manage, and I was not looking forward to the prospect. This "first-morning slump" was a crippling lethargy that invariably afflicted me for the first few hours of yet another tour of Rome.

As the days went on and I got to know the group better, the motivation to show the wonders of Rome would return, I knew, but this knowledge never had any effect on the first-morning slump. Yet, there could be little doubt that part of my job description was to present a chirpy and friendly face to the group, especially at the start of the tour. I am neither chirpy nor friendly by nature, and the results of my efforts have probably been fairly grotesque at times, but I knew that I had little alternative.

"Have a good night's sleep?" I asked Father Michael in my chirpiest voice as I nibbled into the croissant.

"Don't mention sleep!" he growled back. "That is the noisiest hotel room I have ever been in! As for the bed - narrow, hard and lumpy!"

I gulped down some coffee, trying to think of a way of changing the subject.

"We have a nice programme this morning," I offered, making my best effort at an upbeat tone. "The mosaics in Santa Prassede are really impressive, and it has that connection with St Peter."

"Actually, I know this church quite well," Father Michael replied as he sipped his coffee, his demeanour suddenly brightening. "If you like, I could give the description of the mosaics in the apse."

"Great!" I said. "If you do that, then I can say a word about the artwork in St Zeno's little chapel and tell them about the pillar at which Jesus was scourged."

"The pillar? Oh no, I wouldn't bother saying much about that. Rome is full of spurious relics. I wouldn't bother the group with anything so dodgy."

"It could be the genuine column where Jesus was scourged, though, might it not?"

Father Michael scoffed. "Fat chance! Jesus scourged at an ornamental pillar made of fancy marble! There are multiple columns in different places that all claim to be the original. The Gospels don't even say that Jesus was scourged at a pillar."

"Well, all right," I said, a little doubtfully, because I had seen how pilgrims showed great interest in this column, but I quickly tried to put on a cheerful air. "I suppose we will have plenty to talk about with the mosaics. And I can tell the group the story of how Santa Prassede mopped up the blood of the early martyrs and conserved it under the floor of what eventually became the church."

The priest scoffed again. "Mopped up the blood! We don't know if Prassede even existed! I wouldn't mention that stuff to them at all! And, anyway, once a focus is placed on relics, people fail to appreciate the real cultural significance of these sites. I've seen it before with pilgrim groups. One mention of a relic and they gather around it like bees around honey. The meaning of the mosaics will go completely over their heads."

My efforts at chirpy conversation were not having such a good response, but I knew what he was talking about. Tombs of saints, relics, and miracle stories tended to be major sources of fascination for pilgrims. Every time I had taken a group into Santa Prassede, the column and the roundel over the blood always became the central hubs of the tour. Maybe it would be good to do it Father Michael's way this time and focus on the mosaics?

An hour or so later, we had disembarked from the coach and were about to cross Via Merulana to enter the church of Santa Prassede. The group leader, Sheila, was walking beside me. Sheila was the head of a prayer group in her village and had led pilgrimages to many destinations in Europe. I had met her by chance in St Peter's Square the previous year and she had contacted our office afterwards to organise this year's pilgrimage.

"All the times I have been to Rome and I have never been in Santa Prassede before," she was saying to me. "When you put it on the programme and mentioned that we could see the column of the flagellation of Jesus, I was delighted."

Inwardly I groaned. Why did I have to mention the *column* in the brochure? Couldn't I have just stuck to the mosaics? To Sheila, though, I tried to be more upbeat. "Oh yes, the column of the flagellation," I repeated. "And the programme would also have mentioned the wonderful mosaics, right?"

"I don't remember reading anything about mosaics," Sheila replied.

"Maybe I forgot to mention them," I said in a fake hearty voice. "Actually, there's so much to see in this church that people might not notice the column at all! Wait until you see the art!"

Sheila gave a chuckle. "I don't think my bunch will be too interested in art!" she said. "This is a prayer group, not an art class. The main thing they'll want to see is that column, take my word for it."

I started mumbling something about how very special *these* particular mosaics were, but we had already arrived at the side entrance of the church and Father Michael was leading the group in. We gathered in the central nave, members of the group sitting to the right and left while Father Michael gave his explanation in front of the altar. I remained in the central aisle about three quarters way back, standing by the large porphyry roundel marking the site of a well into which (according to legend) Santa Prassede poured the blood of martyrs which she had sponged up.

I had to admit that Father Michael did a fine job describing the mosaics in the apse and on the triumphal arch. Jesus, he told us, is standing among the clouds, being conferred with the wreath of victory by God the Father. Christ's victory gives the ultimate meaning to the death of all the martyrs. On either side of Jesus, saints Peter and Paul are standing, holding their arms round the shoulders of saints Prassede and Pudentiana, who tradition describes as sisters. Father Michael pointed out that we can't know for certain if these ladies ever really existed. The two women have red shoes instead of jewelled ones, indicating their status as princesses, whereas the title of "Empress" belongs to Our Lady. To the left, Pope Paschal is seen holding a model of the church. The mosaic was certainly done during the time of Paschal (died in 824) since he has a square halo (or "nimbus"), indicating that he was still alive when it was made.

After his talk, Father Michael told the group that I would shortly be taking them over to a side chapel to see the wonderful mosaics there. Beforehand, did anyone have any questions? I saw Sheila raising her hand and my heart sank. There could be little doubt about what was coming next. "Where's the column of the flagellation? Kieran said on the brochure that it was in this church somewhere."

Father Michael gave an irritated look in my direction and soon most members of the group had swivelled around in their seats to face me.

"Oh, yes, the column," I said in a bogus cheery tone. "Actually, it's over there on the right, in St Zeno's chapel, which has a *most* remarkable set of mosaics that I wanted to tell you all about."

By this point, Sheila was already on her feet and was heading over to the chapel. The group rose *en masse* and followed her. Some began to cram into the tiny chapel to see the column whilst others began to browse in the little religious gift stall that was set up nearby. I was standing helpless behind the teeming mass of pilgrims when Father Michael arrived over. He glared at me. "You can just forget about describing those mosaics now!" he said. "All they'll want to see is that column! They'll touch it, they'll rub it, they'll photograph it. Above their heads is one of the richest cultural experiences in Rome and they're completely taken with a fake column! I'm out of here! When you're done, I'll see you all over at St Mary Major!"

With that, Father Michael stormed out of the church. I spent the next fifteen minutes trying to shoo the milling pilgrims towards the exit. They had begun quite a frenzy of buying now at the souvenir stall, and the custodian was beaming with satisfaction as he served them. My stress-levels had not abated an hour and a half later when we reached the Basilica of the Holy Cross. It was already 11.20am and the church was due to close from 12 to 3pm, as is the case with many churches in Rome. Our main mission here was to view the relics of the passion which had been collected by St Helen in Jerusalem in the early fourth century, taken back to

Rome and set up here in her principal residence. The title of the basilica is that of the "Holy Cross in Jerusalem" because of the fact that a shipload of clay from Mount Calvary was taken back to Rome and sprinkled on the ground before erecting a custom-built chapel to house the relics.

I felt that it was essential to show the group the paintings in the sanctuary area which describe how St Helen found the relics of the passion, but I was sure that if I asked Father Michael's opinion, he would try to dissuade me, so I studiously avoided him on the walk between the coach stop and the basilica entrance. Time was at a premium, and I marched the group to the front of the church and gave a short description of the beautiful fifteenth century frescos in the apse. These depict St Helen's excavations on Mount Calvary and the identification of the true cross by the fact that a sick person was healed upon touching it.

As I spoke, Father Michael stood at the back of the group with his head down. After the explanation, we trooped out the side door to the left and up the steep steps into the area where the relics of the Passion are kept. This was once the sacristy but was converted into a chapel in order to permit daily veneration of the relics. Only a few people can fit in front of the display case, so I gave a brief description of what there was to be seen and allowed the group to file by in their own time. They viewed the portion of the cross, the nails, the thorn from the crown placed on Christ's head and the inscription written by Pilate. I felt sure that Father Michael doubted the authenticity of all of these relics and this sapped my confidence. My description of the relics lacked any real conviction or enthusiasm.

When everyone had viewed the relics, we lumbered back down the steps towards the basilica. It was 11.50am and the church was about to close. In fact, I could hear the custodian jangling keys near the door as he waited for us. Italy is not always the most punctual of places for many things, but churches close very much on time. I was at the head of the group in the corridor that leads from the chapel of the relics, just about to turn back into the basilica. In front of us, in a separate area at the end of the corridor, was a tomb I knew well, that of six year-old Antonietta Meo. I hesitated. The group should really be told the story of this heroic little girl who died in 1937. Laura's parents lived not far from here and we always took our children and their cousins to visit this tomb at some point every summer. There could be no doubt that the story of Antonietta would interest the group, but I also knew that the custodian would begin grumbling if we didn't leave soon.

On impulse, I turned around and addressed the group. "Come on into this little museum for a moment, everyone! There is something here you really ought to see!"

It didn't take long to summarize the life of Antonietta Meo. She suffered from bone cancer and had a leg amputated at the age of five, all of which she accepted with cheerfulness and serenity. During her years of illness, Antonietta dictated or wrote more than a hundred letters to Jesus and Mary. They display a mature spirituality that is remarkable for her age. I quoted a portion of one of these letters from a prayer card that I picked up in the shrine. "I want to abandon myself in your arms. Do with me what you want. Help me with your grace. You help me, since without your grace, I am nothing."

Shortly before she died, Antonietta finished her last letter to Jesus with the words, "Your little girl sends you a lot of kisses." On the day of her death, she told her mother, "In a few hours, I will die, but I will not suffer anymore, and you shouldn't cry." After the child's death, her mother had a vision of Antonietta in a glorified state that confirmed that the little girl was now in paradise.

Around the room in which Antonietta's tomb is located, there are various exhibits, including some of her possessions, letters and toys. I walked over to Father Michael who was standing with Sheila and looking intently into one of the display cabinets.

"Had you heard of Antonietta Meo?" I asked.

"No!" he replied. "What an amazing child!" His demeanour had brightened up considerably.

"What a great model for young people!" Sheila chimed in.

By this point, the custodian was jangling his keys noisily at the entrance to the room and glaring crossly in my direction. I walked over to him with a new spring in my step. "We'll just be a moment!" I said brightly. "Our group is really taken by little Antonietta!"

He grunted and swivelled around, still rattling his keys as he headed for the main exit. As I waited for the group to follow, I was aware of a sudden sense of complete relaxation. My worries about appeasing the group leader and placating the spiritual director had all evaporated. Little Antonietta had lifted our spirits onto a higher plane.

That afternoon, the group had a couple of hours allocated to shopping and I was relatively free. Laura and the children were in Ireland so there was a chance for me to sit in the hotel lobby and reread my old copy of **The Bones of St Peter** by John Evangelist Walsh. The following day, we would be visiting the *scavi* – the archaeological area under St Peter's that came to light during the search in the 1940s for the apostle's bones.

Space restrictions under St Peter's Basilica mean that the *scavi* tour is reserved to small groups of about twelve to fifteen people at a time. Reservations must be made well in advance and attempts to book a place are often not successful. About thirty people in our group had signed up for the tour if it was available, and the list of names was sent to the *scavi* office a few months in advance. A week before the group arrived in Rome, we received a confirmation email with the group divided into two parts and assigned different entrance times during the course of the same morning. It was only then that we realised that Father Michael, Sheila and I would be assigned to the same slot since our names were together at the top of the list. In hindsight it would have been better if we had been in different groups, but we left the reservation as it was. The common wisdom in Rome in those days was to accept any *scavi* slot that you were lucky enough to get. Try modifying it and it could vanish like a puff of smoke.

Early the next morning, we left the hotel in good time and made our way to the left side of St Peter's square where the Swiss Guard allowed us access. Everyone seemed to be in a rather quiet and sombre mood. Was it my imagination or were Father Michael and Sheila keeping their distance from each other? Did the reconciliation achieved by Antonietta Meo the previous day have such a temporary duration? After presenting my letter to the lady in the kiosk, we gathered in the shadow of the imposing walls of St Peter's and awaited our guide. Ten minutes or so later, a smartly-dressed Italian of about fifty years of age arrived. He introduced himself as "Giacomo" and told us that he was looking forward to being our guide for the next hour and a half. I was a little surprised since my previous tours of the *scavi* had all been guided by American seminarians.

Giacomo informed us that we would be the first tour group to visit the site today. Without any further preamble, he instructed us to follow him as efficiently as possible. He entered through a small door on the side of the basilica and we found ourselves directly in the Vatican grottoes, the low-ceilinged area under the floor of the present basilica. The floor level here is almost that of the original church built by Constantine over Peter's tomb in the fourth century. In the fifteenth century, that church was demolished and the new St Peter's was built with its present floor at a higher level. From that time onwards, the area under the new floor came to be called the "Vatican grottoes." It contained the tombs of some popes (and others) and access to the area beneath the high altar which marked the believed site of the tomb of St Peter.

Standing in this low-ceilinged area just inside the entrance to the grottoes, Giacomo gathered us around the top of a narrow staircase that descended to a still lower level. As he spoke, he was keeping a rather anxious eye on the closed door at the bottom of the stairs.

"In the first century, the area to the left of St Peter's Basilica, where you had been standing just now, was the site of a Roman circus, usually called the Circus of Nero. St Peter was killed at the centre of this arena during a persecution. According to tradition, he asked to be crucified upside down, since he considered himself unworthy to die as Jesus did. His executioners complied. Afterwards, his body was recovered by his followers and buried in the cemetery on the slope of the hill which ran down towards the circus.

"The circus was there," Giacomo said, indicating the area behind us outside the basilica perimeter, "whereas the hill was here." He pointed to the area of the grottoes in front of us directly beneath the centre of the basilica. "Of course, it is not so easy to imagine that now because the hill had to be levelled in order to build the church on top of it.

"When Pope Pius XI died in 1939," he began, "the Holy See wanted to provide a suitable tomb for the recently deceased pope close to the tomb of St Peter, but they also wanted to carry out an important project that had often been considered but never undertaken: to create an underground chapel here directly in front of the supposed site of the tomb of St Peter. The problem was that the floor level in the grottoes was a little higher than it is now, so it was not suitable for a chapel, as the ceiling was excessively low. Therefore, they decided to lower the floor by three feet.

"Sounds simple, right? Just lower the floor a little bit, create a chapel in front of St Peter's tomb and life can go on as usual! But the excavators were about to bring to light some remarkable things that had not been seen since the dawn of Christianity.

"Just under the floor, they came upon various marble and stone sarcophagi, some beautifully made. Evidently, these had been lowered into the floor at various times through history. These were ancient and some were historically interesting, but no-one was surprised at their discovery. After about three months work, however, one of the workmen uncovered what appeared to be the top of a brick wall at a depth of two feet. One side of the wall was plastered and painted a rich emerald colour. An archaeologist was called and eventually a large quadrangle, each side about six metres long, was revealed. When the earth was eventually removed from this building, what stood uncovered was a spectacularly beautiful tomb, with niches containing cremation urns, intricate wall paintings, stuccoes, and entablatures.

"It was determined that the tomb dated from around the year A.D. 150. The archaeologists realized that they had discovered one of the finest examples of Roman funerary architecture existing from that period. Maybe now the workers could return to the original project of lowering the floor of the grottoes to create the underground chapel? It wasn't to be! New walls of further tombs had already been uncovered around the periphery of the previous dig. An archaeological team was assembled, and permission from the new pope, Pius XII, was obtained to enlarge the excavations. Eventually a line of sumptuous tombs was unearthed, some containing beautiful artwork. As the tombs were excavated, the dig approached closer and closer to the presumed site of the tomb of St Peter. The pope was consulted once again and the momentous decision was taken to excavate the most sacred ground in Rome. They would look for the remains of St Peter."

At that point, the door opened at the bottom of the stairs and someone gave a signal to Giacomo. He seemed more relaxed as he turned to the group with a wide smile. Evidently some obstacle to the progress of our tour had been removed.

"We can go down now and view what the archaeologists uncovered. Follow me!"

Shortly afterwards we had descended the steps and found ourselves standing on a narrow Roman road from the second or third century. Giacomo began to show us the various tombs that had only been brought to light during the excavations of the 1940s. Even if you struggled to recall the details, you would never forget the atmosphere of that place - the Roman alleyway, the dim lighting, the sophistication of the artwork, the symmetry and elegance of the tombs, and, most of all, the sense of incredible antiquity.

As we moved along, Giacomo indicated that soon we would begin to see the excavation area that was directly concerned with finding the remains of St Peter. He looked around at the group. "Does anyone have a quick question before we continue?"

"Yes, I do." It was Father Michael. "To excavate this area in the 1940s, huge volumes of clay had to be removed from these elaborate Roman tombs, right? So the Christians who built the original basilica in the fourth century just filled up these buildings with earth and covered all of these art works in order to build a church on top of it? To me, it doesn't sound very respectful. Nowadays we wouldn't dream of covering up an ancient Roman mosaic. Doesn't this prove that those critics are right who accuse the early Church of precipitating Europe into the dark ages with their destruction of classical civilisation?"

I was standing beside Sheila and I couldn't help noticing that she gave a disparaging grunt when Father Michael said the word "mosaic."

Giacomo gave a beaming smile. "That's a great question, but maybe not for the reason you think. When the emperor Constantine decided to build the original church - the old St Peter's - it is true that he made the decision to pack all of these tombs with clay. That was the only way of levelling the hill so that a building could be erected on top of it. And covering these tombs was a decision that couldn't have been taken lightly, but the problem had nothing to do with the artwork!"

Father Michael had a puzzled expression on his face. "But why was the artwork not an issue?" he asked. "That was an amazing floor mosaic we just saw. Did Constantine not appreciate that?"

Sheila gave such an audible snort at the repeated mention of "mosaic" that Giacomo glanced anxiously over at her before responding to Father Michael. "At the time of Constantine, some of the tombs in this area were only a few decades old. Others were more than a century, it is true, but tombs of this sort with a similar quality of artwork would have been found everywhere outside the walls of Rome. There would have been nothing rare or unique about such architecture. The Roman Forum was still standing at this time, remember, and it was filled with the glories of Rome. So when Constantine decided to fill in the tombs, the artwork was not the issue at all. However, the interference with tombs *was* a big issue. All tombs in Rome, even the simplest of them, were strictly protected by law under pain of death. This had nothing to do with art but a mortal fear, perhaps a superstitious one, of disturbing the remains of the dead."

As Giacomo spoke, I recalled the passage I had read the previous day in J.E. Walsh's book which stated that

Constantine must have invoked the full weight of his imperial powers to order the filling in of these tombs. There were strict laws prohibiting interference with human remains. In all Roman history, there is no record of a similar official action against the tombs of Roman citizens.

The smile had returned to Giacomo's face. "I am glad, though, that your spiritual director raised this question! Let us consider again the extent of the disturbance of the Roman tombs and the reason for it. This line of tombs that we have just visited is on an ascending slope. Up there ahead of us, on the higher part of the slope, about twenty-five metres away from the first tomb excavated, is the site of the tomb of St Peter. The tombs here on the lower slope were built in the decades after his burial. When Constantine decided to raise his church on top of the grave of the apostle, it was necessary to fill in these tombs on the lower slope in order to level the hill and make a suitable platform to begin construction. But to construct such a broad platform at the same level of Peter's grave, filling in these tombs wasn't enough! The engineers had to build three giant foundation walls, seven feet thick, running the entire length of the church. These walls become higher as the ground falls away from Peter's tomb, reaching to over ten metres at their highest point. That is why you have to climb a steep flight of steps to enter St Peter's Basilica!"

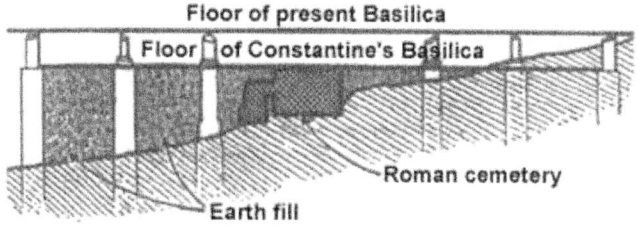

*(From J.E. Walsh, **The Bones of St Peter**, Sophia Institute Press, used with permission)*

Giacomo looked around at us all. "Can you imagine the challenge this presented to the builders? The amount of earth that had to be transported to fill up the slope and create the platform? We are talking about more than one million cubic feet of soil. Why would they do that?" He looked around earnestly. "And it was not only the logistical problem of moving the soil, but also the legal and cultural issue caused by the interference with tombs."

He pointed behind us towards his right. "There was level ground back there where the circus used to be, and the circus no longer existed in Constantine's time. Why not build the church over there?"

There was silence from the group. Eventually Sheila cleared her throat and spoke up. "Because they wanted to build directly on the tomb of St Peter?"

"Exactly!" Giacomo's tone was emphatic. "We will consider shortly the various pieces of data which indicate that the area ahead of us is the resting place of Peter. But the greatest piece of evidence is the fact that Constantine moved heaven and earth - almost literally –

to build a church with its main altar directly above this spot. No-one would have built a church in this crazy position unless he had a very good reason! No-one would have taken the legal, cultural and logistical risks to construct such an enormous edifice over a graveyard – one that was still in use – unless he believed that he had no other moral alternative. The fact that he chose to build here is compelling evidence that he believed this spot to contain the bones of St Peter. In addition, it reveals that he considered it imperative to build directly upon those bones and nowhere else."

As Giacomo spoke, I was still recalling what I had read in Walsh's book the previous day. Until these excavations were done in the 1940s, nobody appreciated how challenging this terrain had been in Constantine's time. The many alterations during the course of history had disguised the grossly unforgiving nature of the site. As the archaeological team uncovered the area, they realised that the construction of the original St Peter's was - incontestably - one of the most stupendous building jobs of ancient history.

"Maybe Constantine was mistaken?" Father Michael was playing devil's advocate now. "Maybe he moved all that earth, but got the location of the tomb wrong?"

I sighed inwardly. It seemed that the battle between Father Michael and Sheila was entering round two, the champion of art and culture versus the defender of relics and tombs. Fr Michael, no doubt, had detected the enthusiasm in Sheila's voice for St Peter's tomb when she gave her replies to Giacomo's questions. He now seemed more than keen to play the sceptic as to the location of the grave.

"It is true, it is true," Giacomo was nodding. "Maybe Constantine *was* wrong, but, still, his opinion on where Peter is buried is not irrelevant. Remember, he stands at a point in history which is more than sixteen hundred years closer to the apostles than we are. He brought an end to the persecutions of the church in Rome. During this period, the Christians had accurately and jealously conserved the memory of where St Peter was buried. At the time of Constantine, Pope Sylvester would have revealed the location to the emperor so that a suitable church would be built in the right place. It was the first time that the secret location of the city's most revered saint was made public knowledge. Thus, Constantine is the very first public heir of the best guarded secret of the Roman church."

"*I* for one would want to know that my church was built directly over the tomb of the apostle, regardless of what mosaics got covered up in the process," Sheila said, looking at Giacomo but leaving little doubt as to where her remark was really directed. The word "mosaics" was practically spat out. "Didn't Christ tell Peter explicitly that he was the rock on which his Church would be built?"

"The establishment of the Church upon the Petrine ministry has *nothing* to do with building a physical church over the bones of Peter!" said Father Michael with a scornful chortle.

This was developing into a squabble between Sheila and Father Michael and I was starting to feel uncomfortable. It was a relief when Giacomo intervened politely to ask their names before continuing his discourse. "Father Michael is absolutely correct to say that the Catholic Church is what it is regardless of whether this basilica is directly over the bones of St Peter. However, neither can Sheila's point be denied that the centring of the altar on the tomb of this apostle has a powerful devotional and symbolic value. It is clear that the Church at the time of Constantine felt that the original resting place of Peter was immensely significant. Let me repeat it again: the gargantuan effort to centre the basilica on this tomb so that it would remain undisturbed is nothing less than astonishing!

"Recall, everyone, how the excavations under Pius XII had proceeded up to this point. After ten months of digging, nearly twenty elaborate mausoleums had been uncovered on either side of the alleyway, containing over one hundred tombs. The question now was whether the investigation should stop there, or if they should proceed into the area under the high altar. The team consulted with Pope Pius XII and he gave his permission. The most sacred area in Rome was to be finally uncovered. Prepare, my friends, to see the assumed location of the tomb of St Peter!"

There was a palpable sense of excitement among most of the group now as we followed Giacomo into a narrow area adjacent to a short flight of steps. Father Michael was walking lethargically at the back, though, as if he wasn't really too interested in what was coming next. As we proceeded, our guide mentioned how the documents from the early centuries provided only scant details about the final resting place of St Peter. According to one of these, Pope Anacletus had erected some sort of shrine over the tomb about twenty years after the apostle's death. The existence of the shrine is confirmed in writings from about the year 200. The task facing the archaeologists in uncovering this shrine was a difficult one. The area beneath the high altar of the present St Peter's had not been touched in centuries and no-one knew what exactly lay there.

"After finding and removing various brick walls that dated from medieval times, the excavators came upon a wall faced with red plaster, the foundation of which went down deep below the level of the Constantinian floor. The wall ran from left to right across the direction of the basilica (the basilica is on an east-west line, whilst this wall runs north-south). Attached to the wall, more or less directly below the present high altar of the basilica, were discovered the badly damaged remains of an elegant shrine with two niches, a travertine table and graceful marble columns."

"The tomb of St Peter!" said Sheila with excitement in her voice.

"Was it though?" asked Giacomo. "The excavators could only glimpse portions of this shrine from behind the various layers of masonry surrounding it, but it seemed more like a pagan monument. It did not have anything recognizably Christian about it. However, it was in the exact place that one would expect to find the tomb of St Peter, and, as we shall discuss shortly, bones were discovered in a grave directly beneath it.

"It is hard to appreciate the challenges that had to be faced by the team. They continued to probe in the area around the red wall, hampered by the construction work associated with altars that had been inserted around the shrine in the sixth and twelfth centuries. Eventually on the right side of the red wall they discovered another shorter wall, in light blue plaster. This ran at right angles to the red wall. Investigations revealed that it had been built in order to shore up a crack that had appeared in the red wall.

"What was remarkable about this wall, though, was the fact that it was covered in crude inscriptions. These took up the entire surface and ran in every direction. They included many recognizable names in Latin, along with the phrases such as *"vivatis in Christo"* ("may you have life in Christ"). Clearly, these names had been scratched on the wall by pilgrims who had come to the shrine and had placed an invocation on the wall for the souls of their dear ones. But what disappointed the excavators is that the one name they had hoped to find – that of St Peter - did not appear even once."

"Maybe he wasn't buried here after all!" Father Michael said brightly, with a mischievous look in the direction of Sheila.

"That was the issue, certainly," replied Giacomo. "If this was indeed the tomb of St Peter, then the non-appearance of his name needed to be explained. Were the Christians keeping the burial place of St Peter secret from the Roman authorities for fear that it might be desecrated? The excavators, though disappointed, were not unduly deterred by the absence of his name. They now proceeded to dig in the area at the base of the shrine.

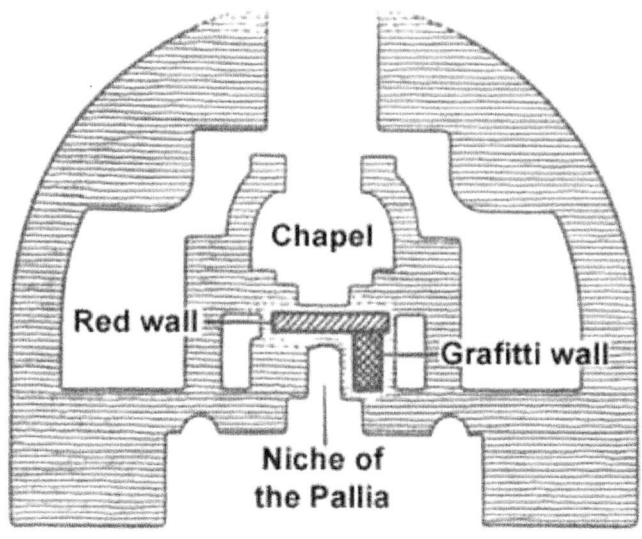

*(Simplified view from above showing the location of the red wall and the graffiti wall immediately beneath the high altar. The graffiti wall was built to shore up the crumbling red wall. From J.E. Walsh, **The Bones of St Peter**, Sophia Institute Press, used with permission)*

"Before going on, I would like to mention in passing that the team found a small cavity in the graffiti wall. This was positioned about two feet above ground and the cavity inside was lined with marble. The archaeologists wondered if it had once held the bones of some important figure in the early Church who wanted to be buried close to Peter? It was a mysterious find, but the work moved on to the more pressing task of digging beneath the shrine. As we shall see, the significance of the cavity only became apparent many years later when the excavations had already been long finished."

We had been standing in a narrow area to the left of the red wall and its shrine over the presumed site of the tomb of Peter, but we could not see either because of the later medieval walls that stood in the way. Giacomo led us around a corner and up a short flight of steps. We were now standing on the other side of the complex, to the right of the shrine. Through a narrow opening, dimly lit, Giacomo told us that we were looking at the graffiti wall. We could just about make out in the dim light a number of Perspex boxes in the wall cavity. Inside, bones were visible. Giacomo invited us to take a moment to venerate the presumed bones of St Peter. Later he would explain why they were kept in these boxes in the cavity of the graffiti wall.

"This is where the climax of all these years of excavations took place! The presumed site of the tomb would have been at the base of the red wall underneath the damaged shrine, directly on the other side of the graffiti wall that we are now looking at, but the archaeologists did not have access to that area because of the other masonry that stood in the way. Therefore, they decided to dig directly down underneath the graffiti wall. When they had sunk a pit about four feet deep, they decided to break through the foundations of the wall. On the other side, they discovered a chamber!"

"The grave of St Peter!" exclaimed Sheila.

"The opening into the chamber was enlarged," Giacomo went on, "and one of the archaeologists, Father Kirschbaum, got onto his back and edged his body, head first, into the space. At first, the chamber seemed to him to be empty, but as his eyes became accustomed to the glare of the flashlight, he realised that the earthen floor was covered with many coins. Some of these seemed to date from Roman times. Over the ensuing months, the soil at the base of the chamber would be sifted painstakingly and would yield nearly two thousand coins."

Upon hearing this, Father Michael gave a low whistle. "Yes, incredible, wasn't it?" Giacomo said with a smile. "The coins were from all over Europe and dated from the fifteenth century all the way back to the very decade of the martyrdom of St Peter. These were proof that Peter's tomb was a place of continuous pilgrimage from the very beginning.

"Then Father Kirschbaum spotted a cavity, shaped like an inverted V, on the side of the chamber that was formed by the foundation of the red wall. He reached into this cavity and found a hard object, which, on examination, turned out to be a bone about twelve centimetres long. His flashlight revealed that many other bones were piled up in the same spot. He replaced the bone he had found and wriggled outside to consult with the others.

"It was inevitable for them to suspect that they had finally discovered the bones of St Peter, even if no-one said so explicitly. Pope Pius XII was informed and he arrived on the spot within minutes. After some discussion with the archaeologists, the Pope gave permission for the bones to be removed. A chair was procured and His Holiness sat there above the pit for some hours while Fr Kirschbaum carefully handed out over two hundred and fifty bones and their fragments. These were deposited in lead-lined boxes at the Pope's feet. The absence of a skull was taken as a very positive sign, since there was an ancient tradition that the skull of St Peter was conserved above the altar in St John Lateran Basilica on the other side of the city.

"The bones were taken to the Pope's apartment and examined during the following months by medical professionals. Their opinion was that they belonged to a robust man of perhaps seventy years of age. Of course, once the Pope and others heard this, it was natural to conclude that the remains were those of St Peter. It must be said though, that the medical personnel were perhaps not the best qualified for this sort of investigation. As we shall see, their conclusion would be seriously challenged a few years later."

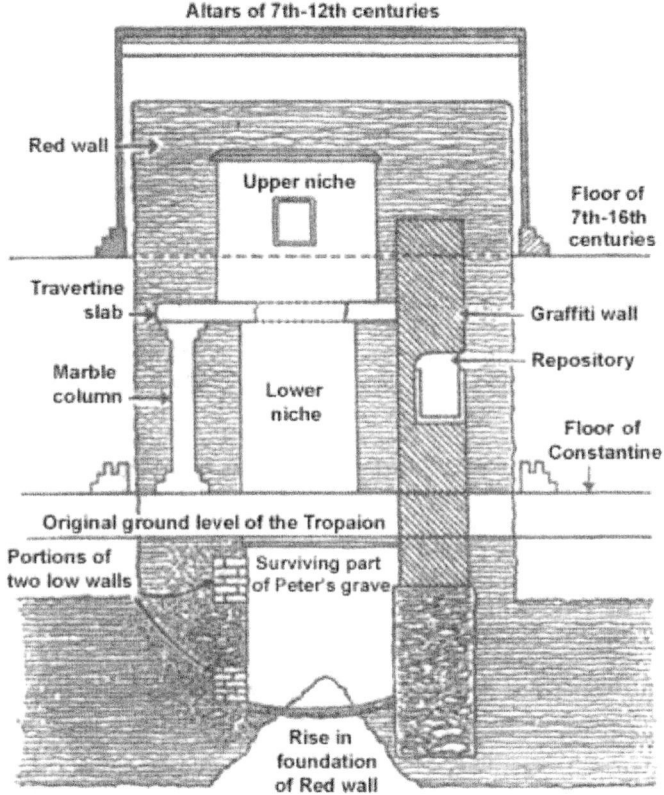

*(Simplified view from the front. The grave underneath is where Peter was originally laid, but his bones were eventually discovered in the repository of the graffiti wall. From J.E. Walsh, **The Bones of St Peter**, Sophia Institute Press, used with permission)*

Vittorio looked anxiously at his watch. "Now, my friends, we are running out of time because the next group will be here very shortly. I must summarize the rest of the information. For the next three years, the excavations continued in the entire area all around the red wall. The surviving portion of this wall is about seven feet wide, but the dig revealed that it had originally been about twenty-six feet wide and that it formed one side of a large rectangular enclosure, twenty-six feet by twelve feet. This courtyard had a tiled floor and the entire focus of the enclosure was the shrine above the tomb of St Peter. It is very likely that the early Church held liturgical assemblies in this courtyard on the spot where we are now standing!"

"That is amazing!" enthused a member of the group.

"An interesting question is when that enclosure in front of Peter's grave had been constructed. Eventually, conclusive evidence was found. A drain covered in terracotta tiles was found underneath the area. The tiles had the embossed symbol of Marcus Aurelius and his wife and could be conclusively dated from between the years 147 and 165.

"The red wall enclosure and its shrine thus dated from only about eighty years after the martyrdom of Peter. About one hundred years later, the red wall developed a crack and the graffiti wall was erected as a supporting buttress. The graffiti wall threw the shrine out of symmetry but, when Constantine's builders came along later, they did not remove it, perhaps because the graffiti on it was already considered historically precious by that time. However, they took the decision to destroy the courtyard. Ten feet were demolished off each end of the red wall, conserving only the central part which contained the shrine of the tomb. The pagan cemetery on the lower side of the hill was filled in, a floor was created over it and this area in which the portion of the red wall was encased became the focus of the new basilica. So the whole lot – red wall, graffiti wall, shrine and grave – were all encased at the heart of the Constantinian church.

"And now my friends we must vacate this area for the next group. Do you have a little more time? Would you like to extend our tour for a few more minutes?"

Not surprisingly, there was a general chorus of "Yes!"

"Wonderful! Please follow me to the Clementine Chapel."

A few moments later we had ascended a small staircase and entered the narrow confines of a beautifully ornate chapel with a magnificent barrel vault. There was seating for about twelve people which meant that all of our group was able to sit down apart from myself and Father Michael.

"Welcome!" Giacomo said. "This is one of the oldest and most sacred places in the building. It was constructed by Pope Gregory about the year 600 directly behind the Constantinian monument that lay above the relics of Peter. Tradition says that the skull of the apostle used to be venerated here before it was moved to St John Lateran. The original investigations that had uncovered the first portion of the red wall and the graffiti wall had begun their dig from here." As he spoke Giacomo pointed to the bronze door at the top left of the chapel. This was the door through which we had just entered.

"Let us return to our subject. We have seen all that was uncovered in those first years of excavations. In 1950, the Pope announced to the world that the tomb of St Peter had been discovered. On the question of bones, he revealed that some had been found in the tomb, but admitted that it was impossible to prove with certainty that they belonged to St Peter. Despite the reserve shown by Pope Pius XII, the belief quickly grew that the bones of St Peter had indeed been found."

Giacomo looked around at the group. "Do you think the story ended there, my friends? Ten years of investigations, a tomb with ancient bones. Surely there was nothing more to be uncovered? But everything was about to change! A most significant investigator was about to enter the story, and her contribution would be assisted by the providence of God. In 1952, a professor of Greek epigraphy, Dr Margherita Guarducci, arrived at the site to decipher an inscription in one of the mausoleums that lay less than ten metres from Peter's grave. Dr Guarducci had a formidable background in Roman and Greek inscriptions. During her first visit, the custodians showed her the graffiti wall. When she saw it, she was shocked. In the spaces between the many names and invocations, there was an elaborate network of apparently haphazard letters and strokes. Never in her long experience had she seen such a confusing pattern of scratches and lines. Intrigued by the mystery, she asked permission to study the wall after she had finished deciphering the writing in the mausoleum. Permission was quickly granted, but it would be more than a year before she could find time to begin work.

"Her method of study involved days spent kneeling in front of the wall with a torch and magnifying glass, with evenings spent studying detailed photographs of the entire surface. After more than a month of intense scrutiny, which included rigorous consultation of relevant works by other experts on ancient inscriptions, she had made no progress at all. The haphazard arrangement of lines yielded no discernible pattern.

"One morning she was standing in front of the graffiti wall with one of the basilica workmen, Giovanni Segoni. She was aware that he had assisted with the original excavations. If you recall, when the graffiti wall was discovered, they noticed that there was a small opening about two feet above ground with a hollow space inside. That was the cavity we looked into a few moments ago and glimpsed the Perspex boxes with the presumed bones of St Peter. Dr Guarducci's eyes now wandered down to this cavity and she asked Giovanni if he recalled finding anything inside which might throw light on the inscriptions outside? It was a chance question, asked with a hint of desperation, in the midst of an unplanned meeting between a scholar of world renown and a humble labourer. What could this workman say that might help her research? Incredibly, his reply would transform the entire story of the search for Peter's bones. Yes, he had found something, and what he found had been stored in a box not too far away for the last ten years. Would the professor like to see the box? He led her to a small storeroom beside the underground chapel of St Columban. The box was opened and Dr Guarducci was stunned to see inside a considerable collection of bones."

Sheila was right up at the front pew close to Giacomo. When he got to the end of his sentence, she gasped audibly.

"A big surprise, right?" Giacomo said with a laugh. "How were these bones removed from the cavity without anyone taking notice? On the day that they found the graffiti wall, the team's real preoccupation was to get access to the presumed site of the grave of St Peter on the other side. They did not examine the contents of the cavity in the graffiti wall on the day that it was discovered and they were concerned about damaging the wall in any way. That evening, when the archaeologists had gone home, Monsignor Ludwig Kaas and Giovanni Segoni came down to examine the findings. Monsignor Kaas was administrator of the basilica. Though nominal head of the excavations, he did not have a good relationship with the other members of the team and felt that, at times, they did not show enough respect for the bones uncovered during the work. He tended to be absent during the excavations, but had the custom of examining the area by night, placing loose bones into boxes, labelling them and storing them away so that they would receive some modicum of respect.

"On the evening that the graffiti wall was discovered, Monsignor Kaas and Giovanni descended as usual to the site. The monsignor instructed Giovanni to search the cavity and place the contents in a box. This was locked and would not be reopened again during the lifetime of Monsignor Kaas - he passed away in 1952. In fact, it would remain closed for more than ten years until the occasion of Dr Guarducci's chance meeting with Giovanni Segoni.

"The day *after* Giovanni had emptied the bones in 1940, the archaeologists led by Kirschbaum finally examined the interior of the cavity and found only a few fragmentary remains. They were not aware of Monsignor Kaas's discovery the day before. The monsignor himself did not appreciate the significance of what he had found, nor that he had withheld significant information from the rest of the team.

"Dr Guarducci, too, did not immediately appreciate the importance of the bones in 1953 when she first saw them. She ordered Giovanni to reseal the box, which was then deposited in a cupboard in the basilica's main offices, considered a better environment than the damp storeroom.

"The professor returned to her difficult task of decipherment. Eventually she managed to individuate about fifty names, many of which included invocations for their eternal life. However, even after spending many months on her knees studying the wall, she could still make no sense of the network of scratches that filled the spaces between the names."

Giacomo shook his head in apparent frustration. "Unfortunately, my friends, time does not permit us to discuss this matter properly. All we can do is allude to the incredible work done by this lady, Dr Guarducci, on her knees in the half-darkness for many months in the tunnel below us. Eventually, sticking steadfastly to her task, she made a breakthrough. The wall, she realised, contained a highly developed form of alphabetical symbolism. The symbolism permitted Christians to express their faith in a way that that did not provoke hostility from the Roman authorities."

"A secret language to communicate their religious beliefs?" Father Michael was very alert now and seemed extremely interested in Giacomo's discourse.

"Yes! It is usually called 'spiritual cryptography'. Virtually every letter of the alphabet stood for a word. For example, 'R' meant 'resurrection', 'V' meant 'vita' (life), and so on. The lines and scratches were used to join letters on the wall so as to express some biblical concept or truth."

Giacomo reached into his briefcase and took out a large sketch showing some of the symbols on the graffiti wall. We could see that a curved line joined the "A" in one person's name to the "R" that appeared later in the same name, and from this a straight line was joined to the "V" in another name.

"The 'A' on the graffiti wall often refers to Christ," Giacomo continued, "since he is the alpha and the omega. So these lines joining the 'A' to the 'R' to the 'V' express the faith that Christ is the resurrection and the life."

Father Michael was nodding in appreciation. "Beautiful!"

"Out of these fifty or so names, Dr Guarducci found statements about Christ, the Trinity, the Cross, Mary as Mother of God, Biblical titles for Jesus such as 'Light of the World', and much, much more. The scratches that once seemed so haphazard and meaningless were actually filled with spiritual significance, a testimony to the living faith of a community."

"Remarkable!" Father Michael's voice had a tone of awe.

"For anyone interested in the search for the apostle's bones, however, a wall this close to the tomb should be expected to have some reference to Peter himself, do you agree?"

"Yes!" said Sheila emphatically. "But maybe they were afraid to write his name for fear of the Roman authorities?"

"It seems they did want to keep the tomb secret from the authorities, but the funny thing is that Peter's name was on the wall in cryptic form more than twenty times!"

"But HOW?" said Father Michael in a tone so loud that the lady in front of me jumped.

"You are familiar with the monogram for Christ?" asked Giacomo.

"Yes, of course," replied Father Michael. "It's a symbol formed from the first two Greek letters for

Christ, which in our alphabet looks like an 'X' superimposed on a 'P'"

"That's it. There are many of these Christ monograms on the graffiti wall, which is not surprising, since they can be found in the catacombs and in any place that you have early Christian inscriptions. But what is unusual here is that the vertical line in the 'P' often had two or three horizontal strokes at the bottom, so that a 'P' and a little 'E' were really being formed together. Dr Guarducci realized that this was in fact a monogram for Peter. In addition, in other instances, the network of lines between the letters of names formed the initials 'PE' or 'PET'. Peter's name was thus represented, either by the spelling out of the initials or by the presence of the monogram, on every part of the surface. If, originally, Peter's name seemed to be absent from the mass of words scribbled on the wall, now Dr Guarducci realised that the presence of the name was all-pervasive."

Giacomo took another sheet out of his briefcase. This had a single large sketch of the Peter monogram, the "P" with the little "E" on its lower stem.

"Does that remind you of anything?" he asked.

There was a pause as the group considered the image. Then Father Michael spoke up. "A key?"

"A key! When the first two letters of Peter's name are superimposed in this way, the resultant symbol is like a little picture of a key!"

Father Michael gave a low whistle. From where I was standing, the look of excitement on his face was evident.

"I think your spiritual director knows what this means." Giacomo said. "Jesus had said to Peter, 'You are *Rock* and on this rock I build my Church. I give you the keys of the Kingdom of Heaven'. When the early Christians drew this symbol here on a wall beside the grave of Peter, they were not just paying their respects to one of the apostles, or simply asking intercession for the souls of their loved ones – though they were doing that too, of course. They were also expressing their faith that Jesus founded a Church, his instrument to bring us all to heaven, and Peter was the keyholder, the rock on which that edifice was built."

Giacomo looked around at us all. "My friends, I hope you can appreciate the beauty of what Dr Guarducci discovered. In one sense, it was nothing new. In fact, it was the oldest feature of the Catholic Church. But to discover it here, under the high altar of St Peter's, and to find it in such a simple and undiluted form, was simply stunning. The early Christians, as evidenced by these scratches on the wall, were attaching themselves to Peter, the rock, the one to whom Christ had given the keys. Salvation was never a matter of direct communication between individual believers and God, but was through the Church, founded by Jesus on particular people invested with his power and authority.

"As Father Michael said, the Church has this power regardless of whether a physical building in Rome is constructed on the bones of Peter. But yet it was a powerful thing that the Roman Church centred its life on the physical remains of the man that walked with Christ.

This fact made the incarnational nature of the faith into a tangible reality for people. God really became flesh and blood. He really established a Church on flesh and blood apostles. Though Christ remains the invisible head, he gives us a visible head, in flesh and blood, till the end of the ages. The Catholic Church is helplessly incarnational!"

"But where the heck *were* the bones?" Sheila's voice had a tone of real exasperation.

Giacomo laughed. "Sheila, it is good that you yearn to find those bones! That is what the pilgrims here have always done, reached for the bones as a physical expression of reaching for Christ. Those troublesome bones! It had taken Dr Guarducci about five years to decipher the code on the wall and to write up her three-volume report. Her discovery of the Peter monogram was of monumental importance. The same symbol had previously been noticed many times on the margins of ancient documents, scratched into Roman monuments, etched onto coins and medals, even painted covertly on the back of public signs. In fact, its presence was ubiquitous in ancient Rome, but scholars had not understood it and had not linked it to Peter until its true meaning was revealed by the fact that the symbol was found in such profusion beside Peter's tomb.

"In 1956, Pope Pius XII agreed that the bones found under the red wall should be re-examined. There was a general presumption, even among the excavation team, that they *must* belong to St Peter. However, that investigation had not been done by specialists in bone identification. Now, a world authority, Professor Venerando Correnti of Palermo University, was asked to make a new study. As he sorted the bones in a room at St Peter's, he quickly realized that they belonged to a number of different individuals. And not only that, about a quarter of the bones were from animals! The next part of his task – the establishment of body parts, gender and age at death - would take much longer. In fact, it would be more than four years before Professor Correnti published his results.

"He announced that there were three individuals present, two males in their fifties and a more elderly female. To say that the findings caused disappointment in the Vatican would be an understatement. The long search for St Peter's bones, begun more than twenty years earlier, had apparently ended in failure. No one had any doubt that the *grave* itself belonged to St Peter. It was easy to imagine how bones from other humans, and especially those of animals, could have been found in the earthen floor of the grave, for this area had once been on the edge of the circus of Nero in which many people and animals had died. The many changes that had occurred in proximity to Peter's grave, such as the building of the red wall, could easily have caused these bones to have ended up there. But, as Sheila puts it, 'where the heck' were Peter's bones?

"In order to furnish a more complete overview of the bones found in the vicinity, Professor Correnti also agreed to examine some other bones found in the dig, including those removed by Monsignor Kaas from the graffiti wall and placed in the wooden box. In June of 1963, while the world awaited the election of a new pope, Dr Guarducci called to see Professor Correnti at the Vatican to see how his analysis of the bones was going. He revealed to her a surprising discovery. The graffiti wall cavity held the remains of a *single* elderly individual, almost certainly male! Virtually all of the bones had been significantly eaten away by decay, but most of the bones in the body were represented, apart from the complete absence of the bones of the feet. Some of the larger bones appeared to be stained by a purple dye, as if they had been wrapped in purple cloth sometime after the body had already decayed. Strands of reddish and gold fabric were found among the remains.

"Dr Guarducci was struck by the fact that the bones belonged to a single individual and she mulled over it during the following hours and days. She recalled one of the discoveries that had been made by the excavators shortly after the original uncovering of the graffiti wall. A senior member of the team had looked into the opening and noticed that a piece of plaster had fallen off the portion of red wall that formed one side of the interior of the cavity. This had a broken inscription in Greek which was interpreted to read *Petros eni* – 'Peter is in here.' The fact that the plaster was from the red wall, which preceded the building of the graffiti wall, had always been understood by scholars to indicate that the inscription *predated* the construction of the graffiti wall. Thus, surely, it referred to the presence of the remains of Peter in the grave below. But now, following the revelation by Correnti that the cavity contained the bones of a single individual, Dr Guarducci began to wonder if the inscription alluded to the presence of the apostle's bones in the graffiti wall?

"For some months, she kept her theory more or less to herself. One person she took into her confidence was Professor Correnti, who responded positively. Providentially, the newly elected Pope turned out to be a friend of the Guarducci family, Cardinal Montini, who took the name Paul VI. In November, in the midst of a meeting at the papal library, she blurted out her theory to him. 'Your Holiness, it seems to me very likely that the bones found in the graffiti wall are those of St Peter!'

"During the following year, the Pope gave Dr Guarducci the permission to carry out the tests she suggested. One of these was the analysis of the mysterious strands of reddish and gold fabric that were found among the bones. These turned out to be made using pure gold applied delicately over wool with impressive skill. Dr Guarducci deduced that the bones had been recognized by Constantine to be those of St Peter. The Emperor wrapped them devotedly in purple fabric interwoven with gold and re-deposited them in the cavity. It must be said, though, that other scholars argue that the bones were already deposited in the wall before the time of Constantine and were not disturbed by him. This raises the question of who could have had access to the purple cloth that was normally reserved for the use of the Emperor, but that discussion is not for us today.

"A second test was the analysis of the particles of soil that clung to many of the bones. This was compared to the soil that lay in the central grave under the red wall. The test conclusively demonstrated that the chemical composition of the soil on the bones corresponded perfectly with that of the soil in the grave. Before being deposited in the cavity of the graffiti wall, therefore, the bones must have lain at length in the soil below the red wall, which virtually everyone recognized to be the grave of Peter.

"A final test involved the examination of the skull preserved in St John Lateran Basilica, long considered to be that of St Peter. This examination took several months and its conclusion was that the bones of the skull in St John Lateran were perfectly consistent with the bones in the graffiti wall."

At that point, a knock came on the door at the top of the chapel and a woman entered. Behind her we could see that she had a group of people in tow.

"My friends," Giacomo said to us, "we must leave it there. Thank you for your attention and your questions!"

A few moments later, we emerged from the grottoes on the right-hand side of St Peter's, under the ramp that descends from the Sistine Chapel. In high spirits after such an enlightening visit, I invited everyone to come for a cappuccino and croissant. They agreed enthusiastically and Giacomo consented to join us as well. We went to a bar outside the left colonnade, across from the imposing entrance to the Holy Office.

Once inside, the group was invited to go to the counter to choose their pastry. In the meantime, I went to the bar and started ordering the coffees. As the group milled in front of the counter, I saw Sheila giving Father Michael a friendly jostle.

"Easy on there, Sheila!" Father Michael said. "No relics or bones on offer here!"

"And not a mosaic in sight!" she retorted.

It was great to see this good-humoured banter between them, but I couldn't quite put my finger on what had happened down in the *scavi*. What was it that had prompted a cessation of hostilities, just like our encounter with little Antonietta Meo had done?

Giacomo was sitting at a table in the corner and I carried a coffee over to him.

"I have seen this often in pilgrims, you know," he said.

"What is that?" I asked.

"The clash between the people who appreciate the art and culture and those who value the devotional aspect. The first group are suspicious of what they consider to be a superstitious attitude to relics and bones. The second group worries that a focus on art obscures the spiritual meaning of holy places."

"That's so true," I exclaimed. "It can be quite a job keeping these two sets of people from each other's throats."

"They seem to be getting on well now, though" Giacomo replied, motioning with his head toward the table behind us. I looked around to see Father Michael biting into his croissant and remarking irreverently how "bone-hunting" was a hungry business. Sheila was laughing heartily.

"These two types of people can learn from each other, I think," Giacomo went on. "The faith is not an abstract or intellectual thing, but neither can it be reduced to touching 'holy' objects in the hope of gleaning some grace from them."

"Maybe what makes the *scavi* tour so good is that it fulfils both of those needs together. There's the scholarly investigation of early Christian symbols, art and architecture, and then we have this tangible proximity to the historical Jesus." Lowering my voice, I said, "Father Michael's mood completely changed after you showed us the meaning of the symbols on the graffiti wall, especially the Peter monogram. It was a revelation for him, I think, that the early Church wrote Peter's name using the symbol of a key."

"Yes," Giacomo nodded. "Scripture and archaeology come together in that ancient etching of the key."

"Amazing."

"Yes, but you know what I think about the most every time I give the tour?"

"What's that?" I asked.

"Towards the end of John's Gospel, Jesus predicts that Peter will follow him all the way, to the extent of 'stretching out his hands' – being crucified like his master. Jesus had said that there is no greater love than for someone to lay down his life for his friends, but it didn't seem likely then that Peter had it in him. Down there at the red wall, however, we have the proof that he eventually measured up."

"Yes," I said quietly, struck by the conviction in Giacomo's voice.

"Even Peter – the one who abandoned Christ at the crucifixion - even he showed higher love."

Chapter Five
Higher Love

"The inordinate attachment to earthly possessions, which can even degenerate into idolatry, is not a greater love, but a lesser, impure, perverted one. The love of creatures, whether it be father, friend, or wife, can reach its full measure only in Christ . ."

Dietrich von Hildebrand

In 2014, a national pilgrimage from Ireland, led by the bishop of Down and Connor, came to Rome to celebrate the opening of the "Year of St Columban," a special jubilee year to commemorate the fourteen-hundredth anniversary of the death of the Irish saint in 615. Many of the group were from the parish of Bangor in County Down, the site of the monastery from which Columban had set sail with twelve companions to bring the Gospel to Europe. The journey of the monk, through huge swathes of what is now France, Switzerland, Germany, Austria and Italy, ranks among the greatest missionary journeys ever undertaken.

I did not know a lot about St Columban before the arrival of the group, even though we had taken coach tours to his tomb in Bobbio numerous times. To get ready for the pilgrimage, someone suggested that I read the little book by Cardinal Tomás Ó Fiaich, **"Columbanus in his Own Words,"** a classic work that contained a good summary of his life and a translation of his writings. It was an ideal resource for the harried courier, short enough to be read in a single sitting, but filled with insights into the character of the monk.

It was surprising to discover the immense legacy of this man who was already over forty years old before he did anything that is remembered. From his five original foundations, about one hundred other monasteries were established in central Europe. Many of these abbeys continued to exist for centuries and had a vital place in the re-civilising of the continent following the collapse of the Roman Empire. The monasteries became vibrant centres of education, agriculture and industry. Most of all, they were bulwarks in defence of orthodox Christianity against the many winds of false doctrine that threatened to corrupt the Gospel during early medieval times. Cardinal Ó Fiaich reckoned that the influence of these abbeys was so significant that Columban could rank with St Benedict as the co-founder of Western monasticism.

The book revealed also that the Irish monk nurtured a constant desire to make a pilgrimage to Rome to visit the tombs of Peter and Paul. In fact, he seemed to conceive of his entire life's journey as that pilgrimage. However, he died in northern Italy at the last and most important of his foundations, Bobbio, a place that would rival Montecassino for centuries as a place of culture and learning.

The pilgrimage in October 2014 for the inauguration of the year of Columban went ahead and the tours, receptions, conferences, concerts and other meetings were negotiated successfully. The most moving event of the week was the solemn procession with the relics of the saint into the Cathedral of Rome in the presence of Pope Francis' delegate, along with cardinals, bishops and thousands of the faithful from all over the continent. The mortal remains of Columban made it to the threshold of Peter and Paul after all.

The following year – while the jubilee was still ongoing - one of the great multinational gatherings happened in Bobbio for International St Columban's Day. The Bangor group wanted to be present and asked us to organise a trip once more. The big question was what else the group should visit during their time in Italy. Should we try to take in some of the other places associated with the Irish missionary scattered throughout northern Italy? After some weeks debating the matter with the group leaders, Fr Joe, parish priest of Bangor, phoned to say that in his opinion there was only one way this trip should be done: begin in France and visit *all* of the original Columban foundations, finishing the pilgrimage in Bobbio for International St Columban's Day. And so it was that in the last week of August 2015, our nine-year old son, Stephen, and I flew from Rome to Zurich to meet the Bangor group and embark on an epic trip.

From the preparation for these two pilgrimages, and the various talks on Columban given by the leaders during the trips themselves, I felt that I had gained some familiarity with the saint. Then, in November 2015, a documentary was broadcast on Irish television, narrated by a former president of the country, Mary McAleese. The picture painted of Columban in this documentary seemed significantly at odds with what I had heard about him. The McAleese account of the monk re-affirmed the traditional view that he was an outspoken figure, unafraid to challenge the powerful and influential. What was new was the claim that a central part of his message was inclusion of the "other," his openness to diversity. This attitude, we were told, made Columban the ideal model for the project of European integration, a project, apparently, that was all about inclusion and respect for diversity.

Whilst the documentary was well-made, eloquently narrated and contained some great footage from the places associated with Columban, this description of his central message was jarring. "Anachronistic" was the word that came to mind towards the end of the documentary when Mrs McAleese spoke from the ancient bridge in Bobbio with a passionate appeal that we follow Columban's example of embracing diversity. Was it really plausible that a man from fourteen hundred years ago should have as his main concern the very issue that most preoccupies the dominant culture of the twenty-first century?

Something seemed awry. Was the McAleese picture correct, or did it involve moulding this medieval figure into a form more agreeable to modern sensibilities? Or worse, was the Irish monk being used to promote agendas that were not his own? I was aware that my own knowledge of Columban was far from complete.

The nature of our job is that the next pilgrimage is nearly always different to the one that went before. There are new monuments to be inspected, different historical periods to be skimmed over, and fresh saints' lives to be perused. Such fevered study is rarely deep. Columban one week, Francis of Assisi the next, Thomas Aquinas the week after, and a quick visit to St Benedict's tomb along the way - if the coach driver's mood permits. Anyone who wanted to hear something profound about a saint wouldn't ask someone like me. I could spin you a few niceties about the saint's life, but not explain the nucleus of his message. Couriers deal in clichés, not cruxes. With my level of historical acumen, I was hardly in a position to dismiss out of hand the accuracy of Mrs McAleese's presentation.

After November 2015, when the events commemorating the significant anniversary of Columban's death were over, it would have been normal for us to have forgotten about the Irish saint for a while. In late November, however, after watching the McAleese documentary, the picture it painted of Columban began to nag at me. I was irked by what seemed an inaccurate portrayal of the Irishman. That prompted a deeper reflection on the Irish missionary's life and character, and this carried over to the new occasions when we took Columban pilgrimages to the continent in the following years. By presenting Columban in a way that did not sit easily with the evidence, that documentary turned out to be a challenge to develop a sharper understanding of who he really was.

These two years had involved a steep learning curve. The 2014 trip to Rome had required organising a whole series of visits, functions and receptions, not to mention the Masses and events necessary for any pilgrimage. The 2015 trip would be even more complicated. We had already visited Bobbio many times with other groups, but the first part of the proposed 2015 journey required a familiarity with the Columban foundations in France and Austria. After Christmas 2014, Laura, the children and I flew to Basel and completed by car the part of the itinerary north of the Alps that would be covered by Bishop Treanor and the Bangor group in the coming year. We visited the four original Columban foundations in France and Austria, and – knee deep in snow - spent New Year's Eve in St Gallen in Switzerland (this city with its magnificent cathedral had been founded by a disciple of Columban, Gall). We checked out the hotels, priced the restaurants, visited the monuments, measured the distances, surveyed the coach parks, but didn't have an opportunity to learn much about St Columban, his character, or his message.

In the New Year, the flights, hotels and coaches for the trip were organised and the bookings began to come in. Even though a large proportion of the group was once again from Bangor, the make-up of the forty-eight strong group this time was very distinctive. As well as two bishops, sixteen priests from all parts of the country booked, evidently eager to follow in the footsteps of

Columban. In addition, a number of scholars of history and Irish signed up for the pilgrimage. Some of them had impressive academic credentials. When the general cultural level of a group is this high, it can be nerve wracking for a courier who is normally quite content to be a couple of pages ahead of everyone else in the local guide book. That wouldn't suffice for a group like this. The ability to bluff convincingly would be absolutely indispensable for this trip.

When August came round, Stephen and I met the group in Zurich Airport and we began one of the most tiring legs of our odyssey. It takes about an hour and a half by coach to drive westwards from Zurich to the French border. Some of this route runs just south of the Swiss-German frontier, with the river Rhine often visible from the road in daylight. After crossing into France, it would take another hour and a half to reach Luxeuil, a provincial town in Eastern France in the shadow of the Vosges mountains.

Road works on the motorway outside of Zurich seriously delayed our progress at the beginning of the journey. Everyone was already tired, having made the journey early that morning from Belfast to Dublin Airport for the flight to Switzerland. It did not seem the right occasion for a lot of talking from me on the microphone, and besides, I did not know the terrain very well. There is no substitute for raw experience of the locality on trips like these, and I had little or none. The entire landscape had been covered in snow during our family visit and now it was dark night, with virtually nothing visible from the coach as we drove along. Not even the great Rhine river could be seen. I had to limit myself to giving the group some information on St Columban to prepare them for our visit tomorrow to his first monastic foundations.

In front of me was Ó Fiaich's, *"Columbanus in his Own Words,"* now well-worn after its first year of use. I read the foreword out to the group, written by Damian Bracken. It describes Columban as a man of firsts in Irish history – the first Irish writer to leave "a literary corpus" behind him, the first Irish person to be the subject of a biography, the first person to describe himself as Irish and to explain what this means, the first Irish person to exert an influence on continental Europe. In one sense he was surprisingly prophetic, looking beyond the tribalism of individual nations to a unity built on Christian foundations. In a letter to the French bishops he writes, "We are all members of one body, whether Franks or Britons or Irish or whatever our race." Famously, Columban was the first person to use the expression *totius Europea* ("all of Europe"), which appears in his letter to Pope Gregory the Great. After the Second World War, European statesmen led by Robert Schuman (whose cause for sainthood was opened by Pope Francis on June 19th 2021) sought to advance the project of a united Europe by gathering various heads of state in Luxeuil and invoking St Columban as a patron for all who strive for European unity.

We arrived late at the hotel in Luxeuil, but were very well catered for with a hot dinner, the stew served to us by the manager himself. The official in charge of the local tourist office, Pierre, was also present. He assured us that he would introduce us to the mayor of the town and other dignitaries during our stay. Pierre seemed very enthusiastic to have a group in Luxeuil that came from the same part of Ireland as Saint Columban. "St Columban is really the founder of this town as it is today," he explained. "The Romans had a spa here from ancient times because of the thermal waters in the place. But this was completely destroyed by Attila the Hun in the fifth century. There was nothing left standing! Then Columban comes along and founds a monastery, school and library that would become world famous and last until the French Revolution. We have a lot to be grateful for! Tomorrow, we'll show you the archaeological excavations which prove that the Irish monks built their abbey on the ruins of the Roman buildings."

After breakfast the next day, we celebrated Mass in the beautiful abbey church of St Peter and St Paul. The parish priest, Fr Étienne Fétel, joined us for the celebration. He had the reliquary with relics of St Columban and St Gall taken out and put on display in the sanctuary for the group. A local man, Philippe, then gave us a tour of the church, which included the stained-glass windows depicting the "Forty Saints of Luxeuil," a testimony to the monks who established a flourishing Christian civilisation in the region. We also admired the exquisite wooden craftsmanship of the organ built in the 1600s.

Outside the abbey, we saw the famous statue of Columban by Grange. This had been unveiled in 1950 in the presence of Cardinal Roncalli (the future Pope St John XXIII), Robert Schuman, Éamon De Valera (Prime Minister of Ireland), and heads of state of eight countries gathered to honour St Columban. It was on this occasion that Schuman proposed his plan for a united Europe, a plan that began to take concrete shape shortly afterwards and that would eventually lead to the EU. As we looked at the fierce expression on the face of the sculpture of Columban, there in the shadow of the church of St Peter and Paul, the most imposing physical legacy of St Columban on the continent, we could sense the driven nature of the Irish monk, his uncompromising zeal to complete what he felt called to do. Standing here on other occasions in the following years, having watched the McAleese documentary, I would wonder how much of the monk's zeal was directed towards inclusiveness and respect for diversity.

After lunch, we gathered at the parking lot and boarded the coach. We had a very exciting prospect ahead – a visit to Columban's very first foundation and thus the first Irish monastic establishment on the European continent. After Columban came to Europe about the year 580, wave after wave of Irish missionaries arrived during the following centuries. As the Roman empire fell and vast areas of the continent came under the control of pagan tribes, there was a general collapse in education, law and order, and the structures of organised religion. Into this chaos came the

Irish missionaries, setting up monasteries, restoring education, building up agriculture and industry. There is overwhelming evidence that the Irish monks made an enormous contribution to preserving Christian civilisation in central Europe.

And here we were, about to visit the very first Irish monastic foundation on the continent, Annegray. This establishment had such success that Columban was compelled to found his second monastery ten miles to the west at Luxeuil and then a third, five miles away at Fontaines. So many monks were present that they had to take turns to sing the liturgy of the hours in the overcrowded chapels.

The half hour drive from Luxeuil due eastwards to Annegray is very scenic. Though the road is relatively level, the surrounding region is mountainous and the area is thickly forested. We were met at the site by Jacques Prudhon, president of *L'Association des Amis de Saint Colomban*, a local group dedicated to preserving the memory of the Irish saint. Jacques showed us the extensive excavations done in recent decades, much of it by the department of archaeology in University College Galway. The archaeologists still hadn't reached the level of the original Irish foundation, which would have had predominantly wooden buildings. Jacques told us that the archaeologists were hoping to find holes in the ground that would mark the place where wooden shafts would have been driven to support the original sixth century structure. We were all impressed by the great natural beauty and the peaceful atmosphere of this place that is so significant for the story of St Columban.

After our tour, as we wandered around the site and gazed at the scenery, I had a strong intuition of something, but I was not able to put it in words until after I had seen the McAleese documentary a few months later. As mentioned already, according to that documentary, one of the distinctive marks of the Irish monk was his openness to diversity. At Annegray, the sense one gets of the legacy of Columban is very different and not so suspiciously modern. Europe was in a state of relative chaos when the Irish missionaries arrived. Those who were ministers of the local Church were lazy and corrupt, preferring sport and hunting to tending their flocks. The knowledge of the faith among ordinary people would have been abysmal, since catechesis was inexistent and educational opportunities few. The local ruling class of Austrasia and Burgundy professed to be Christian, but were living in irregular marital arrangements, bringing the faith into disrepute. As we stood there in the beautiful vale of Annegray, surrounded by the sparse remains of the abbey walls, there was a tangible sense of Columban's foundation as something that was rooted in God. He had not come here to blend in with the corruption, laxity and heterodoxy of the times. He wished to establish something, but not something of his own making. That establishment would be embedded in the divine, in goodness, in truth, in the word of God. Someone who seeks to be inclusive is effectively on everyone's side.

Columban, no doubt, had respect for everyone as a child as God, but by his actions he showed that he was on the Lord's side first, come hell or high water. The high water was not long in coming.

Later, I wondered why I had this particular sense of Columban's spirituality as we stood in Annegray. When some time had passed, I realised where it had come from. I was reading a book by Romano Guardini, a favourite author of both Benedict XVI and Pope Francis:

> *"In the Christian life, faith has consequences, that to 'serve God' we must renounce 'Mammon,' that to be free for God we must break the hold that the world has on us. Faith demands a reconstruction of the inner life, a reforming that can be brought about only by overcoming."* (***The Conversion of Augustine***).

One thing that is clear about the life of Columban is his asceticism and his dedication to prayer. As we stood that day in the peace and natural simplicity of Annegray, we were beholding a foundation that was realised through overcoming the hold that the world has on us so as to be free for God. If Columban had begun his mission with talk about genuinely good things like tolerance, then he would not have gotten very far. Rather, by cooperating with God's grace, he first reconstructed his inner life. Only then could he contribute to reconstructing European civilisation.

On the return journey from Annegray, we asked the coach driver to turn in Sainte-Marie-en-Chanois and take the narrow forest road leading to the cave of Columban, a place of private retreat for the monk. A central element of his spirituality was the habit of spending extended time with God in absolute solitude. Laura and I had driven up here through the snow the previous winter and felt sure that the place would appeal to the pilgrims. Now, with the group, most of us walked the last half mile to the cave, the holy well and the little church dedicated to St Columban. By prior arrangement, members of *Les Amis de Saint Colomban* kindly made their cars available to shuttle group members who had difficulties walking from the coach.

These few minutes spent in Columban's cave, with the little holy well on the slope beneath it, were once again moments of magic for the group. Archbishop Fulton Sheen is quoted as saying that any brotherhood of man that does not place itself under the fatherhood of God results in tyranny. The reign of terror in the French Revolution and the global experience of communism demonstrate the flawed nature of any project that seeks to foster fraternity whilst systematically excluding the transcendent dimension of the human person. It is no accident that Columban's whole way of life was sustained by prayer in places like this cave. As others have put it, the vertical dimension of the monk's spirituality – his relationship with God – was the foundation of a correct horizontal relationship with people around him.

Our last visit today would be to Fontaines, the third foundation of Columban in the area. There is little to see here apart from the site of the original abbey, which is now occupied by a private house. The drive was more than ten miles, so it was an opportunity to recount to the group some more of the life of the Irish monk. The topic for this journey would be the tale of how he came to be banished from the region. The "official" motivation for his exile blamed his insistence that the abbeys be allowed to celebrate Easter according to the Irish method of calculating the date of the feast. This led to an investigation of the monasteries. Columban's refusal to grant the king access to the cloistered spaces of the abbey led eventually to his banishment.

The real motivation for expelling Columban was very different. In 595, a few years after the monk arrived in the area, King Childebert died. His sons became kings of Austrasia and Burgundy, but they were too young to ascend the throne, so their grandmother, Queen Brunhilde, ruled in their stead for a time. As Theuderich grew to manhood and assumed the kingship of Burgundy, he had a number of mistresses living in the royal household and they gave birth to four sons.

On one occasion, Queen Brunhilde asked Columban to bless the four illegitimate children publicly. Her motive for this may have been to validate their future claims to succeed their father. Whatever her reason, Columban refused to go along with the request. He raised his voice and said, "These children will never hold the royal sceptre because they were begotten in sin!" With that he stormed out of the palace.

From that moment, Columban's fate was sealed. Brunhilde began to agitate behind the scenes, petitioning the local bishops to investigate alleged irregularities in the Irish monasteries. Eventually the king's emissaries ordered that Columban, accompanied by all monks of Irish and Breton origin, was to be expelled. The brethren born in Gaul could remain in Burgundy. Columban and his companions were forced to march six hundred miles to Nantes, from where they would be placed on a ship for Ireland. Twenty fruitful years after they had founded Annegray, the sojourn on the continent seemed to have come to an end.

For many years, people have been lobbying that the Church should abandon its perennial teaching about marriage. In the documentary, at times, it was hard not to have the impression that Mrs McAleese was invoking Columban to support this agenda. The uncomfortable truth – supported by historical documentation - is that Columban was uncompromising when it came to the Christian vision of marriage. Far from embracing tolerance, his rejection of what was incompatible with this vision led to his expulsion from Burgundy. The Church's teaching that marriage is between one man and one woman and involves a bond, forged by God, that is indissoluble, is firmly rooted in Scripture and Tradition. It involves a cooperation with what God wants and what he has enshrined in human nature. Columban would hardly have refused a blessing on a child, yet he could not agree to a blessing that was staged by the Queen in order to legitimise the union of her grandson with multiple women. His refusal led directly to his banishment and the inception of one of the great missionary journeys of history.

The next morning, we began a small portion of that journey. We loaded the coach, took our leave of Luxeuil, and retraced the road towards Zurich, skirting around the natural park of the Vosges and passing the towns of Belfort and Mulhouse. This time, with the benefit of full daylight, we had fine views of the Rhine as we crossed the border into Switzerland at Basel.

Columban's banishment did not go as the secular authorities planned. In Nantes, the captain of the ship that was supposed to take the monks back to Ireland lost his nerve when a storm blew up and God himself seemed to be preventing the sailing. The monks were released and they began an epic trek across France. Following the course of the Rhine, they came into what is today Switzerland and Austria.

The next day, following part of this route, we drove past Zurich and arrived at our hotel just outside St Gallen in the early afternoon. There was time to check in and have a short rest in our rooms before continuing to the centre of the city. We were given an interesting tour of the Cathedral of St Gall by diocesan staff. This tour included the crypt, with the skull of St Gall, and the bishop's private chapel, which is believed to stand on the site of the original hermitage of the Irish saint. Bishop Markus Büchel joined in concelebrating the Mass. Afterwards there was free time for dinner in the beautiful town before returning to our hotel.

Next morning, we visited the famous Abbey Library. Bishop Noel had contacted the diocese of St Gallen in advance and arranged for the library to put on display some precious manuscripts of Irish interest that would not normally be available for public viewing. We didn't know in advance which manuscripts would be on view, but someone expressed the hope that they might include the famous **Grammar** by Priscian, the standard textbook for the study of Latin during the Middle Ages. The St Gallen copy was probably made in Bangor about the year 850 and later taken to the continent. The monks who made the manuscript jotted over nine thousand notes in native Irish on the margins about all kinds of things, including short poems and news on everyday matters in the monastery. Incredibly, these "glosses" were to become the most important sources of our knowledge of Old Irish. One of the most famous is an ironic poem about the weather. The monk is taking comfort from the storm since it makes an attack by the Vikings unlikely this evening:

The bitter wind is high tonight,
It lifts the high locks of the sea,
In such wild winter storm no fright
Of savage Viking troubles me.

The Abbey Library is on the UNESCO world heritage list, not only for its wealth of manuscripts, but also for the workmanship in wood of the bookcases and the floor. Before entering, we all had to don large slippers over our shoes in order to protect the antique wooden floor.

Our guide gave us a general description of the library and its significance, tying it in with the legacy of

Columban, who attached great importance to education. His monasteries were centres of learning and became famous for their libraries and scriptoria (workshops in which manuscripts were copied). Since the printing press had not yet been invented, these scriptoria had a vital place in the preservation of culture and learning. She revealed another remarkable fact: nearly *all* surviving manuscripts from continental Europe produced during the seventh and eighth centuries are due to the Columban foundations. These are now in the libraries in Turin, Milan and, especially, St. Gallen.

At that juncture, she pointed to a significant example of one such manuscript on display in the centre of the room. It was Priscian's **Latin Grammar**! The famous work that we had heard so much about had been taken out especially for us, but it was inside a glass cabinet and only one page was visible. Which page would it be? Would it include any of the glosses? Later, when we had some time to look closely, there was a general thrill when it emerged that the page on view contained the very gloss with the poem in Old Irish about the Vikings!

The following days are for me a blur of memories. The sight of Lake Constance at Bregenz, the city in western Austria where Columban established his fourth foundation in the ruins of the old Roman fort of Brigantium; the visit to the church of St Gallus which probably stands on the remains of the original Columban monastery; singing vespers with the Cistercians at Mehrerau Abbey on the shores of the lake and hearing the monks recount the old tradition that St Columban had established his monastery on the very spot where Mehrerau now stands; the drive along the upper valley of the Rhine towards the San Bernardino Pass, with Austria and then Liechtenstein on our left, recalling how so much of St Columban's journeys on the continent involved following the course of this great river; crossing into the Swiss canton of Ticino, the only predominantly Italian-speaking region in Switzerland, through the tunnel below the San Bernardino Pass, over which Columban would have walked on his way to Italy; driving along the spectacular Melide Causeway that spans Lake Lugano and approaches the Italian border; celebrating Mass in Milan's Duomo and recalling that Columban would have preached his sermons against Arianism in an original church that stood on this site; being led in procession with Bishop Noel after Mass right to the tomb of St Charles Borromeo, reforming archbishop and patron of the city; and then the great last few days in Bobbio, the spectacular ancient bridge across the Trebbia river, the prayer vigils, Masses, concerts and gatherings for dinner with thousands of people from all over the continent who attributed their faith to the work of Columban.

In the following years, the renewed interest in Columban prompted other groups to travel with us in the footsteps of the Irish monk. Our itinerary had now expanded to include the city of Zurich, the biggest waterfall in Europe near Schaffhausen on the Rhine, and a boat trip on Lake Constance to the old town of Lindau in Germany. The St Gallen library was still on the programme, though we never again saw the Irish manuscripts on display. On each occasion that we visited Annegray, I wondered at what Columban had built and how his legacy was related to the modern conception of inclusiveness.

Understanding crystallizes slowly in my mind. As time went on, I began to develop a clearer appreciation of how Columban had contributed to European civilisation. He was rooted in Christ. He knew the Bible and the Church Fathers. He was committed to prayer. He was passionately loyal to the See of Peter. It was that loyalty, in fact, that impelled him to challenge the pope to exercise his ministry faithfully. He saw his own life as a pilgrimage in the service of Christ. He was a fearless speaker in defence of what he called "God's cause." The establishments that he was founding were not simply human institutions. They were part of the fabric of the Church, which is ultimately mystical in nature.

The fact that it is probably possible to sum up Columban in relatively few words such as these points to what it is that makes him a pillar of European civilisation. The key to his life was his relationship with God. Upon this grounding on God, other, secondary, principles can be based, such as, for example, tolerance. But principles such as toleration of diversity, or concern for others, by themselves can never be the starting point for a lasting and just civilisation. The tyrannies of the twentieth century, all of them based upon godless visions of wellbeing, are sufficient testimony that a just and humane civilisation cannot be founded on a purely materialistic conception of the human person.

What Columban built at Annegray, and which was then replicated in dozens of other abbeys around Europe, was not founded simply on concern for others. It was based, rather, on the conviction that God is ultimate and that he is everything. In following him, all else finds its proper place. Society is then grounded securely and ordered well. When my behaviour is ordered towards my creator, my conscience will demand that I deal with others in a manner worthy of their dignity as children of God. Looking back on my life, I can see that I did not treat others with respect during those years when my existence was ordered towards myself. Failing to appreciate the beautiful and transcendent nature of the other person, I behaved badly and hurt others. As my relationship with God was purified, so too was my behaviour towards others.

On one of those trips in the footsteps of Columban, we were driving across Switzerland towards the Austrian border. Time was at a premium and I just given the fastest city tour of Zurich in history (though I still made time for my customary cappuccino in the café once frequented by Einstein). It was "quiet time" on the coach. A lady named Anne, who had come on many of our trips, appeared at the top of the bus and passed me a copy of Dietrich von Hildebrand's **Beauty in the Light of the Redemption**. The author converted to the faith from atheism in his twenties and went on to become an ardent opponent of Hitler's national socialism. Anne pointed out an excerpt that she thought was interesting. "It fits in with what you have been saying about Columban's reordering of this region following the collapse of the Roman Empire," she said, and went back to her seat, leaving me with the book. I began to read it then and there, with the panorama of Lake Constance opening up before us.

Von Hildebrand made the point that the more we love God above all else, the deeper and purer is our love for created things. Inordinate attachment to things in this world is a form of idolatry. We are inclined to think that passionate love for creatures is a powerful thing, but it is a lesser love, not a higher love. When I love the things of this world in the context of my relationship in Christ, with the power of the Holy Spirit, then my love reaches its full measure.

This made me think once again of Mrs McAleese's documentary. Prominent voices in our society demand that Christianity change its teachings to accommodate currents in culture, that the Church adapt to the times. If it were a purely human institution, then perhaps it should get with the times. The fact is though that the Church - even if many people might wish otherwise - is of divine origin, is bound by divine revelation, and transmits the power of God. If the Lord taught thousands of years ago that the highpoint of his creation was man and woman - called into a covenant of love that reflects the image and likeness of God - then the Church has no power to alter that teaching in response to the changing currents of culture, even if it must show tender respect towards those that think otherwise.

In any year, most of our trips are to Italy, so these reflections on Columban were being tempered now and then with deliberations on the contribution of Italian figures to the development of European civilisation. St Benedict was the most important of these. Political events in 2016, coupled with a natural disaster, brought the legacy of Benedict into the spotlight (briefly) in a controversial way.

During that summer of 2016, a new law was passed in Italy permitting civil unions between people of the same sex. The first unions under the new law came into being during the month of August. There was little enough public controversy about the introduction of the new legislation and Laura and I were not even aware of it. On account to the special Jubilee of Mercy called by Pope Francis, 2016 had been our busiest season in years and the law regarding civil unions had passed under the radar for us. On the morning of August 24th at about 3.30am, we were awakened by the sound of the door on our sixth-floor bedroom in Rome repeatedly opening and closing, apparently by itself. The chandelier on the ceiling began to swing and the beds began to move. We had experienced earthquakes previously, but nothing as dramatic as this one. Later we learned that, tragically, about three hundred people died in the quake, most of these in the town of Amatrice in northern Lazio.

In the following weeks, there were thousands of aftershocks in central Italy. We were back in Ireland on

October 30th when a 6.6-magnitude tremor hit the very centre of the peninsula. It was the biggest earthquake in thirty-six years, though there were no direct fatalities. A few days later, in a transmission for Radio Maria, Dominican theologian Giovanni Cavalcoli said that the earthquake was divine chastisement for "the offence to the family and the dignity of marriage, in particular through civil unions." Fr Cavalcoli's statement was swiftly and roundly condemned by a host of authoritative figures in the Church, including Archbishop Angelo Becciu of the Vatican secretariat of state. He said that Cavalcoli's remarks were "offensive to believers and disgraceful for non-believers." Becciu apologized to quake victims and assured them they had the "solidarity and support" of Pope Francis.

The ***Osservatore Romano***, official newspaper of the Holy See, described the affirmations as "offensive" and assured the victims of Pope Francis' closeness to all those affected by the earthquake. Radio Maria moved swiftly to distance itself from the transmission and suspended Father Cavalcoli from the station with immediate effect. For his part, the Dominican theologian refused to back down. He told the Vatican to "read your catechism" and insisted that earthquakes were "caused by the sins of men."

Almost two years later, Laura and I were doing more extensive driving than usual in Umbria because we had to prepare for a pilgrimage to the region that would take in Orvieto, Spoleto, Assisi, Montefalco and Cascia. Norcia was not far off our route one day and we decided to drive there, even though we knew the town had been devasted by the earthquake. We parked outside the city walls and walked the short distance to the centre to behold the ruins of the basilica of St Benedict. In a house on this spot, St Benedict had been born in the year 480. The scale of the destruction was shocking. Nothing had yet been rebuilt, as far as we could see. It was a scene of absolute desolation.

St Benedict has always been considered the principal founder of western monasticism, though modern scholarship has rediscovered the crucial role of Columban and his followers. This monastic movement helped to re-Christianize and re-civilize Europe after the fall of the western Roman empire. As well as preaching the Gospel, the monks helped to bring order, discipline, and learning to a continent in chaos. The Benedictine rule, with its emphasis on prayer, manual work and study, became in turn the basis of the rules of other religious orders. It is no accident that St Benedict is one of the main patrons of Europe. Indeed, he and his order can be considered a pillar of European civilisation.

From the twelfth century until the 2016 earthquake, the church built over the birthplace of Benedict stayed substantially the same. Now, all that remained was the façade and part of the apse. The rest had been completely destroyed, along with many other historic buildings in Norcia, not to mention the homes of ordinary families. As Laura, the children and I stood there in Norcia and remembered what we had heard about Benedict's role in the construction of a Christian

Europe, we recalled again Father Cavalcoli's assertion that the destruction of the birthplace of the patron of the continent should be taken as a sign – a sign that we have betrayed our Christian roots and that the Lord is calling us to repentance. The sign seemed real since the epicentre of the earthquake was only five km from here.

It is understandable and perhaps right that Church authorities quickly distanced themselves from the comments. The priority in the aftermath of the earthquake was solidarity and care for the victims. Attributing blame for the cause of the earthquake was hardly helpful to those families who at that moment were acutely suffering its effects. But was Bishop Galantino correct in saying that comments of this sort constituted "paganism without limits"? And was Vatican Radio right to say that the Dominican's position was "not in line with the proclamation of mercy which is the essence of Christianity and the pastoral activity of Pope Francis"?

The central question here is: "Can a God with a merciful nature be compatible with a God who chastises humanity?" After seeing the devastation in Norcia, this question came frequently to mind over the following months. It was clear that there is a difference between punishment for the sake of punishment, and a punishment that seeks to chastise humanity in order to lead it to the fullness of life. The Bible is full of stories of this merciful God who chastises: the plagues of Egypt, the forty years of hard formation in the desert, the punishment of various kings for their infidelities, the exiles, and much more – *"For the Lord chastises those he loves, and scourges the people he calls his own"* (Hebrews 12,6). C.S. Lewis is often quoted as saying that "God whispers to us in our pleasures, speaks in our conscience, but shouts in our pain: it is His megaphone to rouse a deaf world."

Upon rereading the transcript of the transmission by Father Cavalcoli, I saw that the phrase he used more often than divine punishment was "divine chastisement" ("castigo divino"). "Punishment" refers to the retribution received for one's offences, whereas "chastisement" refers to a corrective action with view to amendment of behaviour. Jesus himself, in the discourse at the Last Supper, says, *"I am the true vine, and my Father is the gardener. He cuts off every branch in me that bears no fruit, while every branch that does bear fruit he prunes so that it will be even more fruitful"* (John 15, 1-2).

Surely God does chastise us with the intention of changing us for the better? Has it just become too politically incorrect nowadays to associate the Lord's chastisement with particular behaviour, especially behaviour which is most dear to the cultural establishment such as that which contravenes the biblical teaching about marriage? The real problem, however, regards the suffering of the innocent. We can grant that God chastises wayward people in order to lead them back to himself, but how can we comprehend the claim that a merciful God permits the suffering or death of children?

In August 2016, the diocese of Meath made a pilgrimage to Rome. On one of the days, we went on an excursion to Subiaco, considered the cradle of the Benedictine order. After spending his childhood in Norcia, Benedict had come to Rome to study law. Disillusioned with the corruption and depravity of Rome, the young man had become a hermit in the hills of Lazio about fifty miles to the east of the city. He ended up spending three years here in solitude and prayer before establishing the Benedictine order.

After a few days in the hustle and bustle of Rome, the group enjoyed the scenic drive to Subiaco through the thickly forested mountains of east Lazio. The motorway across the Apennines has some of the highest viaducts in Italy. Someone commented on the lush greenness of the area despite the many weeks of intense summer sun with little rain. During the last stretch of the journey, in order to reach the monastery of St Benedict, we had to drive through the ancient town of Subiaco. This was established in the first century by the Emperor Nero as a settlement for the craftsmen who were working on his sumptuous villa. Later, we passed the ruins of this villa as we began the spectacular climb to the monastery.

During the climb, we also passed another significant Benedictine monastery, Santa Scholastica, named for the sister of Benedict. The Meath group was booked for lunch in the restaurant here. First of all, we would have a tour of the upper monastery and celebrate Mass, before returning down to Santa Scholastica for our meal. The sisters traditionally give us a "digestivo" (after-dinner liquor) at the end of lunch. Made by the monks, its sweet and sticky consistency always reminds me of cough medicine. As we drove past Santa Scholastica, I mentioned to the group that there would be "cough medicine" for everyone after lunch.

The upper monastery is called the "Sacro Speco" (the Holy Cave) because it is centred on the grotto in which the young monk lived as a hermit for three years. The various levels of the building have an important cycle of medieval frescoes depicting scenes from the life of St Benedict, as well as scenes from the life of Christ. In the cave itself, there is a fresco of the Assumption of Mary from the 1300s that is particularly beautiful. Mary is seated with her Son in an intimate embrace. His right hand is around her shoulder, while her right hand is held devotedly in his left. Mary leans her head on Jesus' shoulder. They are surrounded by a group of angels with a dazzling array of musical instruments. This intimate scene of celebration constitutes a deep theological reflection on the event of the Assumption, painted six hundred years before it was formally defined by the Church.

After our tour, we began the celebration of Mass. In his homily, Bishop Smith drew attention to the historical fact that the Benedictine movement, one of the most significant contributors to the civilisation of Europe, began in a cave where a young man put God above everything and submitted himself to the divine will. As he spoke, I thought of Columban in his cave near Annegray and remembered again the saying that a true brotherhood of man can only be forged when we place ourselves under the fatherhood of God.

The Eucharistic prayer began and Stephen (who by now was almost twelve) and I were kneeling in a pew about middle way down the chapel. There were three or four priests concelebrating with Bishop Smith. When it came to the "Our Father" I realised that I wasn't quite myself and had some difficulty standing, but I still managed to receive Communion. After Communion, Stephen and I knelt again on the back pew, but by now I was not feeling well at all. At the final blessing everyone stood up, but I remained kneeling because I couldn't trust myself to stand up. People in the group must have been struck by my uncharacteristic display of piety. I have a vague recollection of Stephen looking over at me apprehensively. Then the priests began to process out with Bishop Smith at the rear. As the bishop approached, I fainted, was caught by someone and dragged out, in the midst of the procession, to a balcony at the back of the chapel. It was a most undignified end to the Mass. Out on the balcony, I came around quickly in the fresh air and found Stephen beside me looking into my face anxiously. Despite the feeling of embarrassment, I couldn't help being struck by the wildness and beauty of the panorama that opened out beneath us. An hour later, down at Santa Scholastica, I was fully recovered and took more than one dose of "cough medicine" after lunch, just to be on the safe side.

With or without the reinforcement of cough medicine, trips like these to Subiaco and Montecassino can only galvanise in the visitor the conviction that Benedict's spirituality was grounded on that vertical connection with God, and it was this that made his order a pillar of European civilisation. But could we accept Fr Cavalcoli's claim that the destruction of Benedict's birthplace was chastisement by God for Europe's betrayal of its Christian foundations?

The question of evil and the suffering of the innocent has echoed through the centuries since the time of Job. Some light was shed for me, however, the following year, when the Gospel was read for the third Sunday of Lent, a day that happened to fall on my birthday that year.

"Now there were some present at that time who told Jesus about the Galileans whose blood Pilate had mixed with their sacrifices. Jesus answered, 'Do you think that these Galileans were worse sinners than all the other Galileans because they suffered this way? I tell you, no! But unless you repent, you too will all perish . . .'

Then he told this parable: 'A man had a fig tree growing in his vineyard, and he went to look for fruit on it but did not find any. So he said to the man who took care of the vineyard, "For three years now I've been coming to look for fruit on this fig tree and haven't found any. Cut it down! Why should it use up the soil?"

"Sir," the man replied, "leave it alone for one more year, and I'll dig around it and fertilize it. If it bears fruit next year, fine! If not, then cut it down."' (Luke 13, 1-8).

It is probably easy enough for us to accept that suffering can be a call to conversion. To some degree or other, we have all encountered illness and bereavement in our families, and we can appreciate that we are not being afflicted for punishment's sake. The Lord is digging around us and fertilizing us, hoping that we will produce some fruit. What makes suffering mysterious, however, is the affliction or death of the innocent, of children who have not reached the age of reason. How can good come out of such suffering? This mystery can be a real obstacle to faith.

As this Gospel was read, though, I felt a chink of enlightenment. Jesus is affirming clearly that the ones who suffer the most should not be considered more guilty or more deserving of God's "punishment." In fact, as we know ourselves, the very opposite seems to be the case. The greatest sinners often have lives of comfort, making people envy them and despair about God's justice. Scripture tells us, however, that the Lord chastises those he loves the most, as the lives of the saints show very clearly. This means that the very comfort enjoyed by sinners can be a sign of reproof by God. When the innocent suffer, we tend to wonder why God would want to afflict them, but perhaps we should view this affliction as a mysterious mark of love. Certainly, it would be wrong to trivialize the death of the innocent, but if a child dies in an earthquake, we can be sure that the merciful Lord has gathered this child into his arms with love and brought him to paradise. In addition, the suffering of the innocent can have redemptive value for others. Our faith should provide us with this absolute conviction.

This fragment of light made me review what Father Cavalcoli had said about the earthquake in 2016 and to imagine an alternative articulation of his point. He was justified, surely, in seeing a link between an earthquake centred in Norcia – which destroyed the church over the birthplace of one of the pillars of European civilisation – and the progressive political and social unravelling of the foundations of a Christian culture. This link is an indication that natural disasters of this sort have a meaning in God's plan. They are not the senseless, atheism-prompting events that many people make them out to be. Instead, they are a call to make God the centre of our lives, to trust no longer in the order of this world which is so precarious and fleeting.

Perhaps, though, instead of presenting the earthquake in largely negative terms as God's affliction of Italy in response to her infidelity, the Dominican could have presented it as God's compassionate plan to correct his people and lead them to himself. Yes, the suffering of the innocent is mysterious, but in faith we can be sure that the Lord cared for them with love, even in the midst of the earthquake.

Having heard this Gospel and reflected on Jesus' avowal that God does indeed dig around us – even the innocent among us - in order to make us fruitful, it was hard not to feel convinced that Father Cavalcoli had indeed made a prophetic statement that was rather too hastily suppressed. The destruction of the birthplace of one of the pillars of Western Civilisation can surely be taken as a sign from God that we turn our backs on our Christian roots at our peril. It stands as an ominous message for Christian Europe, a desperate call from our heavenly Father to repentance and conversion.

Three weeks after the reading of this Gospel, we turned on the news to discover that Notre Dame in Paris was burning. The effects of the traumatic event on France reverberated across Europe. In the aftermath, opinions similar to that of Father Cavalcoli began to be heard a little more frequently. Could the destruction of one of the most renowned buildings in the West be a divine warning that European civilisation was on the brink? Suddenly, the world seemed to be staggering from one ominous event to the next. Less than a year later, humanity was in the grip of a pandemic of biblical proportions. Now, the Dominican priest's warnings seemed less far-fetched as our economic and social supports were being stripped away. Was the Lord calling us back to fidelity to him by detaching us from the securities of this world?

These years of wandering in the footsteps of Columban and Benedict have helped my perspective. If the McAleese documentary was disconcerting back in 2015, now it is no longer so. I have no doubt that it misconstrues Columban's contribution to European civilisation. What Mrs McAleese claims – no doubt sincerely – to be the Irish saint's central message would hardly keep a sports team together, let alone be the basis for a just and humane civilisation.

Columban knew that he was created by a loving God in his image and likeness. He also knew that sin had damaged our nature and that we were in need of redemption. Redemption is a journey in which the Lord refashions us in his likeness, a likeness that we have lost through sin. He does that by suffering for us in our flesh, offering himself to the Father in our place. Columban had no doubt that true life could only be obtained by living with, for and in Jesus. The foundation of his life was prayer and the austere practices by which Christ in him would overcome the sinful tendencies of a fallen nature and reconstruct the heart from within. Built on Christ in this way, Columban could become a genuine builder of European civilisation because his desires and actions had been purified in the crucible of his spiritual life. Once his heart had been rebuilt by Christ, only then could he have the potential to rebuild society.

The Columban of the McAleese documentary did not seem aware of the reality of personal sin and the need for redemption. He was someone decidedly more modern, more concerned with the immanent that the transcendent. He speaks of inclusion, but lacks the radical attachment to the transcendent that – alone – enables us to love the other selflessly. He agitates that everyone should be allowed to achieve self-realisation, yet never considers that our desires are disordered and in need of purification and correction. If I talk endlessly about the inclusion of others, but have not dealt with my personal sin, or allowed grace to rebuild my disordered heart, then my words will remain only words.

It would be incredible if it had not become so commonplace. People everywhere, from inside and outside the faith, are demanding more and more aggressively that the Church change its teachings so that those teachings conform to the spirit of the world. According to the current spirit of the times, the thing that counts the most is the freedom to do what I discern is good for me. The irony is that the bedrock of Christian spirituality is the discernment of what *God* wants for me, as opposed to what I want, or what the world wants. The Church's role is to put God prophetically first in all things, before material gain, before prestige, before comfort. If the Church fails in her task to put God first, then she is guilty of idolatry, the idolatry of that which she has placed before God.

In addition, right discernment involves self-overcoming. A child who has been spoiled, who has never had to delay gratification, how can he make a discerning choice, which by nature requires the ability to see from the point of view of the other? It requires the virtues, strengthened by the gifts of the Holy Spirit.

Ironies abound. Columban had been sent packing because he stood up to the secular powers and held fast to Christ's teaching on marriage. Now, people call on the Church to submit to the secular culture's view on marriage and abandon the teaching it received from Christ. I was struck by this irony in July of 2018, as we listened to a homily from Vatican Radio in the car while driving into Rome. It happened to be the feast of St Benedict, but the homily was for the following Sunday.

The first reading was from the prophet Amos. Amaziah, the official "prophet" at the royal sanctuary of Bethel was telling Amos to go away; they did not want him saying things that were uncomfortable to hear. The task of the prophet, according to Amaziah, was not to challenge people, but to support the status quo.

Amos replies that he has no natural inclination to be a prophet. It was the Lord who took him from his life as a peasant and sent him to preach repentance to the king. In saying this, Amos is underlining something vital. The task of the prophet in the Old Testament is to speak in place of God. The prophet is radically rooted in God's word and this - almost always - places him in conflict with the secular powers. The powers-that-be have their own agenda, and it is generally a materialistic one. The true prophet has no agenda of his own, but only that of God. This was true of Amos, as it was true of Benedict, and of Columban. The message they proclaimed was sown by the Lord. It was not their own. They did not twist it to suit themselves or the spirit of their times. They received it like seed into virginal ground.

Chapter Six
Sown in Virginal Ground

"The stillness of prayer is the most essential condition for fruitful action. Before all else, the disciple kneels down."
St Gianna Molla

A week in Rome can seem a long time. Even if the itinerary each day is different, it is inevitable that we pass certain roads and monuments repeatedly. A courier is expected to keep up an informative commentary all the time, but when you have different groups in successive weeks, it can be hard to remember what exactly you said to who. "Did I already tell them the history of the Aurelian city walls? Oh, what the heck, I'll say it again anyway, just in case. Better to say it twice than not at all."

The power of Rome was built in part on her efficient road system. This allowed the quick movement of troops and goods to all parts of the empire. According to the old saying, all of these roads led to the Eternal City. Many of the old consular roads are still partially visible fanning out from Rome, the most famous being the Old Appian Way. Some of these ancient highways can be pointed out from the coach from a distance because they are lined with the distinctive umbrella pine trees that are so characteristic of Rome. Such trees lined all the consular routes in olden times, providing shade from the sun. They have been continually resown over the centuries and are still to be found on large stretches of the ancient roads.

Given that during a week in Rome, with excursions to places like Assisi, Tivoli and Castelgandolfo, we would often pass stretches of old roads with the pine trees, I would find myself wondering if the umbrella pine had already been mentioned to this particular group or not. If my memory failed me, then I would tell them anyway, just to be sure.

One August day we had two pilgrimages on the move in Rome. One was leaving the city after their week's stay, departing with Ryanair from Ciampino, the small airport that is located to the southeast of the city. The other was arriving the same evening in the much larger Fiumicino airport, located to the southwest. There were about ninety minutes between the check-in time for the outbound group and the arrival time for the inbound one, so the plan was for me to help the first group check in and then make a mad dash for the other airport to greet the second group. However, when I arrived for check-in with first group, we were informed that there was a problem with the aircraft and the flight would be delayed for some hours. Ciampino is very small and, at that time, the seating was completely inadequate for the numbers passing through. People were always left standing for long periods while they waited for boarding. Leaving the group hanging around the airport for four hours didn't seem a good option, but we had the second group arriving at Fiumicino and I needed to be on my way very shortly. What would we do?

Over a hurried phone call with Laura, we decided that we would employ the coach for a few more hours, reload the first group, and take them to Castelgandolfo for dinner to kill some time. In the meantime, we would find a new courier to go to Fiumicino and pick up the second group. Laura immediately phoned Mirella, a trusted courier that we had used on many occasions, but she turned out to be busy. Other couriers that we knew were also unavailable.

"Laura, how about if you go yourself and pick up the second group? It should be fairly straightforward. You just have to bring them to the hotel and check them in. There's no itinerary to be followed tonight."

I tried to sound casual, but was well aware that Laura had no inclination to do the work of a courier. In fact, she preferred to avoid travelling altogether with groups and devoted herself to doing the never-ending office work, which meant I nearly always travelled alone.

"But what will I tell them as we're driving in from the airport?" she asked. "I have no idea what to say!"

"It's not really important so long as you keep talking. Just chatter to them about anything. Keep it as light as possible. You're a Roman, you'll think of something to say about Rome!"

A couple of hours later, Laura had collected her group at Fiumicino and successfully marshalled them onto the coach. As they drove towards Rome in the dusk, she began her commentary. At one point along the journey, a woman a couple of seats back asked a question.

"Do you see that line of pine trees over there off the motorway? What are they called?"

"Well, that's the distinctive pine tree of Rome," Laura said. "You find them in parks and gardens, along the main roads, everywhere in fact."

"I was on a trip a couple of years ago and the courier said they were called 'umbrella' pines. Does that sound right to you?"

"That's the first I ever heard of it. We just call them 'pini' - pine trees."

"I just knew it! The *umbrellicus* pine my foot! I had a feeling that a *lot* of what that courier was saying was just made up! And *you* would know these things, you're a Roman, right?"

"Oh, yes, born and bred," replied Laura cheerfully.

"I'd say a lot of what we were told that time was nonsense!"

"Well," Laura said, "you can't really trust a lot of these couriers. They just say the first thing that comes into their heads and hope that no-one knows any better. Was she Italian?"

"It wasn't a 'she'! And to make matters worse, he was *Irish*. I had a feeling that he had just arrived into Rome for the first time on the previous flight to ours and was completely winging it."

"It takes many years to get to know Rome well," said Laura chattily, the penny refusing to drop. "There's such a long history here and so many monuments."

"Exactly! I would have liked to have heard some of that historical stuff, but instead he must have talked about the umbrella pine at least four times! You'd think there was nothing else to see around here!"

Later, when Laura reported this exchange to me (and after my unsuccessful attempt to strangle her), we came to a mutual decision that she return permanently to her office job.

Remembering what had already been said to groups wasn't the only challenge. Sometimes it was difficult to know just how to pitch the tour, for not all of the trips were pilgrimages - some were holidays organised by retirement groups, choirs or groups of friends. But if the tour was passing by an important sanctuary, then it really seemed essential to give a brief history of the place and a summary of the life of the associated saint. This didn't always go down so well. A few times I could even hear the grumbling from where I was sitting.

"More talk about saints, heaven help us!"

"How many times is he going to mention St Francis of Assisi!"

"If I hear anything about another church, I'm joining the Buddhists!"

Normal grumbling aside, every now and then we would get a person on the trip who seemed to have a more serious grievance with the Christian faith. Sometimes they would manifest their discontent with prickly questions during the tours. Other times they would approach me privately to discuss an issue that they considered to prove decisively that the Church was in error, or that faith was futile.

It was 1997 and I was working in Lourdes for the summer, the junior courier for an established company. A large diocesan pilgrimage had arrived that particular afternoon and we had ferried them in different coaches to the three separate hotels we were using. I was assigned to Hotel Paradis and was going around the tables after dinner to explain the programme for the following day. One of the tables had been set for two, but it had only one occupant when I arrived, a man of about thirty years old.

"The other place there was set for my mother," he explained. "She's really tired though, so she decided to skip dinner."

I began to go through the next day's programme, but the young man soon interrupted me.

"Look, I appreciate your help, but I won't be attending Masses or processions or anything like that." There was a hint of disparagement in his voice.

"Oh?" I said, taken aback slightly.

"My mother has cancer, and that's the only reason she came here to Lourdes - she's looking for a cure. I don't believe any of that stuff, but someone has to accompany her."

"She probably would want to join in the pilgrimage events though, I imagine?"

"Oh no, all she wants to do is go to the baths. We're going to head down there ourselves tomorrow afternoon. You won't see us at any of the other events, so there's no need to look out for us."

I found out soon enough that the young man's name was Robert. Despite his insistence that he and his mother would be doing their own thing, I heard quite a bit from him over the coming days, much of it a diatribe against the miracles that had allegedly occurred at Lourdes.

At the ninth apparition, on February 25th 1858, the lady instructed Bernadette to go and drink at the spring and eat the bitter herbs she found there. The little girl went to the back of the cave to the spot pointed out by the lady, and scratched at the ground until water began to flow. Obeying the lady's instructions, Bernadette washed her face in the muddy water and drank some of it. The three hundred people present were so shocked at this bizarre behaviour that many began to complain openly. In the hours following the apparition, however, the water began to flow more copiously and became perfectly clear. The first miracles of Lourdes were all associated with bathing in the water from this spring. In the century and a half that followed, the majority of healings were linked to the baths.

For many years, the experience of immersing oneself fully in the ice-cold water of the baths was part and parcel of a standard pilgrimage to Lourdes. In 2020, as a result of Covid-19, the baths were closed temporarily. When they were reopened in 2021, their way of operating was dramatically changed. Immersion in the baths was now replaced by a "water gesture." Pilgrims queued up as normal in front of the same cubicles once used for the baths, before being taken in as individuals, or in family groups, by one of the volunteers. With the aid of a jug of water poured by the volunteer, hands and face were washed. Then, with hands cupped to receive the water from the jug, each pilgrim drank. It was interesting that Covid-19 had actually brought the practice at Lourdes more into line with Our Lady's original instructions to Bernadette, which specified only the washing of face and hands, in addition to drinking the water.

In 1997, however, full immersion in the baths was a staple part of a visit to Lourdes, especially for those who hoped to find miraculous healing. It was not surprising that the main interest of Robert's mother was in the baths.

On the morning following the arrival of the group, after breakfast, I was standing in the hotel lobby waiting for the pilgrims to gather. We would have Mass shortly in the sanctuary. As I stood there, Robert ambled over casually.

"Mother's not up yet. I'll just hang around the lobby here until she surfaces."

"Great. We're heading to Mass now and then we're all going to gather in front of the grotto for a prayer with the bishop."

"You know, all this stuff about coming to Lourdes for healing doesn't really add up."

"What do you mean?"

"Well, people seem to think that if they have cancer or some incurable disease then they have a good chance of getting a cure at Lourdes, but the figures don't bear that out. There have only been sixty-something official cures at the shrine. In the past one hundred and fifty years, literally *millions* of people have come here looking for a cure. If you take any group of that many millions of sick people, you'll find that sixty of them get cured unexpectedly or inexplicably, even if they never visited a shrine or believed in God!"

I was taken aback because I hadn't realised that there were so few official cures. Before I could mumble some sort of reply, Robert began speaking again.

"There's a thing called the placebo effect, you know. If we count up all the people that have been cured here compared to the vast numbers who have come, it's something like a one-in-three-million chance of a miracle. Spontaneous remissions in cancer actually happen a lot more often!"

I tried desperately to think of some acceptable response. "We shouldn't dismiss what is happening here on the basis of numbers, though, Robert. Our Lady showed Bernadette the spring and asked that people come and bathe, so it *must* be a good thing. It probably has many good effects that don't show up in official figures."

"'Our Lady showed Bernadette the spring'!" Robert repeated, in a mocking voice. "How can we be sure that this little girl saw *any*thing? Her family were living in abject destitution. If I was living in that situation, I might start wishing for a heavenly visitor myself to lead me out of poverty!"

The conversation was making me uneasy as we were becoming ever more surrounded by group members as they came down from their rooms into the lobby. It was already time to go and I said to Robert that we could continue our chat at lunchtime if he wanted.

"Oh, yes, that would be good," he replied drily. "I have quite a bit more to say about this place and its fatal attraction for people who are terminally ill!"

As I led the group along the river towards the sanctuary, I thought uneasily of my own aunt who had come to Lourdes with cancer and died soon after returning home. A brother of one of my best friends had met a similar fate. In fact, I had heard of quite a few people who had come for a miracle and died shortly afterwards anyway. The only person I knew personally who claimed to have been cured in Lourdes hadn't been suffering from anything too serious in the first place. The 'cure' could easily have been merely in her head. Was Robert right that this place had no great claim to being a place of healing if we compare the vast numbers of pilgrims to the modest record of cures?

Mass was in the basilica of the Rosary, a church with three groups of five chapels arranged in a semicircle. The chapels to the left have mosaics depicting the five Joyful Mysteries of the Rosary, the chapels directly behind the main altar show the Sorrowful Mysteries, whilst the chapels to the right has the Glorious Mysteries. Above the five central chapels is a massive mosaic of Mary with the words "Par Marie A Jesus" – *through Mary to Jesus*.

During Mass, I continued to have the same uneasy feeling. What exactly could I say to Robert at lunchtime when he began assailing me again about the impotence of Lourdes? When the celebration was over, the group gathered with the bishop in front of the Grotto for a few minutes of prayer. Afterwards we all filed underneath the statue of Our Lady, placed in the same niche where Bernadette saw the vision. Following the usual custom, the pilgrims ran their hands along the massive stone sides of the Grotto as we walked along. While we passed through, I could imagine Robert ridiculing what we were doing. It looked like a classic case of a superstitious religious practice - rubbing "holy" objects in the hope of a magical cure.

The group had free time afterwards and I headed up to the basilica of the Immaculate Conception. To get up to the level of this church, you have to climb up the steep steps beside the façade of the basilica of the Rosary. The upper basilica is not built directly on top of the lower one but is situated further back, more or less on top of the Grotto itself. There are quite a few steps involved, so I always found it a good place to go for a bit of quiet time as many of our pilgrims would have difficulty getting up here.

Before entering the basilica, however, I went for a moment into its crypt, which was the first of the churches constructed in the sanctuary. It was built while Bernadette was still alive. Here, to the right, was a reliquary containing some relics of Bernadette and a place for lighting candles. Again, it occurred to me that

Robert would not be impressed with the veneration of relics and the lighting of candles.

Later, as I sat virtually alone in the upper basilica, I gradually became aware of something that would have stood out to any first-time visitor: the walls of the church were covered in plaques giving thanks for answered prayers. Many of the plaques explicitly mentioned cures. The plaques were everywhere, on every interior surface of the church. In addition, there were many "ex-voto" objects attached to the walls. These were usually small silver hearts placed by people in gratitude for blessings received. High up on the walls, there were so many of these little hearts that they were used to form in huge writing the words spoken by Mary to Bernadette, including, "I am the Immaculate Conception" in the original dialect used by Our Lady. There were many hundreds of expressions of gratitude here, perhaps thousands. This meant that all these multitudes of people had come here to Lourdes, received a blessing of some kind, and felt strongly enough about it to go to the considerable trouble of recording it in this way. How many other untold thousands had come, received a blessing, but had not left a record of this sort?

It occurred to me that the lower basilica must have similar decoration on the walls, even though our visits had always focused on the fifteen mosaics depicting the mysteries of the Rosary. Sure enough, when I went down, I saw that the walls here were also covered in plaques commemorating favours received.

It seemed clear that the sixty-something officially recognized miracles at Lourdes were only the tip of the iceberg. Many, many more remarkable events had occurred. Yet, as I walked back towards the hotel, I did not feel like getting into a debate with Robert about relative numbers of miracles. What was happening at Lourdes couldn't be quantified in terms of physical cures - of that I was sure - but I was at a loss to put into words just what *was* happening here. As the junior courier in his first season at the shrine, much of my time here had been spent spinning the illusion to the poor pilgrims under my care that I knew the town and the sanctuary much better than I did. Understanding the real message and meaning of Lourdes was not high on the list of priorities for the travel company I was working with. Yet, it was clear that Lourdes brought blessings in ways that went beyond visible miracles, but how could I explain this to Robert?

There were a number of other conversations with Robert before the end of that pilgrimage. Try as I might, I could not avoid him in the hotel lobby. One evening I was hanging around the reception area after dinner because my job description included being available in the evenings to answer queries and solve problems. When I saw Robert ambling his way towards me, I looked around frantically at the little groups of pilgrims chatting in the hallway. Surely one of them had a question or task for me that would occupy some time and get me off the hook?

"Mary," I called out to an elderly lady seated nearby, "did you manage to use the correct dialling code for calling home?"

"No, actually I didn't get through. Maybe I had the number wrong again," she replied.

"Why don't we try one more time?" I said, motioning to the public phones on the other side of the hall. "Come on, I'll dial it for you."

"Oh, no. It's a bit late now. I'll try it tomorrow."

"Anybody want to head down early to the sanctuary for the procession?" I asked desperately, aiming my question at no-one in particular. "If we head down there now, we'll get a good spot. Somebody? Anybody?"

Silence greeted my suggestion. In the meantime, Robert had arrived over and was standing in front of me with his usual rankled expression.

"You know the thing that really gets me about this place?" he said.

Groaning inwardly, I said aloud, "No, Robert, what is it?"

"It's the fact that everyone treats Bernadette's testimony as if it were the *Gospel*."

"Well, she's a canonised saint," I said with a defensive tone. "To be declared a saint, your life has to be investigated pretty thoroughly. We can take it, surely, that she was an honest girl?"

"I'm not saying she was making the whole thing up, but she might have been imagining things. She was half-starved after all. That's hardly a stable situation to be living in. Hunger can do funny things to your mind. Also, the fact is that *dozens* of other girls in Lourdes after Bernadette started to claim to see visions of Our Lady. Why do we dismiss those visions as hallucinations, but accept that what Bernadette saw was real?"

This was a troubling revelation and it left me speechless for a moment. It was the first time I had heard that other girls from the village also claimed to have visions. Later I discovered that Robert was exactly right. In the immediate aftermath of the visions, many girls of a similar age to Bernadette claimed to have ecstatic visions. But as I stood in front of him in the hotel lobby that evening, I wasn't sure if what he was saying was true or not. If it was true, it certainly seemed to do some damage to the credibility of Bernadette. Why should we consider her testimony to be more believable than these others? As I asked myself this question, however, an answer promptly came to mind. There was one feature of the Lourdes story that powerfully confirmed the testimony of Bernadette, and it had nothing to do with miraculous healings.

The parish priest, Father Peyramale, who was initially very suspicious of the apparitions, told Bernadette that the requests for the procession and building of a chapel could not be fulfilled unless the vision's name was known. On the occasion of the fourteenth apparition (March 3rd 1858), the little girl asked for the lady's name, but the vision only smiled. The following day, Bernadette asked again and received the same response. Finally, on March 25th, feast of the Annunciation, the lady replied

– as always in Bernadette's own dialect – "I am the Immaculate Conception."

It is hard to believe that an illiterate child could have fabricated such a phrase. If Bernadette was making the whole thing up, she would surely have reported the vision as saying something like, "I am the Mother of God." Instead, she gave a title that was both theologically profound yet enigmatic in its particular expression.

Earlier that day I had been thinking of an analogy to share with the group in order to highlight how remarkable Bernadette's case was. In the end, I had refrained from using it because it seemed a little silly and I was not sure if it would be effective. Now, however, I felt that I might as well tell it to Robert. Maybe it would get him off my back for a while.

"Look, Robert, to be honest I don't know what to say about these other girls who claimed to have visions. But Bernadette's testimony is supported by the phrase she attributes to the lady: 'I am the Immaculate Conception'."

"Why is that? There was an alleged vision in Paris just a few years previously in which Catherine Labouré claimed to see a lady who told her that she was immaculately conceived. Couldn't Bernadette have heard about that?"

"Maybe she did, but her family situation makes it unlikely that she heard anything outside of the happenings in her own village. She couldn't even speak French! *If* she had heard about the Paris events, though, the other details of that particular apparition in Lourdes on March 25th 1858 makes it extremely unlikely that Bernadette was fabricating or imagining the visions."

"Oh? What details are those?"

"Do you know anything about the theory of relativity or Albert Einstein?" I asked.

"Relativity? Einstein? No, absolutely nothing. What have they got to do with Lourdes?" Robert looked suspicious.

"Einstein published his theory of relativity in 1916. Let us imagine that he died shortly afterwards and then, in 1919, a boy from an isolated mountain village in France claims to be seeing his ghost. Imagine further that the boy is very poor at school, is virtually illiterate and only speaks his local dialect, which is very different to French. The local people are very sceptical that the boy is indeed seeing Einstein and they demand that he ask the vision to say something. One day, the boy comes back and says, 'The ghost told me that the theory of relativity correctly quantifies the precession in the perihelion of Mercury.'"

"The *what*?" blurted out Robert.

"The general theory of relativity is about gravitation. As a planet rotates around the sun, the shape of its orbit forms an ellipse. The ellipse gradually changes position every year because other gravitational objects in the solar system, apart from the sun, are also operating on that planet, deviating it from its course. This change is called a 'precession'. Newtonian gravitation couldn't account for the magnitude of the precession of Mercury's orbit, but Einstein's theory did."

"Oh," said Robert, sounding a little bewildered as to where all this was heading.

"If an illiterate boy in an isolated village claimed to see the ghost of Einstein and correctly described something that only Einstein (and a very few others) could have told him, then we would consider his testimony that much more credible, wouldn't we?"

"I suppose so," Robert said with a reluctant air. "But what were those details in Bernadette's testimony that you referred to?"

"The title that Bernadette attributed to the lady is about as remarkable as an illiterate boy repeating a correct statement from the theory of relativity. The Church had only defined this dogma as an article of faith less than three and half years previously. This little girl couldn't have had the foggiest idea what the lady's title meant - 'I am the Immaculate Conception' - and had to repeat the phrase to herself over and over as she made her way to Father Peyramale's house. Not only that, the *construction* of the title seems to be simply flawed. A conception is an *event*, not a person. Mary is the *fruit* of the Immaculate Conception, surely? That is what the Church defined three years previously."

"Yes, exactly! What Bernadette said wasn't even coherent. Surely that proves the words couldn't have come from a heavenly source?"

"Quite the contrary, Robert. As theologians began to reflect on these words, they began to realize that they have a profound and mysterious aptness. This title of Mary points to the eternal divine plan in which God would become incarnate and draw us all into the life of God. Mary has a unique role in this, and that is why she was immaculately conceived and can justly be described as *the* Immaculate Conception. St Maximilian Kolbe, in the very last words he wrote before being taken to Auschwitz, gave an amazing reflection on how Mary is the *created* Immaculate Conception, whilst the Holy Spirit is the eternal and *un*created Immaculate Conception. Bernadette had reported something that was deeply true in a way that she could not have grasped."

Robert shrugged his shoulders. "That's all a bit too heavy for me. To be honest I can't see how Mary can be described as the Immaculate *Conception*. Immaculately *conceived*, yes, but not a conception."

There was a small crowd beginning to gather in the lobby to get ready to go down to the sanctuary for the procession. I took Robert by the arm and led him over to a quiet corner before continuing. I had been thinking about the question that very day and felt prepared to give an answer. "Imagine that there is a bitter war between two kingdoms, a conflict that has been going on for generations and has no hope of being resolved. Then, the daughter of one king goes to the son of the other king and betroths herself to him. That son is a self-absorbed egotist and the girl has absolutely no natural inclination to marry him, but she performs this act of self-abnegation in order to end the state of conflict. She gives birth to a son, who manages to unite the two sides and bring peace. Now, we could justly call this girl the 'reconciliation' of these two nations. A reconciliation is an event, not a person, but this girl has given herself so profoundly to bring about this event that we can see how it makes sense to call her 'reconciliation'. Do you see the point?"

"I suppose so," replied Robert grudgingly. "But in what way would Mary have been involved in the event of her conception? Surely that is the *one* event in life where a person is purely passive?"

"Many of the Fathers of the Church have compared Mary to the original Eve. Eve was disobedient to God's word, but Mary, the New Eve, is blessed because of her openness to the word of God. When the Lord created Mary's soul at the moment of her conception, he foresaw her radical openness and obedience. In a sense, already present at her conception is God's knowledge of the utter self-emptying of this girl so that she could be filled with the grace of God. It is an event that has no parallel in the conceptions of other human beings (apart from Christ himself). As a unique event in which Mary's qualities are brought to perfection by God, we can start to imagine why it might be appropriate to call her the 'Immaculate Conception.'"

"So Bernadette used a verbal construction that was unusual and that turned out to be profound when people thought about it. That *could* have been a lucky accident, surely?" Robert appeared to be clutching at straws now.

"It wasn't the only accident that day! When the dogma that Mary was immaculately conceived was defined by the Church a few years previously, the principal Scriptural foundation for the dogma was the scene of the Annunciation in Luke's Gospel. Here, the Angel Gabriel describes Mary as 'full of grace'. St Luke renders the words of the angel in Greek using a very unique term that seems to imply that Mary is made perfect by God's grace."

Robert was looking restless as I continued. "It was March 25th – Feast of the Annunciation – when the vision finally told Bernadette her name. Now, is it plausible that Bernadette could have come up with such a name for Mary on such an appropriate day of the year? It is a well-documented fact that this little girl was virtually illiterate at the time of the apparitions. If she was making things up, or if she was suffering from self-delusion, then we would have to believe that, on the very Feast of the Annunciation – the feast that is most linked to the dogma - she fortuitously reported the lady describing herself as the 'Immaculate Conception', a profound theological term understood by virtually nobody, and with a connection to the Feast of the Annunciation that was understood by virtually nobody."

"Ok, admittedly that would be a very lucky coincidence."

"The first apparition was on February 11th. March 25th was the *sixteenth* apparition and it occurred six weeks later. In the meantime, many people were asking Bernadette who the lady was and were pressurizing the little girl into finding out. Some people presumed that the vision was the Blessed Virgin, but Bernadette is documented as correcting people on this score at various times. In fact, this little girl demonstrated a remarkable precision and rectitude of character in insisting – in the absence of clarification from the vision - that the lady *not* be described as the Mother of God. This admirable restraint only increased the force of the revelation when it came like a bolt from the blue on March 25th.

"Robert, I'm just the junior courier here. I don't know much about the miraculous healings that have happened at Lourdes, but for me the clearest proof that Bernadette saw Our Lady is her repetition of the vision's words, 'I am the Immaculate Conception'. The Church had discussed the dogma for centuries, but in eighteen hundred years of weighty discussion from theologians and doctors of the Church, no one had *ever* used it as a *title* for Our Lady expressed in those terms. *Never*. Then, on the most appropriate day of the year, an illiterate girl, from a destitute family, living in a former prison cell, in an isolated town, speaking an obscure dialect, comes up with 'I am the Immaculate Conception' in that dialect! It's not just unlikely that she could have made it up, it's well-nigh impossible!"

By the next evening, Robert and his mother were gone and I was speeding in from the airport with a new busload of pilgrims. Thinking back on the previous pilgrimage, I realised that the conversation with Robert had helped me put into words what had been on my mind ever since first hearing the story of Lourdes. What Bernadette reported was a phrase that could only have emanated from heaven. It could not have come from her. She was a jar of clay into which had been poured something from another world. The words were comparable to what the Angel Gabriel had said to Mary at the Annunciation. The phrase, "Hail! Full of grace!" could not have been uttered by any human being with the same meaning. Gabriel, as all good heavenly messengers do, was repeating the words entrusted to him by God the Father; words, effectively, that expressed God's own name for Mary. What happened at Lourdes on March 25th 1858 was a second Annunciation. This time the heavenly messenger was the Blessed Virgin, and the recipient was a little girl who did not understand what she heard, but the words expressed were still a rendering of God's own name for Mary. The very fact that Bernadette did not understand what she was saying made her the perfect channel for this revelation. Like a transparent sheet of glass, she transmitted this light from heaven without adding anything to it herself.

I felt a lot of regret as well. It seemed to me that Robert had left Lourdes in a worse state than he had come. The conversations with me had not benefitted him. On the subject of miracles and cures, I had been very vague and hesitant, not knowing what to say. It seemed likely that Robert had gone away with even less faith than when he had arrived. Despite all of his scepticism, he had harboured a tiny desperate hope for a miracle when he arrived originally. Now, even that hope was gone. It seemed wrong that people would come to such a great pilgrimage shrine and leave in a worse spiritual state than when they arrived. Was it my fault? What could I have told him during those conversations?

During the next pilgrimage after Robert's group - as with virtually every pilgrimage that had come my way so far in Lourdes – a couple of members mentioned explicitly that they had come looking for healing. There was a man named Sean accompanied by his wife and thirty-something year-old son. Sean had cancer and had only been given a few months to live. There was also a woman named Margaret who was suffering profound bereavement after the suicide of her daughter. Both of these people were seeking a cure, but there was a marked difference between them. Like Robert, Sean's son made it clear that they had only come to Lourdes as a last resort. They had tried every form of treatment and had now come here in desperation looking for a cure. The bereaved woman was also looking for healing, but her attitude was not at all like that of Sean and his family. She showed all the pain and anguish of her situation, but something was different. What was it, I wondered?

On the morning after arrival, the group celebrated Mass in the chapel of the Poor Clare convent. The priest had chosen special readings for the liturgy, and these were all on the theme of healing. The Gospel was from Luke 17 and recounted the cleansing of the ten lepers.

Afterwards, only one of the lepers came back to thank Jesus. To this man - a Samaritan - Jesus says, "Get up and go on your way; your faith has made you well" (Luke 17,19).

I was thinking about this passage later that morning as our group stood in silence for a while before the Grotto. If his mother had been healed, then - from the impression I had received of Robert - it seemed likely that he would have been happy about the healing, but would have resumed the very same life that he had before cancer struck. Then, all at once, I realised something that had not occurred to me before: Robert was looking for healing, but he was not looking for salvation. He wanted his mother's cancer to be gone, but he did not want his life to be changed. He showed no interest in having a relationship with Jesus or in anything to do with living the life of faith.

With this realisation, the difference between Sean and Margaret seemed to become clearer: Sean and his family wanted a cure but showed no signs of having any interest in being saved. Sean's wife spoke of how her husband was such a popular figure in the local community, passionately involved in music and sport. They just wanted their old life back, unchanged. If he was cured today, he would go back, full steam, into music and sport tomorrow. Margaret, by contrast, seemed to me to be *already* saved. Everything she said and did indicated a lady who had abandoned herself and her family into the providence of God. She had come to Lourdes to look for comfort and strength, and she was willing to be changed in order to receive it. She did not simply want her pain to go away. She was open to enduring whatever it took to help her deal with her pain.

As the season went on, this distinction between being healed and being saved helped me to have a better insight into what was going on in people's lives. On one of the pilgrimages there was a husband and wife in their sixties. The wife had only been given weeks to live. One evening I had a conversation with the husband after dinner. He was really hopeful that the cancer would go into remission for at least a few months after this pilgrimage so that they could make the most of whatever time was left. "Making the most" involved going through a bucket list of the things they always wanted to do. This consisted in a lot of travel and nothing, apparently, of a remotely spiritual nature. The last part of the conversation was about the husband's extensive business interests and his plans to expand the company. The sickness of his wife had really messed up his work and he was looking forward to getting back to normal as soon as possible. To all appearances, this was a man who wanted a cure for his wife but would probably run a mile from salvation.

For a while that season, I became a little bit wary of those who seemed to be in Lourdes for the sole reason of finding a cure. Later, though, I discovered something that made it clear that there was nothing wrong with looking for physical healing. The mother of St Thérèse of Lisieux, Zélie Martin, suffered from cancer and went to Lourdes hoping for a miracle. The cure did not happen and she died just two months later while Thérèse was only four and a half years old. Thérèse had four other sisters, all of who were devoted to their mother. From her letters, it is clear that the search for a cure was done for their sake, not simply so that Zélie could continue in her old way of life. She didn't fit in my category of those looking for healing but not for salvation. This lady was already saved and was placing herself in the providential care of God. Indeed, how much she was already saved became abundantly clear in 2015, for in that year she was canonised a saint along with her husband by Pope Francis.

Some years later, when Laura and I began taking pilgrimages to different Marian shrines, I discovered that this relationship between physical healing and salvation had been mentioned by Our Lady on occasion during different apparitions. A visionary, prompted by a member of the public, would ask Mary if such and such a person was going to be healed. Our Lady would reply in a conditional way: they will be healed only after they have changed their life, or, they will be healed in a year's time after their conversion, or, on a few occasions, the request would be met by the revelation that they will not be healed. God wants our good and, in those many cases like Zélie Martin where serious illness causes terrible suffering for a family, we can be confident that he wants to bless that family with health and long life. However, God's desire for our salvation is much greater than his desire for our health in this life. Sometimes, the suffering and illness can actually assist us in turning to

God in a more radical way. When Zélie Martin died at age forty-five in 1877, a series of events was precipitated that led to her little baby girl becoming one of the greatest saints of modern times. It is possible that Thérèse's radical and childlike trust in God would not have become so great if she still had her mother to lean on.

It is problematic to claim that God afflicts people directly with illness or death. The Church, in grappling with the mystery of suffering, has consistently asserted that suffering and death are caused by sin, but that the Lord can permit suffering for the greater good. In that sense, God can be said to "chastise" us by allowing us to suffer the consequences of sin in order to bless us in a deeper way. It appears undeniable – in fact it seems to be a truth on the level with scientific fact – that suffering has the potential to bring about good that would not have emerged otherwise.

It was a long and hot summer in Lourdes. The more groups that passed through, the more perplexed I became. On the one hand, I could see that many people who came looking for a miracle were barely practicing the faith and did not seem too interested in being saved. Their previous way of life before illness was their idol and they wanted it restored. They did not want to make Jesus their Lord. Some of these people, as far as I could tell, went home in a worse spiritual state than when they came, like Robert and his mum. Other people started off their pilgrimage just like Robert, with the same lack of faith, the same focus on temporal things, but yet they were filled with serenity and peace by the time they had left. Something was happening, something that could not be quantified by the Lourdes Medical Bureau. What was perplexing, though, was the completely unpredictable nature of who ended up being touched by grace. Some people who seemed genuinely devout, and had come looking for healing of some sort, did not experience anything, whilst others were deeply moved at some point of the pilgrimage, either at the baths, or in front of the grotto, or during the evening procession. It became clear that no neat criterion – such as "Is the pilgrim seeking healing or salvation?" would suffice to categorize the outcome of a pilgrimage.

Afterwards, I worked a second season in Lourdes for a different company. Then time passed and I did not return for many years. Laura and I were now working for ourselves and were concentrating most of our trips in Italy, with the occasional pilgrimage to Poland and Fatima. Lourdes was so long in the past that I could barely remember the layout of the town or the names of the hotels. Bernadette is not someone easily forgotten, however, and I would mention her encounter with the Immaculate Conception whenever we had a visit to the Spanish Steps in Rome, or a tour of the basilica of St Mary Major. Near the Spanish Steps is the monument to the Immaculate Conception erected shortly after the proclamation of the dogma, whilst St Mary Major has a kneeling statue of Pius IX, the pope who made the definition.

At this point, I had begun translating the weekly homily on Vatican Radio by Father Rosini. It was almost Christmas, the fourth Sunday of Advent, and the Gospel recounted the event of the Annunciation of the Angel Gabriel. When that Gospel was read, the second annunciation to Bernadette would sometimes come to mind. Something about the entire homily on this occasion, though, reminded me of Lourdes and helped to put my thoughts in perspective regarding the healing of some but not of others.

It is a Gospel passage that can cause a lot of confusion for Catholics. On the one hand, the words of the Angel, "Hail, full of grace!" represent the clearest biblical foundation for the Immaculate Conception of Mary, the belief that she was protected by God from the stain of original sin. On the other hand, the narrative is talking about the *virginal* conception, which is about the incarnation of Christ in the womb of Mary. Father Rosini's homily was all about how God *always* conceives virginally.

In the first reading of that Sunday, David is so grateful to God for his many blessings that he tells the prophet Nathan that he plans to build a temple for the Ark of the Lord. That night, however, Nathan, receives a message from God. David is not to build a house for God - God instead will build a house for David and make the sovereignty of his lineage permanent. In the Gospel, the angel Gabriel appears to Mary and announces the fulfilment of Nathan's prophecy. The virgin is to conceive and bear a son who will take the throne of his ancestor David. Father Rosini tells us that the prophecy of Nathan is not just for David, but for all of us.

David had a noble and beautiful idea, just as we have many noble and well-meaning projects. But our ideas remain merely human ideas. Only God can give life, and he always gives life virginally. In the Gospel, Mary provides the good soil that welcomes the seed of God, but it is only God who can generate true life. We are not the sole generators of anything good. Our mission in our marriage, our vocation, our daily existence, is not to follow our own ways, no matter how good those ways might seem to be. Our job is to bow before the Lord and allow his initiative to bear fruit in our lives. Any initiatives we have must be based on the work of God in our lives. Often, we expect God to bless our projects. We pray to him asking for success. We ask him to shake some holy water over the things that we own and value, but the Lord is not our personal chaplain tasked to assist our worldly designs. The things we do will not bear permanent fruit, will not be blessed, if they do not have their origin in God. Christmas shows us that God's work is always virginal. It always comes from him, not from us.

This made me recall the months spent in Lourdes all those years ago. One of my concerns then was to understand how God was distributing his grace. Why were some people cured and others not? I had a big preoccupation with defending the truth of the apparitions and the honesty of Bernadette, but I struggled to defend God and his apparent reluctance to heal some heart-wrenching cases. Now, things had become a little clearer. The businessman whose wife had cancer wanted that illness gone so that life could go back to the way it was before – he told me so himself. It seemed clearer now that what this man desperately needed – though he didn't know it at the time – was to learn to love his wife in a deeper way. Love requires forgetting oneself, but this husband's concern for his wife was very much dominated by his own affairs and interests. Cancer, this terrible affliction, was an opportunity for the man to let go of those material things that could not bring lasting health or happiness to him or his spouse. It was a call to submit to God, who alone gives life. If the man had relinquished his grasp on those material preoccupations, putting eternal considerations first, allowing the Lord's word to be planted within him, then he would have been purified and deepened in his love for his wife.

Yes, it is ironic that someone like me would look back more than twenty years at this husband and make a judgement of such a sort. Though I might have been concerned to uphold the Church and defend the apparitions, it is fair to say that I was even more self-absorbed and knew even less of love. Yet, suffering of one sort or another can help change even someone like me. It can allow the seed of God's grace to germinate in our fragile nature.

Chapter Seven
Grace and Nature

""Without God, we cannot. Without us, God will not."
Saint Augustine

Laura had had quite enough of working with the hotels in the centre of Rome, at least with the sort of establishment that catered for large groups.

"I wouldn't mind if they provided a good service," she said. "Instead, everything tends to be minimalist, starting with the breakfast."

"You're telling *me* about it?" I grumbled. "I'm the one there in the morning fighting with the staff when the food starts to run out."

"But you know, Laura," I went on, "the advantage of being at the centre of Rome is that the group can just step outside at any time and immerse themselves in the city. It more than compensates when the hotel is a bit shabby. If we were to stay on the outskirts, then the itinerary would have to be really well organised so that people are kept stimulated."

"Well, other tour operators are doing that all the time. Look at the number of groups that stay in hotels on the Via Aurelia and other places on the outskirts. Couldn't we try putting a group or two out there and see how it goes?"

That summer, Laura ended up booking hotels for two groups in the Parioli area of Rome. This is a well-to-do residential district directly to the north of the city centre, not too far by coach from the main sights.

For me, it was an interesting change since I didn't know the area well. The two hotels were within a few minutes' walk of Piazza Euclide. The piazza is dominated by the massive basilica of the Immaculate Heart of Mary, a twentieth-century church that could rival one of the main basilicas of Rome in dimensions. The dome – which would have been second in size only to St Peter's in Rome – was never completed. Most famously, the future archbishop and saint, Oscar Romero, celebrated his first Mass here in 1942.

The parishes booked in these two hotels would arrive together on the same flight. The itinerary was organised so that they would do different visits at slightly different times. Mirella, a freelance guide that we sometimes employed, was an expert on museums and classical monuments like the Roman Forum and Colosseum, while I felt more at home visiting churches and tombs. All the visits would have to coordinated precisely to permit a smooth changeover whenever it was required. The plan was to provide the groups with the best possible visit of each of the sites, Mirella doing the classical tours and me doing the "holy" stuff.

It was going to be an intense few days. The fact that we were staying outside the city centre had prompted us to put together a very busy itinerary. Staying in a residential district meant that there was little to do in the area of the hotels during free time, so the "solution" was to give the groups virtually no free time at all. Of course, this meant no free time for me either. I would regret that by the end of a hectic week.

It was already gone 8pm when I arrived at Fiumicino airport. Mirella was standing waiting for me with an anxious look in the arrivals hall. I handed her the rooming list for her group. "You're going to be with Fr Brian's group this evening, and you'll take them tomorrow to the Vatican Museums before we do our change over. The parish is from the south of Ireland. I'll be with Fr Philip's group. They're from northern Ireland. I've never met either of them before and have no idea what they even look like. What's important is that we keep the groups separate when they come out and make sure everyone gets onto the correct bus."

Mirella and I took up position about ten yards from each other, holding up signs with the names of the respective parishes. About half an hour later, the first members of Mirella's group started to trickle out, but there was no sign of any of mine. A man in his forties wearing brightly coloured Hawaiian-style shorts emerged and made his way over to Mirella with a beaming smile. Snatches of the conversation wafted over in my direction. This, evidently, was the parish priest, Father Brian. The group continued to swell and Mirella could be heard saying to Fr Brian that there were only a couple more to come. None of my group had yet emerged from within and I was starting to get a bit anxious. I ambled over to Fr Brian, introduced myself and asked him if he had spotted another parish group waiting for their bags at the conveyor belt.

"Oh, yes, they're there all right," said Fr Brian, rolling his eyes. "The priest leading them is like something from the nineteen fifties! He's marshalling his poor parishioners like foot-soldiers. They were terrified to come out without him."

Just then a youngish man dressed in full clerical outfit emerged with an entire group in tow behind him. I dashed back to my original position and held aloft my sign.

"We've done a roll call inside," Fr Philip said as he approached me, his tone very serious and business-like. "All present and correct. Onwards to the coach."

On the journey to the hotel, all went smoothly. I gave my usual riveting talk on how to survive in Rome for a week: dodging pickpockets in the city, avoiding mosquitos in the rooms, ordering a proper hot cup of tea in an Italian bar. There was also a description of appropriate dress code in the Roman basilicas. At that point Fr Philip motioned to me that he would like to take the microphone.

"Yes, this is something very important," he said. "In summertime here in Rome, tourists go around dressed in all sorts of outlandish outfits, but it is essential that we show respect when we enter a church by being dressed in an appropriate way. In my opinion, even shorts that go to the knees are inappropriate. These are holy places we're entering! We can save the shorts for next time we go to the beach!"

The next morning, I took Fr Philip and his group to celebrate Mass at the church of Sant' Anna dei

Palafrenieri, which is located just inside the main car entrance to Vatican City. One of the first oval churches ever built, it is the parish church of Vatican State and a very convenient place to celebrate Mass for pilgrim groups before they visit St Peter's. By this point, Mirella had already entered the Vatican Museums with Fr Brian's group and was heading towards the Sistine Chapel. The plan was for me to take my group to the basilica for a tour after Mass. Our tour would end as Mirella was exiting the Sistine Chapel with her group. We would meet up at the fountain to the right of the basilica just under the ramp descending from the Sistine. The groups would be switched and we would do it all again. This time, I would take Fr Brian's group for a tour of the basilica and finish with a celebration of Mass at midday in the church of Spirito Santo not far from St Peter's Square. Mirella would take Fr Philip's group directly to the self-service restaurant in the museums for an early lunch and then continue to the Sistine Chapel.

I had just begun the tour of the basilica with Fr Philip and the first group. We had seen the Holy Door, entered the basilica and beheld the round slab of porphyry inside the central entrance. On this slab, Pope Leo III had crowned Charlemagne Holy Roman Emperor on Christmas Day, 800. Now we were standing looking into the magnificent space of the basilica and I was trying to express why the Church would have gone to such trouble and expense to create this building. It was a thorny question. Over the years, pilgrims had often complained at just this point that the entire edifice was a scandal, a blatant betrayal of the Church's mission to care for the poor. These reservations were entirely understandable. After all, the methods employed by the Church to raise money for the construction of this very structure were among the factors that triggered the reformation, the fragmentation of the Church and a century of religious wars.

Having heard critical comments about the opulence of St Peter's on more than a few occasions, I had come prepared. It was important, I said, to understand this building in the correct religious context. Unfolding a sheet of paper, I quoted a passage from John's Gospel:

Mary took a pound of costly perfume made of pure nard, anointed Jesus' feet, and wiped them with her hair. . . But Judas Iscariot, one of his disciples (the one who was about to betray him), said, "Why was this perfume not sold for three hundred denarii and the money given to the poor?" (He said this not because he cared about the poor, but because he was a thief; he kept the common purse and used to steal what was put into it.) Jesus said, "Leave her alone. She bought it so that she might keep it for the day of my burial. You always have the poor with you, but you do not always have me." (John 12, 3-8)

This passage, I said, tells us two things. Firstly, Christ is not against us spending money to honour him, even if that money could have been spent on the poor. Secondly, some of those who complain about the Church's use of money don't care at all about the needy. Like Judas, they use care of the poor as a way of undermining the Church's legitimate veneration of Jesus. Leaving aside the question of the morality of the original decision to build this elaborate basilica, I went on, there is the more pressing question of how we should act today. Every now and then people say that the precious materials and furnishings found in churches should be sold off and the money given to the poor. Only this, they claim, is consistent with the demands of the Gospel to care for the marginalised.

Claims like these, I commented, fail to take into account the fact that the demolition or stripping of a building like this would cost much more than would be earned from it. More importantly, such demolition would involve the destruction of irreplaceable works of art that lift the human spirit towards the good and the beautiful and form an important part of the world's heritage.

As I spoke, Fr Philip was nodding vigorously, clearly agreeing with these sentiments.

"The most important reason for maintaining and cherishing the beauty and grandeur of this basilica," he interjected, "is that it gives glory to God. When the artists of the sixteenth and seventeenth centuries built and decorated this place, they did so with a passion for excellence and beauty. The beautiful works they created give us a glimpse into the beauty and perfection of God."

A very small and thin woman named Bernie was standing at the front of the group and it was evident that she had been hanging attentively on every word that was being said. She nodded and murmured constantly, but at this last statement of Fr Philip she began shaking her head as if she disagreed. Fr Philip noticed this and turned to her immediately.

"Is there something I said that you disagree with, madam?" he asked in a brusque tone.

"Well, actually there is, now that you mention it." Bernie had a very pronounced northern accent. "When I got in here just now and looked up at the size of this place, I didn't think about God. I thought about the engineers and builders that built it, so I did. If you ask me, it gives glory to them more than to God, if you know what I mean?"

"I most certainly do *not* know what you mean, madam!" Fr Philip replied, clearly irritated. "God is the author of everything good. When we see a great work of art, we naturally give credit to the artist, but God is the ultimate source of that person's talents. It's our choice, we can choose to give glory to people who are mere instruments of the Lord, or we can give the glory to the Lord himself. I know who I'll choose!"

"Well," said Bernie, chuckling, "if you ask me, the poor critters who slaved on this place were more instruments in the hands of the pope than the Lord! And it looks like the pope got his money's worth out of them!"

"Well, fortunately, we don't need to ask you, madam. That's the reason we have Kieran as our guide." Fr Philip said pompously. Then, looking pointedly at me, he said, "Lead on, please!"

Feeling a little taken aback by the priest's rebuke to Bernie, I hesitantly led the group towards the *Pietà* of Michelangelo. As we gazed upon this most famous work of art in the basilica, completed by Michelangelo when he was only twenty-four years of age, Fr Philip quickly regained his composure and seemed to become very invigorated. He exhorted the group to behold the youthfulness of Mary as she held her dead son in her arms. "Mary is always young," he said, "because she is filled with the life of God."

Bernie was standing close to Fr Philip and remarked immediately (probably referring to her own wizened face and stooped figure), "If anyone looks at the state of me, I think they'll have trouble finding any of the life of God!"

Fr Philip turned to her with a cold smile and said loudly, "Indeed." As he turned away, Bernie stuck out her tongue like a schoolgirl and then tittered silently into her cupped hands. She seemed to be enjoying her new role as a foil for Fr Philip. There was a general chorus of suppressed sniggers from the group, but Fr Philip was already on the move and didn't seem to notice anything.

Later, as we approached the tomb of John XXIII, I gave the group a short biography of this pope who called the Second Vatican Council.

"But that can't be his real body?" someone said incredulously. "It looks like a wax figure. When did you say he died?"

"In 1963," I replied. "Yes, that is indeed his real body! Popes are not embalmed when they die, but a preservative would have been applied to the body on account of the protracted nature of the funeral. However, when the exhumation took place nearly forty years after his death, everyone was surprised at the perfect state of preservation."

"Is it some kind of miracle then?"

At this point, Fr Philip interjected. "The preservation of a body from decay has often been understood by the Church to be a heavenly confirmation of the sanctity of the person. After all, if sin is the ultimate cause of death and corruption, then the absence of decay could well indicate holiness."

"When I pop off, it looks like I'll be decaying fairly quickly then!" said Bernie, this time sniggering openly into her cupped hands in front of Fr Philip. There was a general ripple of laughter through the group.

The priest raised his hand with the palm facing downwards and looked crossly around at the group. "Hush! This is a sacred spot, not a place for irreverent wisecracks!"

The body of Pope John XXIII is located at the altar of St Jerome at the back of one of the great pillars that supports the dome of the basilica. There are five or six pews in front of the altar reserved for those who wish to pray. We were standing about ten yards back from the pews, outside the barricades that fence off the area.

Fr Philip turned around to look at the tomb and then spun back to face the group. "I'll tell you what," he said in a condescending tone. "Seeing that some of us have been a little irreverent, let's all go inside and pray for a few moments. Maybe John XXIII might intercede for us and help us to conduct ourselves a little more appropriately for the rest of the tour."

A few minutes later, Fr Philip stood up and our tour resumed. Around the corner of the same pillar supporting the great dome, there is an ancient bronze statue of St Peter seated in a chair. We stood a few yards back from this statue while I described it to the group. Some experts wonder if it might date to the fifth century, but a more common opinion is that it is a thirteenth-century work of the great Florentine artist, Arnolfo di Cambio. The distinctive "snail" curls of the hair and beard are characteristic marks of Arnolfo's works. St Peter holds the keys of the kingdom in his left hand while his right hand is raised in blessing. I told the group how the statue is always dressed in beautiful vestments for the feast of Saints Peter and Paul on June 29.

As we stood there, we watched other pilgrims file by the statue, each one touching the extended right foot. This has been worn completely smooth by centuries of passing pilgrims.

"Why is everybody rubbing that foot?" someone asked.

"This is a very normal part of Catholic devotion," Fr Philip replied in a somewhat exasperated tone, as if the answer should be obvious. "In the Catholic Church we pray with our bodies. Why should prayer be confined just to thoughts or words? These pilgrims are genuinely expressing devotion to St Peter by touching the foot in a reverent way. Now, why don't we all line up and follow suit?"

Fr Philip began shooing the pilgrims into a double line and soon he had the entire group lined up dutifully before the statue.

The high-point of the tour of St Peter's generally comes when we descend into the crypt and stand in front of the tomb of St Peter. There are often stewards in this area who ask people to maintain silence. They keep pilgrims moving along so that others too can venerate the tomb. Fr Philip gathered the group around him and intoned the Creed in Latin. Nobody else seemed to know it and he was left to sing it by himself. By the side of my eye, I could see the steward standing meekly in an alcove across the way. Usually, these officials would be very pro-active in hustling tarrying pilgrims along, but it would have been a brave steward indeed who would have tried to hurry the tall gaunt figure of Fr Philip, dressed as he was in full clerical outfit, singing sombrely in Latin in front of the tomb of St Peter.

A short time later, we emerged from the crypt and waited at the fountain on the right side of St Peter's Basilica, underneath the statue of St Gregory the Illuminator of Armenia, a statue placed here in 2005 in one of the final public acts of the papacy of John Paul II. We didn't have too long to wait. Mirella appeared shortly afterwards, descending the ramp from the Sistine Chapel with the group behind her. After an exchange of some pleasantries and a bit of banter between the groups, we switched positions and Mirella began to lead Fr Philip and his pilgrims towards the Vatican museums. With some trepidation I led Fr Brian and his group into the basilica. This would be my first real encounter with them and I could only hope that the tour might go a little more smoothly than the one that had just been completed.

We prayed before the Holy Door, entered the basilica, and viewed the porphyry slab upon which Charlemagne was crowned. Then I invited everyone to contemplate the enormity and grandeur of the basilica. A few of the usual anecdotes about the huge dimensions of the building were presented. For example, I told them, if the average golfer teed off from underneath the Holy Spirit window in the apse of the basilica, he would have great difficulty driving the ball out one of the entrance doors, nearly two hundred and twenty metres away. Then I said a few words about the controversy that erupted in the sixteenth century over the methods used to raise funds for the construction, particularly the sale of indulgences.

"Oh, yes," commented Fr Brian, shaking his head incredulously. "Cash payments to shorten your time in purgatory and buy a fast ticket to heaven!"

"Even if some people in the Church can legitimately be criticized for certain practices at that time," I said, "we can still today rejoice in the grandeur of this place. When we enter, we can be struck with awe and see here a glimpse of the beauty and glory of God." Then I began to read the passage from John's Gospel in which Mary venerates Christ with the costly ointment. As I finished, I could see that Fr Brian looked a little peeved.

"The anointing of Christ before his passion was one thing," he said, "but what we have here is completely different. The opulence of this place is a permanent countersign, in my view. It only helps to reinforce the idea that the Church is inward looking, focusing on its own business and doesn't care about the poor."

It didn't seem like the place or time to get into a discussion, but I felt I had to muster some sort of reply. "Granted, at the time it was built there were genuine issues about neglect of the poor and the manipulation of the fear of purgatory, but nowadays, given that we can hardly dismantle the place, we can surely look on it as a gift from our Catholic heritage that helps us lift our hearts to the majesty of God."

Fr Brian looked up into the vast space above us in silence for a moment. "Naw," he said, shaking his head. "It doesn't do it for me. The very opposite in fact."

Not knowing how to reply, I slunk over towards the *Pietà* with the group following behind. Soon afterwards, we were standing a few yards back from the body of Pope John XXIII. I summarised his life, his heroic work saving thousands of Jews during World War Two while he was papal nuncio in Hungary, his surprise decision to convene the Second Vatican Council and his enduring popularity among Italians of all political persuasions. Then I described his exhumation in January 2001, a few months after his beatification.

We didn't have long to wait for the question that often arises in this spot. One of the younger members of the group asked, "So, that's his real body?"

"Yes!" I replied. "We can't say for sure that the perfect preservation is miraculous because there could well be a natural explanation, but many people believe that it's the Lord's way of confirming that this man was in a state of holiness when he died."

Once again, I could see that Fr Brian was looking ill at ease. "Personally, I'm not one for the cult of relics or tombs," he said. "We can go directly to the Lord with our prayers. Some of this paraphernalia to do with saints are just distractions. They draw people into superstitious kinds of behaviour." He was frowning as he looked intently towards the glass case holding the body of the pope. "Let's continue with our tour. I find this all a bit ghastly!"

Needless to say, we did not enter the closed-off area for prayer in front of the altar. Instead, we turned the corner and beheld the ancient bronze statue of St Peter. I recounted to the group the history of this statue and the various theories as to its origin. As we stood there, other pilgrims were passing by and rubbing the foot. While one pilgrim was rubbing the foot particularly vigorously, Fr Brian stepped to the front of the group and raised his voice.

"By the way, let's have none of this rubbing of the statue that you see going on here. Objects of devotion are not lucky charms. We don't absorb blessings or benefits by wielding objects in a superstitious manner.

What our faith is about is prayer from the heart! I guarantee you there are people rubbing this statue who don't even know who St Peter was and have no notion of his significance for the Catholic Church."

As Fr Brian turned away, he suddenly had an afterthought and wheeled back towards the group again. "Oh, and by the way, just think of the amount of bacteria and viruses that must be present on that foot! Thousands of people are touching it daily and scores of them surely have the cold, or the 'flu, if not something much worse! Let's just skip this part of the tour and continue along to our next point of interest. Kieran, lead the way."

Shortly afterwards we were standing in the crypt in front of the tomb of St Peter. Fr Brian said a short but reverent prayer, asking for the intercession of St Peter for the renewal of his parish. He also prayed for the intentions of the Holy Father. Our visit was over and we made our way out of the basilica. I felt mentally wearied. Never had I been involved in two such contrasting tours of St Peter's, all on the same day.

Mirella was staying in the hotel with Fr Brian's group, while I lodged with my in-laws across the city and commuted each day to Fr Philip's hotel. This involved taking the metro from home to Piazzale Flaminio (near Piazza del Popolo), and from there boarding the train to Piazza Euclide. The journey took the bones of an hour, giving me plenty of time to reflect on the curious situation that was unfolding before me. It was evident that Fr Philip had certain strengths, but it also seemed clear that something was "lacking" in the way he dealt with his parishioners. Similarly, Fr Brian had great qualities, but he too seemed to have some shortcomings. Did Fr Philip need to take on some of Fr Brian's qualities, and vice-versa? Fr Philip celebrated the Mass with great devotion. One could have been in no doubt that something supernatural was happening and that the sacred host should be received with humility and reverence. Fr Brian, on the other hand, had the common touch. He was constantly interacting with the group in a friendly manner and trying to get everyone to participate and feel welcome. Was the ideal priest a sort of hybrid of these two men, I wondered, combining the best qualities of Fr Brian and the best qualities of Fr Philip? For a time, it seemed that way to me, but before the trip was over, I had changed my mind entirely.

Logistically, it worked out better for Mirella to accompany Fr Brian's group on the first excursion of every day, since she was already in the hotel with them. I, on the other hand, after my daily commute, would begin with Fr Philip's group. We usually returned to the hotel for about an hour after lunch so that people could rest and change, if necessary. At this point, I would take the shortcut on foot from Fr Philip's hotel, coming down the flight of steps from Via Francesco Denza towards Piazza Euclide. Sometimes, I would meet Mirella on the steps coming in the opposite direction. There was no time for niceties during these brief meetings. We would exchange a few notes about our respective groups and then hurry on our way.

A week's programme in Rome usually included a coach tour by night on one of the evenings, complete with a dinner that included musical entertainment. When we began working in Rome, the restaurant we used for these musical dinners was located on the Old Appian Way, close to the site of the ancient Quo Vadis church. According to a very old tradition, St Peter was fleeing Rome during the persecutions of Christians when he had a vision of Christ at this point along the road. "Quo vadis, Domine?" he asked ("Lord, where are you going?") "I go to Rome to be crucified a second time," Jesus replied, at which point Peter himself returned to the city, was arrested and martyred. For years, we took groups to the beautifully-located Quo Vadis restaurant, just a stone's throw from the place where this event is said to have happened, but a fire led to the closure of the restaurant about 2007 or 2008. The manager, Paolo, asked us if we would consider taking our groups for the following season to a new place he was managing out near the Olympic stadium. Laura and I thought long and hard about this proposal, worried about the journey time and possible delays getting there with traffic. Eventually we decided to give it a go. It turned out to be an overwhelming success. The restaurant was much calmer and more elegant than the ones at the city centre. The quality of the food was consistently good. We took dozens of groups there from 2008 until the restaurant eventually closed for family reasons about ten years later, not long before the pandemic.

A deal had been worked out with Paolo for the groups of Fr Brian and Fr Philip. The restaurant could hold well over one hundred people, so our two groups could easily be accommodated at the same time. The fact that it was a larger number of people than a normal group, all arriving at the same time with a fixed menu, would earn us a discount of a few euro per person. The usual musicians would easily be able to entertain everyone since it was their custom to perform in one part of the restaurant and then in another, moving continually so that people had periods of music alternating with moments of peace and quiet.

By the time the evening of the dinner arrived, however, I was regretting my penny-pinching scheme of combining the two groups for dinner. At lunchtime, I was descending the steps towards Piazza Euclide when I met Mirella on her way up.

"Mirella, there you are, I wanted to talk to you about tonight's dinner."

"Oh, yes, how nice it is that we will all be eating together! It will be a chance for the two groups to get to know each other."

"I'm not so sure about that, Mirella."

"What do you mean?"

"Well, you know how the musicians, Enzo and Sonia, go around singing at the tables during the meal?"

"Yes?"

"Well, what they sing and how they sing it depends on what I tell them about the group as soon as we arrive.

But the trouble is that I don't know what to tell them about these particular groups!"

"What do you mean?"

"When we have a happy-go-lucky group that is not too pious, I tell them to go ahead and sing whatever they like. They sing all the usual Neapolitan songs, but they also add in stuff from Abba, the Beatles, Elton John. By the time they're finished, people are up dancing and it can get very lively sometimes.

"Then, we have the other extreme. Some groups – and especially their spiritual directors – are more serious. They enjoy music, but they want arias from the operas, like *Nessun Dorma*. They ask for sacred music, like *Panis Angelicus* or an *Ave Verum.* The idea is to have an enjoyable evening, but to retain the recollected mood of the pilgrimage. Fr Philip is the most marked example of this type that I think I've ever met! How will Enzo and Sonia get the balance right?"

"Don't worry, Kieran, just tell them to tone it down a bit. Also, you make sure that your coach arrives first at the restaurant. Have a good chat with the musicians and I think they'll be able to strike the right balance."

"I hope you're right," I replied, trying to shake off a feeling of dread.

A few hours later, our coach pulled up in front of *Da Benito* and I led the group inside. Enzo, as always, was standing in the entrance strumming his guitar while Sonia sang something melodic. I instructed Paolo on how to assign the tables. Mirella, the two drivers and I would be seated separately at a table furthest in from the entrance. Fr Philip's group would take the tables adjacent to ours, with Fr Brian's group (when they eventually arrived) seated at the tables immediately inside the door of the restaurant. I made sure to position Fr Philip at a table adjacent to where I myself was sitting. His mood would need to be monitored closely as the evening progressed.

As the waiters began serving the drinks, I took Enzo and Sonia aside, explaining that we had two very different groups sharing the room. One of the priest leaders would appreciate a reflective, classical style of music, whilst the other priest leader would probably be open to everything.

"I don't want to ruffle Fr Philip's feathers, you see, so it is best if we keep things very dignified. All of that dancing and carousing that went on with the last group would definitely not be appropriate tonight. Also, Enzo, you will have to leave out some of your usual jokes."

"Carousing and dancing? *My* jokes?" Enzo broke into a laugh. "Kieran!" - his voice had now taken on a very soothing tone - "After *all* this time, you know you can trust us! How many times have you brought groups here? Did any of them ever leave unhappy?"

At that moment the door opened and the other group began pouring in to the room. I sighed. "Ok, Enzo, I'll leave it to you to gauge the mood of the group." The musician's words hadn't left me feeling very reassured.

I went over to our table where Mirella was already seated with the two drivers, Salvatore and Gianni. They were the two longest serving drivers for the Terrenzio coach company and they had been here with us on many occasions previously. Gianni was no ordinary driver. He was not content just to drive the coach, but felt it was part of his job description to entertain the group at every opportunity. On more than one occasion I had to rein him in, such as the time when we were ascending the hairpin bends towards the Abbey of Montecassino. As we went around each hairpin bend – at fairly high speed – Gianni would bounce from his driver's seat into a standing position, then he would bounce back down to a sitting position once we were around the bend. He continued to do this as we negotiated the bends up towards the monastery. Some members of the group started whooping in delight, but others had looks of terror on their faces. I asked Gianni to stop but he didn't hear me amid all the noise, so I eventually roared at him to sit down and concentrate on driving his bus. He was so offended by my shouting at him that he sulked for the rest of the day, but was back to his usual self – pranks and all – by the following morning.

"Gianni," I said, as soon as I sat down. "The priest on my coach, Fr Philip, is someone who likes peace and quiet. I've asked the musicians to keep the tone fairly mellow this evening. This means that we are not going to be inviting people to do party pieces, nor suggesting racy tunes for the musicians to perform, like you did last time we were here."

"Kieran, Kieran," replied Gianni, with the same pacifying tone that Enzo was using earlier. "*Racy* tunes?

You know me. You know all I want is for people to have a good time. Don't worry! All will be well."

Salvatore gave me a knowing look from under his bushy eyebrows, shaking his head slightly. Always conscious of the importance of keeping the group leader onside, he knew exactly the kind of antics his colleague was capable of. "Yes Gianni," he said. "Let's all have a *very* quiet evening this evening, shall we?"

The waiters were already serving the starters and the musicians were playing softly in the background. By the time the main course was over, things seemed to be going really well. Sonia had sung a beautiful version of *O Mio Babbino Caro* and had received a standing ovation from Fr Philip.

"See how our friend is enjoying the evening?" Gianni commented to me. "He certainly seems to appreciate the music."

"Yes, Fr Philip seems to be enjoying it, thank God, but we don't want things getting too enjoyable, Gianni, *understood*?"

Gianni gave an animated laugh, but there was a worrying look of devilment on his face.

The wine was really starting to flow at this stage. The waiters had started replenishing the bottles at all the tables. I couldn't help noticing that there were more bottles being carried towards Fr Brian's group. Evidently there were more empties down that end.

There was a pause between songs and Fr Brian stood up and clapped his hands for attention. I immediately stiffened and looked worryingly towards Fr Philip, but he was busy eating his food and didn't seem to be paying much attention.

"Listen up, everyone!" Fr Brian was saying. "Why don't we give the musicians a break and we'll sing one for them?"

Then he launched into a version of *Oh Danny Boy* in a powerful voice, with most of the group joining him. It wasn't so bad after all. When he sat down, Enzo and Sonia gave him extended applause and Gianni shouted "Bravo!" a few times. At that point, the manager, Paolo, called me over to his desk, asking if the bill could be settled now in case there was little time later. This was our usual practice. It was a fixed fee per person regardless of how much wine the group drank, and we nearly always settled the bill at about the halfway point in the meal.

When I got back to the table a couple of minutes later, Gianni was gone. Feeling uneasy, I saw that he was down the other end of the restaurant with Fr Brian and he was engaged in an animated conversation with Enzo. Then Fr Brian turned to the group and spoke aloud.

"Gianni, our driver, tells me that a song that is often performed here is one from the *Sound of Music*. Please join in!"

Enzo struck up a tune on the guitar while Gianni and Fr Brian began singing in unison, "*Doh a deer, a female deer . . .*" Soon virtually everyone had joined in from both groups, though I could see that Fr Philip was just watching with a sombre look. At the end of the piece there was loud applause. Fr Brian and Gianni were slapping each other on the back and seemed to be really getting warmed up.

Gianni was not returning to his seat and began speaking again in Enzo's ear. Clearly, he had another request in mind. I hopped out of my chair immediately and made a beeline for the guitarist. "Enzo!" I called out. "Why don't you come down this end and see if anyone over here has any requests for you and Sonia to perform?" Then I glowered in Gianni's direction, hoping he would get the message, but he was so busily engaged in banter with people around him that he didn't even notice my glare.

As Enzo, Sonia and I came back towards our table, I whispered to Sonia to make sure to ask Fr Philip if he would like her to sing anything.

"Does anyone over here have a special request?" Sonia said as she looked around innocently. "An aria from an opera? How about an *Ave Maria*?" As she said this she was looking towards Fr Philip. He responded immediately.

"Oh, yes, an *Ave Maria*, that would be perfect! Do you know the one from Schubert?"

"Of course, it's my favourite!"

Enzo called for quiet and began plucking the distinctive arpeggio of Schubert's *Ave Maria*. The room had quietened somewhat, but there was still chatter from the far end where Gianni and Fr Brian were joking with the pilgrims. Fr Philip stood up suddenly, an annoyed look on his face, and began tapping his glass with a spoon.

"Quiet down there! *Quiet*! We have a beautiful piece of music being performed here! We need complete silence! *Please!*"

A complete hush fell over the room. Enzo began plucking again and Sonia gave a beautiful rendition of the piece. I could see Fr Philip with his eyes closed as she sang. A warm applause from the room followed, although it wasn't at nearly the volume that had greeted "*Doh, a deer.*"

While Sonia had been singing, I had nipped into the kitchen and instructed Paolo to get the desserts served as soon as possible. Even though this *Ave Maria* was settling things nicely, it was important to be out of here quickly before things got out of hand. Once dessert had been served, we would have our customary farewell song – *Arrivederci Roma.* Then it was just a matter of rounding the pilgrims onto the coaches. All in all, or so I consoled myself, the evening hadn't been *such* a disaster.

As the waiters wheeled out the dessert trolleys, I saw that space had been made for Gianni down at Fr Brian's table. They had set an extra place for him and pulled up another chair. "Oh well," I thought to myself, "that might have been worrying an hour ago, but those two partners in crime can't do any great harm at this point. We'll soon be out of here."

Mirella was chatting flirtatiously with Paolo over at the kitchen and I was very intently scraping the last of my dessert from the bottom of the bowl when Salvatore touched my plate with his fork. "Oh-oh," he said. "I think you need to see this."

I looked up in alarm. Gianni was back on his feet and was whispering in Sonia's ear, who then began speaking to Fr Brian. Once again, the priest addressed the group in a loud voice. "Gianni and I need two partners for the next number! Who would like to volunteer?"

I stood up and called over to Enzo, "Sorry, we don't have time for anything. We really need to go soon!"

"Don't worry," said Enzo, smiling broadly. "It won't take long. You'll enjoy this one, Kieran, I promise! Now let's have those volunteers!"

A woman from Fr Brian's group arose and went over to Gianni, while Bernie from Fr Philip's group got up and went to Fr Brian. Fr Philip's table was adjacent to ours and I could hear him say, "Well, *really*!" as soon as Bernie stood up. She was determined to be his nemesis right to the end.

Enzo began strumming and Sonia broke into "*I could have danced all night*" from *My Fair Lady,* while the dancers twirled around the open space in the centre of the restaurant. The response from the combined groups was thunderous in volume. Virtually everyone stood up and began clapping and shouting. The sight of the priest dancing with one woman and the bus driver dancing with another had an electrifying effect on the pilgrims. It was a once in a lifetime spectacle. In addition, no doubt, they were stimulated by the fact that they had just downed a quantity of wine comparable to that of the wedding feast at Cana. As the dance progressed and

Bernie was being twirled around by Fr Brian more and more rapidly, the group was becoming ever more raucous. The noise rose to a fever pitch. Suddenly, Fr Philip stood up and turned to me with a furious look.

"I have had quite enough!" he shouted. "As soon as you can get these wild animals under control, let's be on our way back to the hotel!"

With that he stormed towards the exit, Salvatore trotting pathetically behind him to open the coach. I slumped in my seat. My hopes for a relaxing evening and a contented Fr Philip had gone up in smoke. When the song ended, Enzo began strumming happily again and there was no doubt that he was going to launch into *"Arrivederci Roma."* I managed to interrupt him in time and, with Mirella's help, began herding the tipsy pilgrims towards the coaches. As we drove back to the hotel, the group was in an animated mood, but Fr Philip sat in a sullen silence. This evening's debacle, I feared, could tarnish the entire trip for him.

Next morning, we had the visit that I had done most often with pilgrimages to Rome, the tour of the Lateran Basilica. While Fr Philip's group and I made our visit and celebrated Mass, Mirella was to take Fr Brian's group to the Colosseum about a mile away. Afterwards, I would lead my group towards the Colosseum while Mirella led hers towards the Lateran. We would meet along the way, switch groups, turn on our heels and do it all again. It promised to be the easiest morning of the week. I was keen to do a particularly good job on the tour of St John Lateran. The history and the artwork of this church was always inspirational for people and I felt that it could be just the thing to get Fr Philip's pilgrimage back on track.

The tour went swimmingly well. After we had finished in the nave, Fr Philip made sure that the pilgrims understood the significance of the presence of the heads of Peter and Paul in the canopy above the altar. He stood with the group for a moment in front of the Blessed Sacrament in the left transept and sang the *Tantum Ergo*, asking the group to consider the privilege of standing here beneath the relics of the table of the Last Supper, which, according to tradition, is conserved above the tabernacle. Then we all proceeded into the Choir Chapel, with its beautiful wooden choir stalls of the 1600s, normally reserved for private Masses.

As the group took their seats, Fr Philip and I went into the sacristy. Here we were greeted by Sister Lucia, the affable sacristan who had been greeting our groups for as long as I could remember. Fr Philip vested and then he and I went into the chapel to sort out the readers and make final preparations for Mass.

"Of course, we'll need a thurible," he said, referring to the metal vessel suspended from chains used for the burning of incense during worship.

I was surprised. Whereas incense was often used at public Sunday Masses, no one had ever requested it during a pilgrimage.

"I'm not sure if it's an option on a week-day," I said hesitantly.

"As you told us so eloquently during the tour, this is the mother church of the world and the Pope's own cathedral! I don't think thuribles or incense will be in short supply around here!"

Fr Philip didn't sound like he was in the mood for nonsense, so I dutifully disappeared into the sacristy. "Sister Lucia," I said, "we have an unusual request, a thurible for incense."

"A *thurible*?" she said in a tone of disbelief. "On a *weekday*? It's not something we do, you know, unless it's a Sunday Mass or a big feast, and only for public ceremonies usually."

"Yes, I know. It's hard to explain but it's something very important for this particular priest."

Sister Lucia had noticed the imploring tone in my voice and she gave me a concerned look. "Oh, *va bene*!" she said suddenly with a laugh, throwing her hands up in the air. "We'll make an exception this time! But don't burn the place down!" Her words would turn out to be strangely prophetic.

A few minutes later I was armed with the thurible at the top of the chapel and Fr Philip was giving me instructions.

"I'll leave a pack of charcoal on this little table here beside the altar. If you don't add a piece about half way through Mass, the whole thing could go out. At that point you need to swing it to let air in and get the charcoal burning. You can add a little incense, if necessary, but generally I'll be the one adding the incense when you approach me with the thurible at the beginning of Mass, before the Gospel and during the preparation of the gifts, got it?"

"Yes, should be no problem," I said confidently, feeling that I had been transported back to my altar serving days.

The first incensing went well. Fr Philip took a spoonful of incense from the metal "boat" that acted as a repository, sprinkled it on the charcoal, and the smoke began to rise as I passed the thurible to him.

About half-way though the rather long and rambling homily, Fr Philip looked towards me and raised his eyebrows a few times, which I took as a signal to add more charcoal. The thurible at this point was hanging on a special stand behind Fr Philip, to the side of the altar. I rose, went to the front, added a piece of charcoal and swung the thurible for a minute or two while the homily continued. No smoke was emerging though, so I turned my back on the congregation, lifted the chain and had a peek inside. The new piece of charcoal had not ignited and the older piece looked like it was on its last legs. Something had to be done fast. If there was no smoke when Fr Philip took the thurible during the offertory, there could be hell to pay. The pack of charcoal on the table had just three pieces left. I added one, but then, on impulse, threw them all in. Would that do the trick, though? Earlier I had noticed that the incense had crackled when Fr Philip had added it. Maybe that was what was needed to help ignite the new pieces of charcoal? The problem was that I had the thurible in one hand and the incense boat in the other. Another hand, ideally, would be needed to spoon in the incense. Then I spotted with satisfaction that the boat had a beak-like spout on it, evidently devised by some clever inventor of church equipment for pouring incense whenever predicaments such as the present one arose. Delicately balancing myself, I tipped the boat over the open thurible. To my alarm, a colossal amount of incense poured into the vessel, completely quenching any few wisps of smoke that had been rising previously. Now I was in real trouble. This homily could hardly go on for much longer and Fr Philip's face would not be a pleasant sight when I presented him with a smokeless thurible a few minutes from now. There was nothing for it but to resume swinging the vessel, in the hope that some sort of combustion would take place, but now I was doing it much more vigorously than before, fervently hoping that the faster passage of air might help. I was faced away from the congregation and the swinging was so wild that I must have looked like Jesse James trying to lasso a stray horse that had wandered into the sanctuary. All this time, Fr Philip was standing at the ambo giving his homily, his back turned to me, oblivious to the experiment in chemistry that was going on a few feet behind him.

Suddenly, the thurible started crackling and profuse clouds of smoke began emerging from it. In a moment of panic, I wondered if I should bring it into the sacristy and douse some water on it, but then I reasoned that it would surely calm down as soon as the swinging stopped. As discreetly as I could, I hung it back on its stand and tiptoed back to my place. Fr Philip was just finishing the homily. Smoke was still billowing from the thurible behind him but he didn't seem to notice.

A few minutes later, it was time to incense the altar before the Eucharistic prayer. Fr Philip gave me a signal and I went to the front, took the thurible, approached him sheepishly and handed him the boat. Then I pulled the chain to lift the lid, revealing a glowing mass of red coals inside. We could have been looking into the crater of an active volcano. As he stooped over the thurible, I bent down and spoke into his ear, "Sorry Fr Philip. By accident I think I overdid it. There's probably enough incense in there already."

He looked up and gave me a merciful smile. "Don't worry, smoke is good," he whispered benignly, adding another generous spoonful.

When we eventually staggered out into the main part of the basilica a half hour later, Fr Philip seemed extremely satisfied. Visibility had been severely impaired for the last part of Mass and the sound of muffled wheezing was coming from every corner of the smoke-filled chapel, but the pilgrims had devotedly stood their ground. Fr Philip was in a good mood, though, and temporary pulmonary impairment seemed a small price to pay.

Just before we exited the mother church of the world, I looked back towards the Choir Chapel. Sister Lucia was opening the huge glass doors. Smoke was billowing out of the chapel into the basilica. Anyone who did not know what had just transpired might have been inclined to call the fire brigade.

Half way down the Via dei SS Quattro Coronati towards the Colosseum, the two groups met and I was soon heading back to the Lateran to do it all over again. The visit had to be more efficient this time round as Sister Lucia expected us for our Mass in the Choir Chapel by 11.30am. Needless to say there would be no incense. Fr Bryan also indicated that he didn't intend to do a homily.

"Have you the readers sorted out?" I asked him as he vested in the sacristy.

"Yes, all four of them have been chosen," he said.

Four readers seemed a lot, but I thought that he intended one person to do the readings and three to say prayers of the faithful. When it came to that point of the Mass, though, Fr Brian didn't do any prayers of the faithful at all. He went immediately from the Gospel into the offertory of the Mass. "Looks like he forgot to do the prayers," I thought to myself. However, after the blessing of the gifts and the reading of the collect prayer, Fr Brian invited three members of the group – two women and one man - to come forward. Each was armed with a sheet of paper. The priest read the first section of the Eucharistic prayer. Then the three who had come forward read sections of the prayer in turn. When it came to the doxology – the high point of the Eucharistic prayer that ends with the great Amen – Fr Brian gave one of the women the chalice, the other a ciborium with the hosts, while the man held aloft another ciborium.

One did not have to be an expert in the liturgy to know that what was happening here was an aberration of a serious kind. The Church has clear ordinances about how the Mass must be offered. These are not simply conventions, or regulations for their own sake, but are grounded in the Church's understanding of what the Mass is, its relation to the Last Supper and to Christ's sacrifice on Calvary, and to who the priest is when he is offering the Mass. The Mass is a participation in Calvary. As Fulton Sheen used to say, when we go to Mass, the veil is drawn back and we are present at the culminating events in the history of salvation. St Paul says, "For as often as you eat this bread and drink the cup, you proclaim the Lord's death until he comes" (1 Cor 11,26). The priest represents Christ in a unique way when he stands at that altar and makes this offering that the Church has faithfully been making since the first Pentecost. Lay involvement in the Mass is good, but the consecration of the body and blood of Jesus and the offering of the Eucharistic prayer is the very thing that the priest has been ordained to do. In fact, only he has the power to do it, a power given by Christ to the Church and passed on from Peter and the apostles to their successors. It is not a power that Fr Brian had the authority to confer on anyone else. When the Mass was over, however, no-one in the group showed any signs of noticing that something highly irregular had just happened.

The way the day was planned, it was my turn to spend lunchtime with the group of Fr Brian. It so happened that he and I ended up in the corner of a café with a coffee and a sandwich, while the rest of the group were spread out in a few different places along the Via San Giovanni.

I said a quiet prayer for courage and mentioned to him that I was bothered by the fact that he had asked laypeople to carry out a part of the Mass that they couldn't legitimately perform. His response was fairly predictable.

"These people feel left out by the Church! They see a few stodgy men like myself doing everything important. We give the homilies, we consecrate the Eucharist and we say all the important prayers! Look, I wouldn't do this in the parish so as not to give scandal. But here we have a fairly exclusive group of 'insiders,' so to speak. I wanted them to feel included and to give them a sense of having a real role in the Church."

"It's only the Church that can give that role though, isn't it?"

"Precisely! And the Church is simply not going to give that to a married man or women of any sort, so I let them have it, just for a moment. And when they're up there at the altar saying the prayers, they make all members of the group, women and married men alike, feel that they are participating."

I sighed. Did I really want to get one more time into a debate about the priesthood? A layperson offering the prayers of the Mass doesn't in any real way increase the participation of those present. Quite the opposite, in fact. It is only Christ that can represent all the baptized because Christ alone has joined himself to them by his incarnation, passion, death and resurrection. Jesus is the ultimate everyman because he has bought us with his blood. And when the Church ordains priests, it confers on them the capacity to identify with Christ - to "image" him – so that they, and they alone, can legitimately and validly offer him in sacrifice.

Before I could say anything, however, Fr Brian put his hand on my shoulder in a fatherly way. "What I did there in that chapel was just a gesture, that's all, so everyone in the group would feel valued, included," he said. "Don't worry, it's not something I would necessarily be repeating."

As often happens, it is only afterwards that you think of the thing that you could profitably have said at that particular moment. It is repeated in many ways in the New Testament that Jesus is the bridegroom who comes among us and lays down his life for his bride, the Church. This image is found in the Old Testament too. In Isaiah, we read, *"For your Maker is your husband, the Lord of hosts is his name; the Holy One of Israel is your Redeemer"* (Isaiah 54, 5). Jesus offers himself on Calvary and gives his life for his bride, the Church. When we celebrate Mass, we participate in Calvary as surely as if we were standing there in the flesh. The priest, by the power conferred on him through the Church, images Christ himself, and says the priestly prayer of Christ, the prayer of the bridegroom's self-offering for the Church and the world. Now, if laypeople are asked to read part of this prayer, the whole event becomes incoherent. Christ is offering himself for his bride, the Church, but here we have members of the Church saying the prayer of offering, as if *they* were the redeemer instead of being the redeemed. Yes, it is true that priests are in need of redemption too, but the Church has the authority to ordain them so that they can offer this sacrifice *in persona Christi*, imaging the bridegroom, regardless of their personal holiness, or lack of it. As John Paul II put it, when the priest says the words of consecration, it is not so much he who is speaking; rather he is putting his voice "*at the disposal of the One who spoke these words in the Upper Room* and who desires that they should be repeated in every generation by all those who in the Church ministerially share in his priesthood."

For the last couple of days of the pilgrimage, I took out a sheet of paper on my train journeys to and from Piazza Euclide and wrote down the contrasts between Fr Brian and Fr Philip. Mirella had said to me on one of our meetings on the steps that she wished they could learn from each other. Was that what was needed? Fr Brian needed to move a little towards the right and Fr Philip towards the left? Fr Philip needed to become more pastoral and Fr Brian needed to become more faithful to clerical discipline? As the days went on, the table was getting longer and longer:

	FR BRIAN	FR PHILIP
Concern for lay participation	Yes	No
Reverence towards the Eucharist	Lacking	Present
Seeks to interrelate with people	Yes	Not really
Feels that he has the right to dispose of liturgical discipline	Yes	No
Appreciates cult of the saints and relics	No	Yes
Appreciates sacred music and art	A little	Very much
Concern to reach out to people	Yes	No
Good knowledge of sacramental theology	No	Yes
Good knowledge of the lives of the saints	Yes	Yes
Listens to his flock	Yes	Not really
Emphasizes the need to teach truth	No	Yes
Emphasizes the need for Church to show mercy	Yes	Yes
Concern for the poor and marginalised	Yes	Not so much

On one of these journeys, I again asked myself Mirella's question: did each one just need to embrace the best of the other? As the pilgrimage was drawing to a close, I had become quite absorbed with this question. All of us in the Church want to have good priests to lead us, but what is it that makes a good priest? It didn't seem that Fr Brian or Fr Philip were just lacking some of the qualities of the other. It appeared more likely that the items on this list were rather superficial manifestations of deeper issues. At one point, I took out my pen, crossed out the table altogether and wrote under it, "These qualities are not the crux of what makes a good priest."

As soon as I wrote the word "crux," I felt that an answer had presented itself. A month earlier, while in Krakow on pilgrimage with a group from St Patrick's Parish, Belfast, the first place we had visited was St Mary's Basilica in Market Square. During lunchtime, I had sat inside for a while in front of the stone crucifix from the 1490s by German artist Veit Stoss, one of the greatest sculptors of his day. The crucifix is startlingly life-like. It graphically depicts the suffering and death of Jesus in a powerful way. We can see that Christ has exhaled his last breath and his side has been pierced. It is clear that the self-offering of the God-man is utterly complete.

Now, in Rome, on the train from Piazza Euclide, I remembered what I had felt in front of that crucifix. In Krakow that day, the psalm of the Mass had been:

Happy are those
  who do not follow the advice of the wicked,
or take the path that sinners tread,
  or sit in the seat of scoffers;
but their delight is in the law of the Lord,
  and on his law they meditate day and night.
They are like trees
  planted by streams of water,
which yield their fruit in its season,
  and their leaves do not wither.
In all that they do, they prosper. (Psalm 1, 1-3)

Jesus is the ultimate example of the man who delights above all in the word of the Father and is obedient to that word, right down to embracing the cross. He is the tree planted beside the flowing water which yields its fruit. The cross, with its vertical and horizontal beams, is the great symbol of this vertical rootedness in God which yields immeasurable "horizontal" fruit for the wider world.

This is what we needed in a priest, not simply the "clerical" qualities of adhering to the norms, nor the "pastoral" qualities of walking with people at their level. What was essential, above all, was cruciform rootedness in God. Radical adhesion to the Lord would spontaneously give rise to a pastoral care for people and a reverent respect for the norms of the Church.

Yes, Fr Philip was a good man with a genuine sense of the divine. On the surface, it looked like he had the "vertical" component of the cross in place, but he did not seem to allow this adhesion to God to penetrate into his heart so that it influenced his behaviour towards those around him. He passed beggars on the street with complete disdain. He treated his own parishioners as pesky irritants who really should just take the graces he was dispensing and leave him in peace. His love for the ritual aspect of the sacraments risked becoming a way of holding the Lord at bay, keeping Jesus in the tabernacle or the monstrance, something to be adored at a distance, not something that would transform his relationships or the inner workings of his heart.

Yes, Fr Brian was a good man with a genuine concern for people. On the surface, it looked like he had the "horizontal" relationships of his life in order, but his good deeds for others seemed to be all about what *he* did with his own efforts, what *he* could do to make people feel welcome. If Church teachings or norms had to be ignored or denied to make people feel welcome, then he was willing to do it because he knew better. Proper rootedness in the vertical relationship with the Father, by contrast, should entail respect for the voice of the Church expressed in its teachings. Fr Brian would still seek to be inclusive and welcoming, but now his actions would be grounded in the power of God transmitted through his chosen instrument, the Church.

On the last day, we had planned a tour of St Mary Major Basilica with the celebration of Mass. The day's programme was a little tight and Mirella suggested that the two groups celebrate Mass together to make things more efficient, one group having their tour before Mass and the second group afterwards. I had a momentary vision of Fr Philip frantically circling the altar with incense while Fr Brian lined up a motley crew to say the Eucharistic prayer.

"Wouldn't it be a nice way to finish?" Mirella was saying in her bright innocent way. "The two groups having Mass together like one big happy family!"

Needless to say, this encounter of the Council of Trent with Woodstock wasn't allowed to happen, but we nevertheless managed to get the programme completed before heading to the airport. Some days later, still mulling over the contrast between the two priests, I began thinking of them in terms of their attitudes to grace and nature. Fr Philip was very aware that the Church is a conduit of divine grace. The church teaches that this grace is received through the sacraments, *ex opera operato*, which is a way of saying that the sacraments effectively transmit grace regardless of the disposition or holiness of the priest performing the act. As he saw it, his job was to provide the sacraments, to open up this conduit of grace. The faithful just had to avail of it.

Fr Brian placed little emphasis on the necessity of supernatural grace. He admitted to me during the week that his busy regime of work meant that he had minimal time for prayer. Salvation was about being in right relationship with those around us, the planet, and those on the margins. It was up to us to cultivate those right relationships with our efforts. Grace from above was a bonus, but didn't seem the primary thing.

By contrast, Fr Philip emphasized the grace of God and the need for faith. When speaking to a man in the group whose wife had a spiritual illness of some kind, he told him that, with reception of the sacraments, or by doing a novena, or by visiting a shrine, she could confidently expect healing, but he never mentioned the need for personal conversion. It was as if grace alone was all that mattered. Nature, the natural disposition of the person receiving the grace, had a very minor role to play.

Taking a completely different line, Fr Brian once described healing as involving transformation using natural means. If someone has an addiction, then the first recourse should be corrective therapy which involves investigation of the addiction, understanding its source, and coming to terms with those personal issues. Let's get the human dimension of the problem sorted out – that is our domain after all - and there'll be no need to worry about grace.

Against these two extremes, the Church has always taught that grace builds on nature. A search for natural integrity that does not acknowledge our vital need for the grace of God will have limited success, at the very most. Spiritual growth is a cooperation with the Lord. It is true that I must use all human means available to come to terms with my wounded memories and damaged relationships, but it must all be done hand in hand with the Lord, seeking his guidance, his strength, abandoning myself to him, trusting in his providence.

Using an analogy, grace is like a supernatural seed planted in natural soil. If the soil is deficient, badly prepared or outright barren, then the seed, no matter how potent it is, will not be able to bear fruit. On the other hand, if I cultivate my soil perfectly, remove the weeds, fertilize the ground, but omit to allow that seed to be planted, then there will never be a harvest.

Fr Philip believed in the potency of the seed, but disregarded the importance of the soil. In fact, he didn't even seem to allow that seed to penetrate into his own heart. The sacred was reverenced and honoured, venerated industriously with incense, but kept safely at arm's length.

If it is true that grace is directed towards the transformation of nature, it is also true that it can only operate by building on the nature that is already there. Our nature is fallen, our memories wounded, our spiritual vision impaired, our wills weak. When we approach the Eucharist well, nurturing that divine seed with trust and abandonment, then our memories can be healed a little, our spiritual vision corrected a little, our wills strengthened a little. Thus, the next time we receive the Eucharist, our nature has been enriched by the fruits of divine grace from the previous reception. The new grace we receive from this new encounter with the Eucharist will have an improved nature to build upon, even if that improvement is imperceptible to us. In this way, each one of us cooperates with the Lord in our own salvation, in our own bearing of fruit for our own good and that of the Church.

On the Feast of the Presentation, a passage from the prophet Malachi is read. First, we are told that *"the Lord whom you seek will suddenly come to his temple."* The temple to which the Messiah comes is none other than our hearts. He comes at baptism and his presence within us is renewed each time we receive the sacraments. But then, shockingly, the prophet's tone changes. The happy coming is not simply about the Lord being present within us. He doesn't come to affirm us in our weaknesses or leave us as we were. *"But who can endure the day of his coming, and who can stand when he appears? For he is like a refiner's fire . . . and he will purify the descendants of Levi and refine them like gold and silver, until they present offerings to the Lord in righteousness"* (Malachi 3, 1-4). God wishes to transform us and to do that we must be chastised. It is not enough for Fr Philip to incense him on the altar, we must also incense him in our hearts. It is not enough for Fr Brian to affirm him in others, we must dialogue with him personally in that interior crucible and be changed. What is true for us laypeople is especially true for the priest. If we are to present a worthy offering to the Lord, then we must permit ourselves to be changed and purified within, chastised by his love.

Chapter Eight
Chastised by Love

"I did not then believe in the living God, not even when I was a child. In fact, I remained in death and unbelief until I was strongly chastised and humiliated by hunger and nakedness daily."

St Patrick, ***Confession***

It was St Patrick's Day, 2011 and I was experiencing a familiar sense of frustration. As a nation, we seemed to have difficulty marking the memory of our patron in a meaningful way. The true story of Patrick was a compelling one, but the most common image in the popular culture was that of an old man in green banishing the snakes from the island. This was despite the fact that, unlike most figures from such an early period, we actually possess an authentic autobiography of Patrick, his *Confession*. It can easily be read in one sitting, but its revelatory power is dramatic. The picture that emerges is of a passionate and courageous man, committed utterly to God and to the Irish people.

It might be true that most Irish people have heard the broad details of his life - the capture into slavery, his dramatic escape, and then the most unlikely of returns to Ireland, bringing with him the Gospel - but, during the annual commemoration of his feast, the great personal qualities of Patrick that stand out from his *Confession* are rarely mentioned. In many quarters, little more than a caricature remains. In others, the situation is even worse – the image and name of Patrick are used to promote agendas that are completely at odds with the faith.

As usual, in the lead up to March 17th 2011, a St Patrick's Festival was organised nationally. This is really a celebration of certain aspects of Irish identity, where "identity" is often reduced to particular habits of music, dancing and drinking. In the midst of all this, many valuable cultural events take place. The problem is that - apart from a few exceptions - the festival seems committed to the studious ignorance of Patrick's real life, achievements and legacy.

That morning, we attended the parade in a village not too far from home. It was light-hearted and entertaining, but it did nothing to evoke the life of the man who had transformed the very social fabric of Ireland. In the evening, when the kids were gone to bed, I reread the *Confession* once again. As well as being the most ancient historical document to come out of our land, this deeply personal testimony has a directness and humility that strike the reader from the very first line: *"My name is Patrick. I am a sinner, a simple country person, and the least of all believers. I am looked down upon by many."*

When I had finished reading, I said to Laura on impulse, "Wouldn't it be great to make a proper documentary on the life of St Patrick? You know, one that presented him as he really was."

"How could we do that, though?" replied Laura. "We have no expertise in filming. And we don't know anyone who does."

Laura was right. How could we do anything of the sort? Yet, I couldn't shake off this feeling that the real life of Patrick should be made better known somehow. A few mornings later, I opened my emails and found one from an Italian called Luigi, a film director working with a religious television channel. He had been commissioned to make a documentary on pilgrimage sites and wanted to come to Ireland to do some filming, with particular emphasis on places related to St Patrick. He needed help choosing the locations to shoot, obtaining necessary permissions, sorting out accommodation for the crew, interviewing local people and translating the eventual audio into Italian. With a sense of amazement I wondered if maybe we were going to make that film on St Patrick after all.

As it would turn out, Luigi's documentary was mostly interested in the theme of pilgrimage to sacred places. Caught up in the fervour to promote the true story of Patrick, I signed up for the job and spent weeks later that year organising the shooting, travelling with the crew and translating the interview transcripts. It was intense work, and intensely disappointing - the final result did not devote much attention to the saint's life at all.

One of the most memorable moments, however, occurred on the lake island of Lough Derg in County Donegal, at a pilgrimage site known as "St Patrick's Purgatory." For centuries people have come here to carry out the exercises of a most severe pilgrimage. It involves three days of intense prayer and fasting. Only one meal is allowed per day, consisting of dry bread or oatcakes. Sleep is not permitted at all on the first night and pilgrims must remain barefoot for the entire duration, regardless of the weather. The prayer exercises consist of a demanding and rigorous series of prayers, done mostly outdoors whilst walking and kneeling.

Having done the pilgrimage many years previously on a number of occasions, I still remembered lucidly how challenging it was. Now I would be on the island wearing shoes, taking coffee breaks in the staff lounge, and leaving in time for a good night's sleep. The business of filming other people doing those penances would be slightly surreal.

When we arrived at the pier, we were told that all the new pilgrims for that particular day had already been transported to the island. We had the boat entirely to ourselves, so Luigi wasted no time in getting the camera equipment set up on the bow so that they could film the approach to the island. It was a grey and cloudy day. The rain began to fall before we arrived and it would continue for the entire duration of our time at the sanctuary. For the next few hours, we were given a free run of the island and dedicated ourselves to filming all of the different pilgrim exercises from various angles. The rector of the shrine also did an interview with us. The weather continued to deteriorate. Towards the end of our visit, we were set up at the edge of the lake, trying to find a good angle to film the pilgrims performing one of the last acts in each round of pilgrim exercises. The earlier exercises consisted largely in walking in circles around a series of "penitential beds" reciting a long series of Our Fathers, Hail Marys and the Creed. These beds are the remnants of the beehive cells of the ancient monastic community that lived on the island. One of the final acts in each station required kneeling at the edge of the lake and making a sign of the cross with the lake water. We were set up at some distance away so that people would not feel intimidated by the cameras. The pilgrims came forward to kneel, one by one. At one point, the cameraman, Giuseppe, turned towards the sound technician, Emanuele, and muttered under his breath, "Sono tutti pazzi!" ("They're all crazy!") Luigi, however, was very quick to respond. "No!" he said firmly, shaking his head. "Un popolo così è imbattibile" ("A people like this will never be beaten").

As Luigi spoke, there was a moment of rare lucidity. What is it that makes a people unbeatable? Surely, the extent to which they place themselves in the hands of their maker. For as long as we rely on ourselves and our own limited powers, we will only get so far. But when we open up to that which utterly transcends us, then we begin to live a different kind of existence, a life that cannot be taken from us. A pilgrim drenched to the skin, on his knees, making the sign of the cross with water from the lake, this was a person who was living for something that went far beyond simple material wellbeing.

The events of recent years, however, seem to cast doubt on the thought that the faith of the Irish people will never be beaten. Governments with aggressively secularist policies, the wholehearted embracing of consumerism by a majority of the population, partisan journalism devoted to a one-sided condemnation of our Christian heritage – all these factors point to a nation that is losing its faith in the God of the Bible. The only life that matters is the life that we are living, here and now. That which is unseen and unheard has no significance or rights.

Yet, it was also clear from the people we met through our work that there persists a stubborn remnant of the faith that Patrick brought. There are few countries where the faith of virtually its entire people can be connected to the heroic testimony of a single man. He was a most unlikely deliverer of the Irish people. Patrick's childhood was unremarkable in its mediocrity. Though nominally Christian, he admits that he did not know the true God. He was, he said, "like a stone lying deep in the mud." His days would have been spent as the children of our age tend to spend their days, centred on himself, devoid of meaning or direction. When he was sixteen, he was captured by a raiding party and taken into slavery to Ireland. A life of utter mediocrity had now become a life of complete misery. He was put to work tending sheep on the side of a mountain. It was here, amid snow, ice and rain, that Patrick changed, against all the odds. He could have given in to bitterness and despair, but instead he responded to the divine grace that for years had sought to touch his soul. Having no earthly pleasures or comforts to distract him, he looked within himself and discovered something that was much greater than himself. He began to pray more and more frequently. The attachment to God increased within him. He started to burn with wonder at the sense of the divine. He would rise before dawn in all weathers to pray with a zeal and an energy that could only have come from outside himself – a power that he would one day recognize to be the Holy Spirit. Though suffering great deprivation, he understood that his captivity had bestowed an enormous blessing on him. In his *Confession* he would say that he remained in death and unbelief until his capture brought upon him hunger and nakedness daily. From this hunger and nakedness of the body, he discovered the nourishment and riches of heaven. The chastisement of captivity had awakened in him the knowledge of divine love.

After six years of this existence, Patrick was a man transformed. He was no longer an immature boy, wallowing in self-absorption. His masters could not have realized that the ragged youth on the hill tending their sheep was a spiritual giant, filled with the strength and wisdom of his divine Master. Around this time, he heard a voice in his sleep, providing him with instructions on how to find the ship that would take him out of Ireland. The journey was not direct, but he was eventually reunited with his parents, who pleaded with him to remain with them forever. Patrick tried to settle down at home once again, but he soon had a dream in which a man called Victoricus came to him from Ireland. He carried with him a great number of letters that could not be counted. The letters began with the words "The voice of the Irish People . . ." As Patrick began to read, he heard the words of those who lived "near the western sea." They called out with one voice: "We beg you, holy boy, to come and walk among us once more."

Just a dream, surely, Patrick! Would you *really* return to a place of misery and hardship on the basis of a dream? But this was now a man deeply in touch with the realm of the Spirit, someone who was not following the ways of human wisdom or earthly calculation. He recognized in this voice of the Irish the call to fulfil his deepest destiny before God. *"Before I formed you in the womb I knew you, and before you were born I consecrated you; I appointed you a prophet to the nations"* (Jeremiah 1,5). It would take some time, but eventually he attained the necessary education, was ordained a bishop and received the mission to preach the Gospel in Ireland.

The traditional account of the return of Patrick to Ireland in the year 432 held that, with some brief resistance, the country was converted to Christianity relatively swiftly and comprehensively. Revisionist historians of the twentieth century questioned this account, doubting that the process was completed so quickly, and questioning the central role of Patrick. These scholars, however, tend to undervalue the precious historical record contained in the *Confession*. No-one seriously doubts that this document is original and comes from the hand of Patrick himself. A controversy with the bishops of Britain motivated Patrick to write in defence of his character and his mission. In these circumstances, Patrick had to be very careful to state his case plainly and transparently. At times, it is almost like a deposition for a court of law. He is forthright about a previous misdemeanour at the age of fifteen (a deed that was subsequently used against him by the British bishops). Given his rather bracing candour, there is little reason for doubting Patrick when he refers to the success of his mission in Ireland. He says: "How has this happened in Ireland? Never before did they know of God except to serve idols and unclean things. But now, they have become the people of the Lord, and are called children of God. The sons and daughters of the leaders of the Irish are seen to be monks and virgins of Christ!" Such statements would easily have been contradicted by his readers if they were not true.

The testimony of the *Confession* is clear: that St Patrick preached the Gospel widely in Ireland; that his preaching was successful and led to an enormous number of converts; that he appointed ordained ministers throughout the land; that he developed a zealous love for the people who had once taken him into slavery. *"If I have ever imitated anything good for the sake of my God whom I love, I ask that he grant me to be able to shed my blood with these converts and captives."*

When Luigi and his crew returned to Italy, the many weeks of editing the documentary and translating the various interviews began. The finished result may not have done much to promote knowledge of St Patrick, but organising the logistics for the filming turned out to be a valuable experience. We had to correspond with the National Museum and other institutions, the Office of Public Works, many diocesan offices and the rectors of some of the principal pilgrimage sites in Ireland. This gave us a whole new body of contacts, as well as knowledge for accessing monuments, but would we ever be able to put any of it to use? Our work usually involved taking groups in the other direction, from Ireland to the continent.

Later that very summer, however, out of the blue, we were asked to organise a trip for an Italian diocese to Ireland. The bishop himself would lead the group and there would be many priests and seminarians present. Their main interest was to visit sites associated with the principal saints of Ireland - Patrick, Brigid and Colmcille. Having arranged the filming for Luigi, we had already studied and visited most of the places that this group wanted to see. It seemed like we just had the ideal preparation.

The pilgrim group was from a part of Italy where poultry rearing was a big industry. One of the diocesan initiatives included a chicken-rearing unit run by the seminarians to raise money for their studies. I discovered this during the pilgrimage as we crossed County Cavan on the way to Croagh Patrick in Mayo. Cavan has many poultry farms and some of these were spotted by the seminarians as we were driving through.

As we passed by, one of the students came up to the front of the coach, "Could we call in to visit one of those chicken farms?" he asked.

I didn't think he was serious. "Oh, I get it," I joked. "You're just trying to avoid climbing Croagh Patrick!"

But the students had a genuine interest in poultry and they went on to tell me how the bishop had recently expanded their own chicken farm in order to raise funds for the seminary. We had no time to stop, though, as the visit to Croagh Patrick and the nearby Marian shrine of Knock was going to take all day. At the time, I didn't think too much more about the bishop's chick-rearing enterprise, but it was to figure significantly in the pilgrimage before the end of that week.

We had organised the trip around the figures of St Patrick and Brigid and some of the other important saints. This meant visiting places like Downpatrick (tombs of Patrick, Brigid and Colmcille), Kildare (St Brigid), Glendalough (St Kevin) and Clonmacnoise (St Ciaran). We also called into sites of lesser importance that we were passing along the way. Many of the ancient monastic sites of Ireland are in the care of the Church of Ireland. At the time of the reformation, these properties were seized by the English crown from the original monastic orders and they became the property of the established church. We found the rectors of these churches very accommodating. In all cases, they gave us full access to the sites, and opened up the churches so that the group could pray inside.

When I phoned one of these sites of lesser importance to organise our visit, I was surprised to be greeted by an American accent. The minister explained to me that she had been raised in the United States but had moved to Ireland a few years previously when the Church of Ireland had put the place up for sale.

"Oh?" I replied. "I thought the site was still in the care of the Church of Ireland."

"Not any more. The place became very run down and the congregation was virtually non-existent, so it came up for sale. Our denomination bought it. We're still in the process of forming a regular congregation. Some Sundays I have two people at my service, if I'm lucky!"

We had just finalised the arrangements for our visit when the minister suggested, "Why don't we have a sort of ecumenical service while you're here? We did something of the sort last Christmas with the local Catholic clergy and it went down a bomb."

"That's very kind of you," I replied, "but we will be a little under pressure for time. We're just calling by in passing."

"Does your group understand any English?"

"Almost none, as far as I understand."

"Well, I can meet you in the church, explain a little of the history while you translate, and maybe then we could say a little prayer together?"

"That sounds good to me. Ok, let's do a little ecumenism! Thanks for offering to meet us!"

We arrived at the churchyard on a wet and windy day, at the height of one of the wettest summers in years.

The minister met us very graciously, standing at the gate with an umbrella in the windswept conditions. The bishop instructed me to get the coach as near as possible to the entrance. Being Italian, they were not too enthusiastic about having to brave this sort of elements in the month of July.

The pilgrims took their seats in the worn pews and the bishop came with me towards the front where the minister was standing. The bishop said how pleased he was to take his group into this historic church. He then took a seat and the minister turned around to welcome everyone and describe the history of the place. She tended to forget that the group did not speak English, so I had to interrupt her every now and then to translate her words into Italian. During the talk, she described how she had been raised in Texas in a "gunslingin'" family that really made the most of the liberal gun laws in the United States. "From the Wild West to the West of Ireland – it was a huge change for me!" she said.

As I was translating her entertaining talk, I began to think how easy and wonderful it was to do ecumenism. This encounter with such a colourful figure from another faith was good for our group, I felt, and the minister herself could only benefit from meeting committed pilgrims like these. This, in fact, was my first participation in an ecumenical event and I really began to feel that I had a certain flair for it. I knew when to shorten her contributions, what bits to emphasize and which parts to omit altogether. There was much laughter from the group and everyone seemed to be enjoying my rendition of her discourse. I couldn't help thinking that all those years of talking before groups were really benefitting me now.

Then the minister said something that took me slightly aback. She had begun to describe the particular denomination to which she belonged. It was quite different to the Catholic Church, or even to the more established protestant churches, she said. "In our denomination, we believe that it is important to respond to the signs of the times. We don't believe it is right to be bogged down in the traditions of the past. The Gospel must be presented in a fresh way that takes into account the spirit of our age, and this requires shelving the old staid traditions."

I glanced nervously over at the bishop. He had just given a homily the previous day that said more or less the diametric opposite. According to *his* homily, the Church's task is to interpret the signs of the times, but not change its teaching in order to accommodate the spirit of the age. I cleared my throat as I desperately sought a way to make her words more palatable to the Italian group. After all, that was the kind of ecumenism that was called for here, wasn't it? This wasn't a situation for a deep theological debate. The best we could do in these circumstances was a business of patching over differences and making the most of common ground, surely, and then heading for a cup of tea afterwards? But how could I find common ground in what the minister had just uttered?

"It is important to respond to the signs of the times in the light of tradition," I said in Italian, after clearing my throat at length. "The traditions of the past don't bog us down. They can assist us in presenting the Gospel in a fresh way that speaks to the spirit of our age."

The bishop began to nod vigorously as I spoke these words. No doubt he was surprised to find such a kindred positivity towards tradition in a protestant minister, and a female one at that. But the agreeable expression on his face did not reflect what I was feeling inside. This situation was becoming distinctly uncomfortable.

Encouraged by the positive reaction from the bishop to her attack on tradition, the minister really began to get into her stride. In fact, all reservations seem to leave her instantly. She gave a sort of cowboy whoop and went into full blown reformation-mode: "You need to admit women to your ranks, man! Look at all these glum male faces around here. It ain't healthy! Show some initiative! What you need in your seminary are a few chicks!"

The bishop's secretary was a relatively young priest and knew some English, but he seemed to be struggling with the sense of what she was saying. He looked around bemusedly and repeated the word, "Chicks!" Some of the seminarians began to chuckle and repeated the word also. The bishop angled his head to one side and looked at me inquisitively, waiting for my translation.

"Oh yes, Bishop," I said, desperately racking my brain for something to say. "The minister was just saying how good it was to hear that your seminary raises chicks to help with the finances. She is very impressed by this initiative."

"Thank you. Thank you," the bishop said in English, repeating the only words that he knew.

After the talk was finished, the group gave a warm round of applause, to the obvious delight of the minister. She and the bishop gathered on either side of me and shook hands.

"I was surprised at how well he took my admonition to consider women priests," the minister said in my ear, looking across at the bishop as he nodded his head agreeably. "I expected much more resistance, but maybe Italians are not as fanatical as some of the Catholics we have around these parts."

Despite the inclement weather, the temperature in the church seemed to have risen considerably. I could feel my face redden.

The bishop tapped me on the shoulder and spoke into my other ear. "It's wonderful to see how positive they are towards us and the esteem in which they evidently hold us," he said, using the royal "we".

"Wonderful, Bishop, wonderful," I replied, my face turning a deep shade of purple.

From the other side, the minister indicated to me that she wanted to ask the bishop a question.

"So, when does he think the ranks of his seminary will be expanded to include women?"

I turned to the bishop and said unblinkingly in Italian, "When do you plan to expand the chicken-rearing capacity of your seminary?"

The bishop looked at me and then looked over at the minister earnestly, once again surprised at this apparent fascination with his poultry enterprise.

"We hope to expand very soon," he said with a warm smile.

"You don't need to translate that for me!" the minister cut in excitedly. "I heard him say 'molto presto'. I know that means 'very soon'. Wow, I really feel we're participating in something historic here! Maybe the bishop could make some sort of official statement and I would be happy to pass it on to our local newspaper? It would be good for our fledgling congregation if we could say the announcement was made here!"

The bishop was looking at me intently again, expecting my translation. But I ignored him completely, turned my back on him and faced the minister. This situation was getting out of hand. "Hold on a second, minister! He could get in trouble if he makes an official statement ahead of time. You know how the Catholic Church is, all protocol and procedure! They can't go from an all-male priesthood to accepting chicks in the seminary just like that!"

I looked at my watch officiously. "Oh, look at the time! We really must get going! Thanks for your hospitality, but my job is to keep this show on the road!"

I turned to the group who were standing around the church chatting. "Ok!" I said loudly, clapping my hands. "Everyone on the coach! Time to go!"

At the door of the church, I met the bishop's secretary. As he thanked me for my job of interpretation, it occurred to me that he may have understood more English than I gave him credit for. "An admirable job of diplomacy," he said with a cryptic smile.

As we boarded the coach, I said to the driver, "Let's get to hell out of here!"

"What happened in there?" he asked concernedly, looking at my flushed countenance.

"Ecumenism!" I replied. "And I don't think I'll be getting involved in it again anytime soon!"

Two days later, my nerves had just about settled back to normal and I was looking forward to what I hoped would be one of the highlights of the trip – the visit to the hill of Slane, a really important place for the story of St Patrick. The documentary of Luigi might have failed to give much attention to our national patron, but I intended that full justice would be done to his life and legacy today. Unfortunately, the weather was still miserable, so I decided to explain the story of the site entirely on the coach. That way, the group wouldn't have to stand on the hill in the rain listening to my description. We could simply climb to the top between showers, remember the great importance of the place, say some prayers and be on our way.

"The hill of Slane is the most significant place in the country for the conversion of the Irish to Christianity," I began. "It is like Mount Horeb to the Jews, or Mount Calvary to Christians in general. On this hill, the light of faith in Christ was lit definitively for the first time in Ireland." I then went on to recount the events that happened on the occasion of the Easter Vigil the year after Patrick arrived in Ireland. At that time, Easter was celebrated on March 25th, and the year in question (according to tradition) was 433. At that time, the high king of Ireland, Laoghaire, was resident at the royal dwelling in Tara, a few miles from Slane. During the pagan feast of the spring equinox, a fire was lit on Tara in honour of the sun god. By order of the king, no other fires were to be lit in sight of the pagan fire. Patrick defied the order, climbed Slane hill with his band of followers, and began the celebration of Easter, complete with the Paschal fire. When the druids at Tara saw the fire on the distant hill, they went to the king and prophesied that if the fire was not put out that same night, it would never be extinguished. Soldiers were sent to Slane and Patrick was arrested. In the presence of the king, he challenged the druids to a trial by fire. The eventual upshot was the conversion of the king and the mass conversion of his subjects.

As always, the historians will question the accuracy of this traditional account, but the story has a beauty that transcends the scruples of the tedious academic who assumes that all traditions were invented after the fact. How appropriate that the light of the faith of a nation should begin with the lighting of the Paschal fire at Easter! At Easter, Jesus died for us and rose again that we might die to sin and live for him. *"Do you not know that all of us who have been baptized into Christ Jesus were baptized into his death? We were buried therefore with him by baptism into death, in order that, just as*

Christ was raised from the dead by the glory of the Father, we too might walk in newness of life" (Romans 6, 3-4). When St Patrick lit the fire of Easter at Slane, he was performing the most vital act in the history of our nation: the Irish people were being initiated into the life of God.

I finished my account and put down the microphone. There was complete and utter silence behind me on the coach. I took this to indicate that the group was impressed by my impassioned description. It was also pleasing to see that the rain had more of less stopped and that there was a bit of light in the eastern sky in front of us. Things were really looking up. My description of Patrick at Slane *was* quite impressive, I had to admit. It had just the right blend of zeal and gravitas, a delicate balance that not all tour guides could manage with such aplomb. The debacle with the protestant minister was becoming a distant memory.

"What exactly is there to see at Slane?" It was the bishop, sitting in the front row, addressing the question to me.

"There are some medieval ruins, and an ancient cemetery. From the hill, there are beautiful views over the landscape of County Meath. We've asked a local priest, Father Seamus, to meet us. He's the parish priest of nearby Nobber and he knows the Slane site really well."

"How long exactly before we arrive?" the bishop asked. He sounded a bit edgy.

"About forty-five minutes."

There was a pause for a few minutes. The bishop and his secretary were having a short conversation in low tones.

"Is there a shopping centre anywhere around here?"

"Yee-es, Bishop," I replied, not sure where this conversation was going. "There's one at Athlone, about forty-five minutes in the other direction."

There was another bout of low conversation with the secretary.

"Let's turn the coach around," the bishop said. "The pilgrims need some retail therapy. The weather has been awful and I don't think they'll benefit much from climbing a hill in the rain to look at a few medieval ruins."

"True, there's not a lot there to see, but it's the *significance* of the place that matters, Bishop!" My voice was becoming a little agitated. "This is where the light of faith was first lit in Ireland! Everything Patrick had suffered up to that point suddenly began to bear fruit in that place at that moment!"

"Yes, yes, very significant for the Irish, but we are Italian and we are just not used to being cold and wet in the month of July! I really must insist that we turn back and visit the shopping centre."

Jacky, our ever-accommodating coach driver, dutifully did an about-turn. "Slane, Athlone, it's all the same to me!" he said, with a shrug of his shoulders. There was silence on the coach as we sped towards the shopping centre with the coach's windscreen wipers at full tilt, for the rain had once again reached torrential proportions. I mulled gloomily on the abject failure of my passionate discourse. Maybe my Italian was the problem? Or was it my squeaky voice? There had to be some reason why, after all that fervour, a shopping centre had greater appeal.

We were quite a few miles closer to Athlone, and I was still wondering if I would live long enough ever to do a decent pilgrimage in honour of St Patrick, when it dawned on me with a shock that Father Seamus was waiting for us in his battered car at the base of Slane Hill, and he had no mobile phone, being a bit old-fashioned in that respect. The rest of the journey to Athlone was spent on the phone with Laura trying to find someone in the parish of Nobber who would be willing to take the word of a stranger and drive all the way out to Slane to rescue Father Seamus. He was the loyal sort and I had no doubt he would wait there in the rain until Kingdom come unless we got word to him that the visit was cancelled. Eventually, Laura found someone in Nobber to do the job. As for me, I spent the next hour walking around the mall lamenting what might have been. While I wandered aimlessly, it was hard not to notice Italians at every turn – bishop included – on an unbridled shopping frenzy. Never had so many winter woollies been sold in the Irish midlands in the month of July.

By the end of the second decade of the twenty-first century, the faith that Patrick had planted so deeply and successfully in our nation seemed to be well withered. What remained in many places was a cultural Catholicism that seemed worse than no Catholicism at all. We knew this at first hand because our children received First Communion and Confirmation in these years. The majority of children in their classes presented themselves for the sacraments, but most parents were not practicing and the preparation for the sacred day seemed virtually non-existent. It was unsettling to see the extravagant manner in which families dressed for these occasions and celebrated afterwards, with apparently no interest in what was really happening. Sadly, many of the children who received First Communion seemed unaware that Jesus was truly present in the Eucharist.

So how did Ireland get reduced to the kind of apathy that has become normal in our time? You hear various answers to this question. The influence of the wave of consumerism that hit the developed world during the twentieth century; the focus in many quarters on an exterior conformity to religion; the lack of an interior relationship with Jesus; corruption and laxity within the priesthood; the huge fallout of the child abuse scandals; and many other factors, have all been cited. In addition, there was the general deficiency of catechetical instruction. This left ordinary Irish people very vulnerable in the face of the global attacks on Christian values from the nineteen-sixties onwards.

In the end, the basic mechanism for the loss of the faith in Ireland is the same one generally present when people lose the faith anywhere: individuals cease to be attached to God in their hearts. The reasons for the lack of attachment can be many - the lure of materialism, the bad example of others, the scandals of the priesthood, habitual sin, poor catechetical instruction, a torrent of anti-Christian propaganda by the dominant culture – but the upshot is that attachment to eternal life is replaced by attachment to something else, and that something is much more immediate and self-directed, my self-realisation, my advancement, my pleasure, my familial interests.

Before his captivity, Patrick lived the kind of materialistic mediocrity that is the hallmark of Western culture, and in which many of us – author included - have floundered for long periods of our lives. On the hill of his captivity, in nakedness and hunger, Patrick no longer had the comforts of the body to rely on. Though purified by deprivation, he still could have kept his heart set on material consolation, as most other people in his situation probably did. Patrick, however, listened to the movement of the Holy Spirit within him and, turning to God, discovered a source of life that was more liberating than the charade that he had known before. Today, in affluent Ireland, many Catholics seem quite happy with the charade, the cultural Catholic approach to First Communion and everything else pertaining to the faith, not realising that what we neglect in church is the true bread, He who comes down from heaven to give life to the world.

Those who travel often to Italy cannot help hearing about the many young Italians in modern times who have lived Christianity to a heroic degree. In recent years, we have taken pilgrims to the tomb in Assisi of Carlo Acutis, the teenager and computer whizz kid who died in 2006. Carlo had great devotion to the Eucharist and managed to bring his parents back to the practice of the faith. In Turin – just a few yards from the box containing the Shroud - we see the tomb of Pier Giorgio Frassati, an avid sportsman who lived a hidden life of prayer and care for the poor before his untimely death at age twenty-four. Modern figures of this inspirational sort abound in Italy, such as Chiara Luce who died in 1990, and Chiara Corbella Petrillo, the self-sacrificing wife and mother from Rome. I would sometimes ask Laura why Italy had so many models of the faith whereas modern Ireland seemed to have so few. We knew that there had to be Catholics throughout the country who lived exceptional lives. Why did so few of these become well known? Were we Irish just not inclined to speak about our great exponents of the faith?

Then, about 2018, the story of a girl from the north of Ireland began to come to public attention. The vivacious Clare Crockett was born in Derry in the midst of the political unrest of the nineteen-eighties. Like so many Irish families, the Crocketts were Catholic in little more than name only. During her teenage years, Clare no longer attended church and lived what many people would describe as a "wild" lifestyle. From her childhood, she dreamt of becoming a film star. She seemed the ideal candidate for a career on the silver screen: natural acting ability, an almost complete lack of inhibition, a beautiful voice, and a very attractive personality. By the age of fifteen, she was already hosting a show for young people on British Channel 4.

In the year 2000, when Clare was seventeen years of age, a friend approached her and asked if she wanted to go on a trip to Spain. The friend was unable to travel and a free place was now available. Clare, expecting the trip to involve sunshine and fun, was none too pleased to discover that it was a Holy Week retreat being hosted by a congregation called Home of the Mother. Far from the parties and frivolity that she had hoped for, she found herself with a group of people intensely celebrating the passion, death, and resurrection of Our Lord.

Clare spent the first days of the retreat sunbathing and smoking. On Good Friday, someone said to her, "Clare, today you have to go into the chapel. It's Good Friday." She entered the chapel, but remained at the back, curiously inhibited for a girl that rarely showed hang-ups about anything. During the ceremony, the congregation was invited forward to adore and kiss the crucifix. As she reluctantly approached the cross, Clare spontaneously became full of regret for her previous actions. She was convinced that it was her behaviour that had nailed Jesus to the cross. The act of kissing the crucifix was a simple gesture, but it marked a turning point in her life. Afterwards, one of the sisters found her in tears. "He died for me. He loves me! Why hasn't anyone ever told me this before?"

For the first time, Clare began to consider the possibility that she was being called by God to live the consecrated life. She had always wanted to be famous, but now she wondered if she should become a nun. She joked to the other participants of the retreat that perhaps the solution to her dilemma was to become a famous nun. Little could she and they have imagined that this was exactly what was about to happen.

The experience she had on Good Friday was a crucial moment in her life, but the next step was a difficult one and she was unable to take it. When she went back to Ireland, she got caught up again in the superficial and sinful existence that the world of acting offered her. Regarding this period, she later said, "I lived in mortal sin. I drank a lot, I smoked a lot, I began to take drugs. I continued with my boyfriend in the same way. I didn't have the strength to break with all these things, because I didn't ask the Lord to help me."

Clare may not have been following the Lord, but he was following her. One night, drunk at a party, she went to the bathroom to get sick. In the midst of this desolation, she felt the Lord Jesus saying to her, "Why do you continue to hurt me?" She felt the presence of God in a powerful way, but didn't know how to respond. Shortly afterwards, whilst going over her lines in a London hotel for the following day's shooting, she realised profoundly that her life was utterly empty and would continue to be if she did not give it to Jesus.

When her family heard of her intentions, they pleaded with her to reconsider. Her manager, in his turn, foretold glittering success if she would only stick to her course, but it was too late, the Lord had won Clare over. A decisive interior decision had been made. On August 11th, 2001, the decision was formalised publicly as she offered her life to God as a candidate in the Servant

Sisters of the Home of the Mother. It was the feast of her patron, St Clare of Assisi, the girl who had once scattered the mighty army of the Holy Roman Emperor with only the Eucharist as her weapon.

As her online biographer recounts, Clare Crockett had a deeply wounded heart in need of healing. Yet, once she had surrendered to Christ's love for her, there was nothing that would stop her. She herself explained, "At first, I was tempted to look over my shoulder and say, 'I want it all back,' but I understood that I had found an even greater love."

Then followed the preparatory years as a candidate and novice before taking her first vows in 2006. One of her early assignments was to the new community in Jacksonville, Florida, where the sisters worked at a parish and school. Sister Clare was in charge of preparing children for First Communion. The documentary on Clare's life, **All or Nothing**, shows the reverence with which those children presented themselves for the Eucharist – a stark contrast to what many Irish parishes experience on First Communion day. Each child moved forward for Communion with eyes averted as they tried to focus exclusively on the Lord that they were about to receive. Sister Clare had imparted to these children a devotion to the Eucharist that few adults could emulate.

In October 2012, Sister Clare was assigned to the recently founded community in Guayaquil, Ecuador. The sisters worked in different schools and parishes in very poor areas, with a focus on youth and children. Several times throughout the year, the sisters would visit villages in the Ecuadorian Amazon to evangelize. Sr. Clare also took part, trekking for hours with mud up to her knees and crossing the tributaries of the Amazon in chest-high water, until they reached the humble villages of the Shuar. These people live in small communities amid great poverty. On some occasions, the sisters reached villages where the indigenous had never heard the Gospel and still practiced polygamy.

For the sisters of the congregation, the abiding memory of Clare is with a guitar in hand. She would sing constantly, even to the point of losing her voice, in the face of heat, fatigue and severe migraines. Her way of singing was a reflection of her character. Sister Kelly Maria Pezo recalls, "When she sang, she kept nothing back. And when she lived, she kept nothing back." Despite the joy and buzz that always surrounded her, however, Sr. Clare's need to be alone in silence with the Lord increased as time went on.

In April 2016, strong floods devastated Playa Prieta where Sister Clare was then stationed in Ecuador. It was just two weeks before the start of a new school year, and the sisters discovered that their school was in a state of total ruin. As soon as the water level began to recede, the sisters got to work to try to restore the school to normal. The work was arduous and involved removing the water and mud that covered the floor to a depth of some feet. The sisters also had to assist the many poor families in the area that had lost almost everything as a result of the floods. Afterwards, when they recalled the events of these days, it seemed as though the Lord was preparing them for the ultimate act of self-giving.

On Saturday, April 16, 2016, shortly after the sisters returned from Mass at the parish church, an earthquake struck. Sister Clare was on the first floor where she had just given a guitar class to a group of girls. They were about to pray the Rosary with the rest of the community. The quake caused the building to collapse, with four sisters and seven girls inside. Only five were rescued alive. In a remarkable "coincidence," the conversation at lunch that very day had been about death. Sister Clare had said with great conviction, "Why should I be afraid of death, if I'm going to go to the One I have longed to be with my whole life?"

Sister Clare's body was flown back for burial in her native Derry. In April 2021, five years later, the process for her canonisation was opened. Her tomb quickly became a place of pilgrimage, with many accounts of miracles and healings. In November of that year, we heard a news report in which the Crockett family called on people to show respect to the other graves in the cemetery after hundreds of people visited Sister Clare's tomb on her birthday. The vivacious girl, with a bottle in one hand and a cigarette in the other, not knowing if she wanted fame or the religious life, had indeed become a famous nun.

In 2022, during a pilgrimage in Fatima, an American Catholic asked me, "What ever happened to Ireland?" It was not the first time in recent years that I had heard this question posed. People are curious to know how a nation that kept the faith through centuries of persecution could surrender it after a few decades of affluence. Prosperity seems to have dulled our innate longing for God, sapped our adhesion to what is eternal. In response, I told him about Clare Crockett and added (a little defensively), "Maybe Ireland is not finished yet."

As I was recounting Clare's life in brief to this affable American, I realised that her conversion – occurring as it did on Good Friday in front of the cross – was very similar to the conversion of St Patrick. All at once, in different circumstances, both became filled with the utter conviction that Jesus' suffering and resurrection were intimately personal events. To each, it was as if - for them and them alone - Christ died, shedding his blood, and rose.

Chapter Nine
The Blood and the Rose

"Behold, I make all things new."
Revelation 21:5

Laura was fretting about the negative reviews of the hotel we had booked over by the Vatican. A few months previously, when the booking was made, the reviews seemed to be a bit more positive, but some very negative ones had been posted recently. Today was August 3rd and the group was due to arrive in the airport that very evening.

"Don't worry, Laura," I said. "The location is good, and we'll be so busy for the next few days that the pilgrims will only be in their rooms to sleep."

"The review that appeared yesterday said to avoid room thirty-six at all costs. It's small and pokey, apparently. The only window is so high up that you would need a ladder to see out of it, while the bathroom looks like it was last decorated in the nineteen-twenties. The bed is creaky, and the television has a funny stain in the middle of the screen."

"Why don't we email the hotel now and ask them if they have the room numbers already allocated? That way we can see if we have been given thirty-six."

Laura wrote the message and a short time later an email arrived with the rooming list. When we pored over it, sure enough, the dreaded thirty-six had been ominously allocated to a member of our group. Laura immediately phoned the hotel to ask for a change, but the receptionist informed her that they were completely full. We would have to accept the room for the first few nights, though other rooms would come available later in the week.

"We saw a very negative review about that room," Laura explained. "Its size, the bed, the bathroom, the television."

"The television has been changed today," the girl cut in. "Apart from that, there is not a lot that we can do. Rooms are being redecorated periodically, but room thirty-six will not be redone until next winter."

When Laura put down the phone, she looked over at me worriedly. "Who will we allocate this room to? Maybe we should give it to Father Pat? He's the spiritual director, after all. Surely, he'll be open to enduring a certain lack of comfort?"

"No, Laura, it wouldn't be fair!" I replied, shaking my head vehemently. "Father Pat works so hard during these trips. He extends himself all over the place to try to pacify some of these fussy pilgrims. Let's try to give him a decent *room*, at least."

"But who can we assign to room thirty-six then?"

"I'll tell you what, when the group arrives this evening, I'll size them up and start to get to know their names. As soon as I spot someone that seems easy going and not too bothered about creature comforts, then I'll allocate that room to them before we reach the hotel and all will be well."

"But what if you don't manage to identify anyone suitable?"

"Laura, after all these years, I can size up these pilgrims instantly. As soon as they emerge into the arrivals hall, before they ever open their mouths, I already have a fair idea if they're going to give me a hard time or not."

"And if you don't manage to find anyone?"

"All this experience has given me the laser eye," I replied, trying to sound modest. "I'll find a suitable candidate for room thirty-six, don't you worry. Over my dead body will we put poor Father Pat in that room. No way!"

Laura did an initial allocation of rooms, provisionally assigning Father Pat to room thirty-six. That evening, once I had found a suitable "victim," a simple switch would be done, allocating that person to room thirty-six, and giving Father Pat the room originally assigned to them.

A few hours later, I was leading the group out of the airport towards the place where the coach was parked. When we reached the bus, I directed everyone to pass their suitcases to the driver and then to hop on board. While helping one lady lug her enormous suitcase over the kerb, she gave a wide smile and thanked me profusely. As she went to board, I asked for her name. While other people were boarding, I nipped around to the front of the coach, discreetly took out the rooming list, found her name and wrote 'thirty-six' beside it.

The last few suitcases were being loaded and I noticed that a gentleman from the group was helpfully passing bags to our driver. This was quite unusual, as most people just deposited their luggage on the sidewalk and boarded.

"Thanks for your help!" I said. "What's your name?"

He only gave me his first name – Gregory - but this seemed sufficiently unusual to identify him on the list later - should we need another candidate for room thirty-six.

During the first ten or so miles in towards the city, the group was given the usual discourse on the dress code for churches in Rome, the dangers of pick-pockets, the procedure for ordering food in bars and restaurants, the layout of the hotel, the order of the itinerary, and other matters. Then I stood up and asked if there were any questions.

The lady assigned to room thirty-six raised her hand.

"What's for breakfast?" she asked.

"Well, it's a continental buffet: cereals, croissants, yoghurt, bread, coffee and tea. By Irish standards it's a bit light, but it would compare well to other Rome hotels."

"With the busy programme you have in store for us, I would have thought that a more substantial breakfast was in order."

"Oh, no, I wouldn't be too concerned at all, madam," I said soothingly. "With the heat of Rome, people don't really eat all that much, I find."

"Well then, I hope the air-conditioning in the hotel works properly!" she replied sourly, the earlier winning smile nowhere in sight. "By the way, is there air-conditioning in the breakfast room?"

"Actually, there isn't," I said, my voice faltering somewhat. "You see, the breakfast room is in the basement, which is naturally cooler anyway."

"Oh, yes, I see their wicked plan now!" she exclaimed. "Give us breakfast in a stifling hot room so that we have little appetite to start with, and then hope that the burning heat will drive us out of there fast before we gobble up the meagre rations on offer!"

There was a ripple of laughter down the coach. Not sure of how to respond, I made a big show of taking out my phone, while mumbling into the microphone, "Pardon me everyone. I just need to call the hotel to say we will be there shortly." With that, I sat as far down as I could in my courier seat, snuck out the rooming list, crossed off "thirty-six" after the lady's name, scanned the page for Gregory and assigned him to the problematic room.

"Any more questions?" I had made the phone call and was standing up facing the pilgrims again.

There were a couple of queries about details on the itinerary. Then Gregory put up his hand. "What time does the hotel bar close at?"

"Well, actually, they're not really running a bar service in this hotel at the moment," I replied, cringing inwardly.

"You mean there's no bar?"

"Oh, no, there *is* a bar, with a counter and seats, and even a few drinks on shelves behind the counter. But, like many Rome hotels, they don't really bother staffing it. You see, there are so many bars around the city that the hotel bars just don't do enough business to justify allocating personnel."

"I've heard of a pub without beer, but you're saying that this bar actually *has* drinks and no-one to serve them?"

"Yes," I replied, with an overly hearty laugh. "It's kind of strange, isn't it?"

"Well, I like a drink before I go to bed. Does this mean I have to go wandering out on the street looking for a bar at some ungodly hour?"

"There's a little mini-market across the street that sells alcohol. Maybe you could buy something earlier and then have it in your room?" I said in a helpful tone.

"Drinking *alone* in my room?" replied Gregory in a tone of shocked disbelief. "No thank you!"

I looked around at all the faces a little uncomfortably. This question-and-answer session wasn't going too smoothly. "Well, if there are no more questions, I'll just take my seat. We'll be arriving in about five minutes."

With my back to everyone, the rooming list was shiftily produced again and "thirty-six" was crossed off after Gregory's name.

Just then the phone rang. It was Laura. "Did you find someone for that room?"

"Sorry Laura, I can't talk right now," I said in a loud whisper.

"I know, you have the entire group behind you listening in." She was speaking in a loud whisper herself now. "But you'll have surveyed the group at this stage to find our victim, you know, with that 'laser eye' of yours. Just tell me who it is."

"It's . . . ," I paused, desperately trying to find an answer. Suddenly, it was clear that there could only be one solution. "It's Father Pat," I croaked.

Next day was the feast of the Cure d'Ars, the simple provincial pastor who is patron saint of priests. In the hotel lobby that morning, someone showed me a quote from him which ran roughly as follows: "When one wants to destroy religion, one begins by attacking the priest, because where there is no longer a priest, there is no longer a sacrifice, and where there is no longer a sacrifice, there is no more religion."

Coincidentally, the centrality of sacrifice in the Catholic faith was to come into relief as the pilgrimage went on. There were two members of a protestant denomination on the trip who had come along because of the positive appraisal they had heard of Father Pat. Usually, our trips were Catholic pilgrimages where Mass was celebrated every day and virtually everyone participated. It was rare to have people on board who held completely different views on the Eucharist.

Towards the end of the first full day, the protestant wife was commentating on the Mass they had attended before dinner, celebrated by Father Pat for the feast of the Cure d'Ars. "At the beginning of the Mass, it was very like one of our own liturgical gatherings," she was saying. "Father Pat welcomed everyone, told a funny story, recalled the places we had visited today and introduced the Scripture readings. But after the Scripture, everything became completely different. It all became very solemn and turned into more of a ritual."

"Are your gatherings very different?" a lady at the table asked.

"Yes," replied the protestant wife. "We don't always have the bread and the wine, only on special occasions. And for us, the sharing of the bread and the cup is all about fellowship with each other in Christ. I notice that Father Pat's prayer after he raised the chalice and host was all about asking God the Father to accept the sacrifice of Christ. What a curious thing! We believe that the sacrifice has already happened two thousand years ago, so why would we need to offer it again? However, we *are* able to share in the fellowship that was won by the sacrifice."

"How about the idea that Jesus is present in the Eucharist?" the same lady asked. "Does your church believe that?"

"Well, in a way," said the protestant wife, turning her head to the side pensively while she searched for words. "For us, he is present in a kind of symbolic manner. The bread signifies the fact that he supplies all our needs. The chalice signifies his passion and death for us. But to claim that he is *actually* present in the bread or the wine wouldn't really make much sense to us."

It was evening time and I had spent virtually the entire day talking in front of the group. I had no desire to enter into a debate, but still it seemed obvious that a Catholic should have quite a bit to say in response to these statements. The Eucharist was not simply a celebration of fellowship won by a sacrifice that happened way back in the past. Whether it was out of tiredness or ignorance or lack of interest, however, nobody mustered a reply.

I did think about the matter later that evening, though. The Catholic understanding of the Mass is often couched in various ways, but which way would provide the best response to the claims that the sacrifice is in the past and that the presence of Christ is merely symbolic? I recalled that Archbishop Fulton Sheen had once said that, at the Mass, "the veil is drawn back" and we are standing at the foot of the Cross on Calvary. That might sound like some sort of time travel, but it is not the case that we are transported *back* in time to the event of the crucifixion. Rather, the event of the crucifixion transcends history. The suffering of God in human flesh is of such cosmic significance that it stands over and above time. The Mass is the means by which we participate bodily in the event. It is not *as if* we were present at Calvary: we *actually are* present at Calvary, for Calvary *becomes present to us.*

The presence of Jesus in the host is not to be thought of in terms of, say, the presence of a genie inside a bottle. Jesus is not hidden *inside* the host. The host *becomes* him, even if it retains all the appearance of bread. Furthermore, the presence is not of a static sort, like some sort of silent ghost inside an inert physical object. Christ in the Eucharist is the Christ who offers himself to the Father on Calvary for our salvation. When we gaze on the consecrated host, we are beholding the Son of God giving himself to us in self- sacrificial love.

How could that be explained to our protestant friends in a convincing way, however? It is true that St Paul says, *"For as often as you eat this bread and drink the cup, you proclaim the Lord's death until he comes"* (1 Cor 11,26). Scripture can be interpreted virtually any way you like, though, since interpretation involves many elements that are themselves non-biblical and are conditioned by the person or group who is doing the interpreting. Catholics interpret the Bible using Sacred Tradition, which is the body of teachings handed on by the apostles and enshrined in the teachings of the Church and the earliest writings of the Fathers. St Ignatius of Antioch, for example, writing just a few years after the death of the apostle John, identifies the Eucharist with the flesh of Christ. In fact, he says unambiguously that to deny this reality is heresy. Maybe it was my shortcomings as an apologist that was the problem, but I felt from previous discussions with protestants that invoking Sacred Tradition as expressed by early Fathers such as Ignatius was unlikely to be very convincing.

The next morning, however, a perfect opportunity seemed to present itself to defend the sacrificial nature of the Mass. When I arrived at the hotel, some members of the group were sitting in the lobby waiting for the signal to board the coach, which was due in about fifteen minutes. Among the group, chatting amicably, were the protestant husband and wife. I pricked up my ears when I realised that they were talking about a book – **Heaven is for real** - written by an American pastor, which our children had read recently. The pastor's son, Colton, had been taken to hospital with a burst appendix. In a dramatic sequence of events, he seemed to die for a short time before reviving. In the weeks and months after this event, the boy gradually began to reveal what had happened to him during that time. In an apparent visit to heaven, he had encountered Jesus, Mary and other figures, including his own grandparents.

As I stood in the lobby and listened to the conversation, I recalled one of the more striking features of Colton's experience. He had recounted to his parents afterwards that the Jesus he had met in heaven had peculiar *marks* on his body. After discussion with the boy, it became clear that these were the marks of the passion. Colton's testimony, coming from a protestant family, was a curious affirmation of a line of reasoning used by Thomas Aquinas in his *Summa Theologica*. St Thomas was considering the views of those who claimed that the resurrected Christ no longer had the marks of the passion. Such wounds would not be compatible with the perfection of a risen body, these critics claimed. In response, St Thomas reasoned that Christ will *always* bear these wounds: they are not a sign of deformity but of beauty; they are not a mark of incompletion but of greater perfection; they remind the Father of the sacrifice he made for us, while they remind humanity of God's love for them.

This debate by St Thomas about the persistence of Christ's wounds had come to my attention just a few weeks previously when we had taken a group on a tour around Tuscany. On the day we went to Florence, a couple of hours in the afternoon had been dedicated to shopping, which provided me with the opportunity to visit the Dominican monastery of San Marco. In the 1400s, over forty of the monastic cells had been frescoed by Fra Angelico, the saintly Dominican friar who always prayed fervently before painting. He was beatified by John Paul II in 1982 and named patron of artists. Among the paintings in San Marco was one of the most famous depictions of the Annunciation in existence. Fra Angelico's *Annunciation* was on a long bucket list of masterpieces that I was getting through gradually.

Having paid the admission to San Marco and followed the route of the frescoes, I discovered that the *Annunciation* was not in one of the monastic cells, but on the corridor of the first floor. Though a very average connoisseur of art, it was still moving for me to observe the humble submission of Mary and the pronounced reverence of Gabriel.

Another fresco, however, ended up attracting more of my interest. In the first cell upstairs, Fra Angelico painted *Noli me tangere* ("Touch me not"), showing Jesus in his meeting with Mary Magdalene after the resurrection.

*(Fra Angelico, **Noli Me Tangere**, public domain)*

At first, Mary thinks he is the gardener and asks if he knows where the body of Jesus has been taken. When she recognizes him, Jesus says, *"Do not hold on to me, because I have not yet ascended to the Father. But go to my brothers and say to them, 'I am ascending to my Father and your Father, to my God and your God'"* (John 20,17). The painting was striking, but there was something perplexing about the red spots dispersed in groups all over the greenery between Christ and Mary Magdalene.

Later, on the internet, I found references to a work by Georges Didi-Huberman from about 1990 which discussed these marks. They were not simply attempts to represent flowers, since Fra Angelico was well capable of painting flowers properly if he wanted to. Something more profound was being signified here. Tellingly, many of the marks were in groups of five and resembled the stigmata, the five wounds on the body of Christ. It was as if these "roses" in the garden of the resurrection were constituted by the very blood of Christ. Fra Angelico wanted to show that Christ sows his stigmata in the garden of this world (in fact, he is depicted as a gardener in this painting). Sin had defaced creation, but the wounds of Christ lead to the rebirth, the flowering of the world.

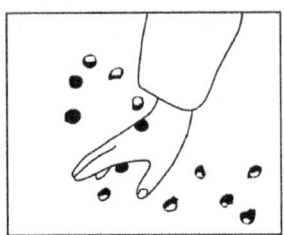 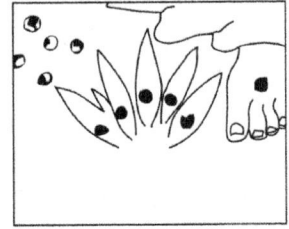

(With permission of Georges Didi-Huberman, **Fra Angelico: Dissemblance and Figuration,** *p20)*

Some years later, I spotted a stained glass at the left back of Killarney Cathedral on the same theme. The window on the left showed Mary Magdalene on her knees, one hand on the jar of ointment with which she intended to anoint the dead body of the crucified one, the other hand held up to her face in a gesture of surprise at recognizing Jesus. The window on the right showed the risen Christ, with the wounds of his passion still visible, in a garden surrounded by flowers in full bloom! Maybe the artist of the window had been influenced by the work of Fra Angelico? Or, perhaps both artists were drawing from a more ancient spiritual work that meditated on the regenerating power of the resurrection? The Killarney windows dated from 1911, nearly eighty years before Georges Didi-Huberman wrote his tract on *Noli me tangere*.

As I stood there in the lobby of the hotel in 2011, I quickly worked out how I would make my point about the Eucharist. As Colton witnessed, the wounds of Christ endure in heaven. That makes sense because the sacrifice of Christ is not just a historical event that is finished, but something that changes all of history. It is as if you had a clock that once worked according to a certain defective mechanism, and then you completely renewed the internal workings of the timepiece. The change you wrought in the clock is not simply a process that ended at the moment you made the repair. It is something that affects how the clock performs right now and into the future. Analogously, Christ's sacrifice alters the inner dynamics of the world and its inhabitants for all time to come. The relations between the world and its creator have been transformed by his sacrifice, and these relations continue to play out in the lives of the inhabitants of the world. The consequences and healing effects of the sacrifice will continue to be worked out until everything is finally consummated in Christ.

Then I would wax eloquently on Fra Angelico's masterpiece. Through the resurrection, the life-giving sacrifice of Christ was imprinting itself on creation, renewing it and causing it to bloom. When we celebrate the Mass, we are participating in this ongoing restoration of the world to right relationship with its creator by the blood of Christ. The disorder that was introduced into creation by the original disobedience of humanity is now being put right by the sacrificial obedience of Christ. The ruin is not put right in an instant, but, from the moment of the resurrection onwards, the process of renewal begins. Creation, bathed by his blood, begins to bloom. *That* is what Fra Angelico wished to represent with the blood upon the flowers.

It would be a masterclass in apologetics. *If* there existed a handbook for that discipline, then it would surely recommend that the would-be apologist start his discourse from common ground. I would begin from something that our protestant friends already accepted – Colton's testimony that Christ still bore the marks of the passion. From there my talk would move onto something that people often found inspiring – the illustration of a spiritual truth by means of a religious work of art. By the time I was finished, it would be abundantly clear that the Catholic view of the Mass as a sacrifice made eminent good sense. "Oh yes indeed," I thought to myself as I ambled over towards the little group, trying with difficulty to suppress a swagger. "If I had been around at the time of the reformation, things might not have turned out so badly after all."

"Did you know that Colton and Thomas Aquinas have something in common?" I asked, directing my leading question at no one in particular.

"Sorry?" replied the protestant husband. "Thomas who?"

Just then, the ever-helpful Gregory stuck his head in from the street. "The coach has arrived, everyone!" he called out loudly. With that, the group arose *en masse* and headed for the exit. I was left standing in the lobby with my mouth open.

A golden opportunity for first-class apologetics had gone down in flames. As the morning went on, I wondered how to get the subject of conversation turned back towards the Eucharist. Even if we managed to restart the discussion, however, what argument could be used to defend the Catholic position? Would a mention of the Eucharistic miracles be helpful? There were many such miracles in history in which the bread and wine were really transformed into human flesh and blood. These miracles, though, only indicated that the Catholic view of the Eucharist is *right*, whereas what I needed to do was to *explain* the Catholic view.

It occurred to me that a good analogy or narrative of some sort might be useful. During our free time for lunch, I took out a pen and paper and wrote the following:

Consider how we human beings since the time of the Fall have been preoccupied with satisfying our appetites. It is appropriate that the Fall is described in Genesis in terms of disobeying God and consuming an apple, for sinful humanity is dominated by hunger for pleasure, entertainment, power, the esteem of others. Jesus in his Passion is a human being of an entirely different sort. He foregoes his own appetites in humble obedience to the will of the Father.

In a way, then, we can speak of two parallel realities: firstly, there is the reality of fallen humanity dominated by self-directed appetites; secondly, we have Christ who renounces himself for the Father and for the entire human race. From the Fall until the end of the world, the first reality will play itself out as human beings succumb to self-centred tendencies. However, that is not the end of the story, for from the time of the Last Supper until the end of time, the second reality is also playing itself out. Christ has entered our story and taken on our flesh. The grace of redemption wrought by the passion is being incarnated in our daily lives, as we join our renunciations to his. This occurs above all in the Eucharist. Here, incredibly, God tells us that we can only truly satisfy our appetites if we consume him. Nothing else will satiate our hunger.

At first, I felt extremely satisfied with my tome, but then, after rereading it, I shook my head. If our protestant friends were not going to relate to talk of

Eucharistic miracles, neither were they going to be impressed by time travel or parallel universes. Their approach to the faith, when all was said and done, was grounded in *Scripture*. What we needed was a biblical explication of the Mass. As it turned out, that very afternoon we were about to embark on a full immersion into the history of salvation from a scriptural perspective.

It was August 5th, the anniversary of a famous event in the city's history, even if many people considered it nothing more than a legend. According to the story, in the year 352 A.D., Our Lady appeared and requested that a church be built in her honour wherever it snowed on the following day. The next day happened to be August 5th and it snowed on the city's Esquiline Hill. The church is called the Basilica of St Mary Major, but is also known by the title of "Our Lady of the Snows."

It was the best of days to visit the church, but also the worst of days. There would be crowds of visitors and a busy series of ceremonies. At 4pm, a solemn rosary would begin, followed by Mass and evening prayer during which white rose petals would be showered from an inner dome to recreate the miraculous fall of snow. Our aim was to avoid getting "snowed in" at the ceremonies, but still visit the church for the feast. At about 2.30pm I began my usual tour from the back of the basilica, a tour that basically consisted in repeating what I had read elsewhere, or recycled from some of our more knowledgeable group leaders over the years.

The walls on either side of the nave and the surfaces of the triumphal arch over the altar have ancient fifth century mosaics which depict crucial events from salvation history. It is very difficult to make out what is represented with the native eye. In the absence of binoculars, any tour of the mosaics must confine itself to a few general points. As I spoke, I was conscious of the presence of our two protestant friends among the group and wondered what they were making of such a Catholic setting.

The mosaics in St Mary Major are among the oldest extant artworks in the world that were created - not just to decorate a basilica - but with the specific intention of *teaching*. When faithful Christians entered this church, they were not just being sheltered from the elements, or being provided with a space to gather as a community: the *decoration of the building itself* was announcing the Good News. As the Christian entered the space and moved towards the altar, his mind and his heart was being drawn by the art into the reality of the liturgical sacrifice that would soon be celebrated here. As the Middle Ages progressed, what we see for the first time on a grand scale in St Mary Major in Rome would become standard in the Christian world: the decoration of church buildings took on the roles of revealing, instructing and inspiring; in short, *forming* the believer in the faith.

During any tour in a busy setting, it can hard to keep the attention of your group unless you are particularly good at your job, something of which I have never been convincingly accused. As I scanned the distracted faces looking at me, it was clear that things would have to be kept short and snappy. It was time to move right to the crux. The mosaics on the nave walls depict events in the history of salvation, events that attain their fullest meaning only in the light of the incarnation of Jesus. For example, if the sacrifice of Isaac is read solely from the point of view of the Old Testament, then it is a great story of the faith of Abraham in the face of the bewildering request to sacrifice his son. But from the point of view of the incarnation, we see it as a foreshadowing of the offering by God of his only Son as our sacrifice, a sacrifice that the Lord does not ask from Abraham, nor anyone else, but only from himself.

Similarly, in the crossing of the Red Sea, we see the Lord lead his people out of slavery in Egypt and towards the Promised Land. In the light of Christ, though, the event becomes a foreshadowing of something that is not just a liberation of a *single* people from a *particular* state of slavery. Rather, it points to the liberation of all people, including you and me, from the much more insidious slavery of sin and our restoration to the Promised Land of union with God himself.

In short, God was already disclosing Christ to us in the figures and events of the Old Testament. As the Christian enters this church and makes his way to the altar, *God's nature* is being progressively revealed to him by the biblical art, a nature of self-giving love. A walk in the church is an incredible thing: a walk through the history of God's communication of himself to us.

As I looked at the many blank faces in front of me, it felt as if I had already lost the attention of the group. The protestant husband and wife, however, were still making eye contact with me, which was more than could be said for many of my Catholic pilgrims. "To heck with it," I said to myself. "This might not be the time or place, but I'll say it anyhow." It was now or never to mention the sacrificial nature of the Mass.

After clearing my throat, I began, "Down here below the altar is a precious reliquary containing fragments that are believed to come from the crib of Bethlehem in which Christ was born. They are a testimony to the fact that God became flesh. All of the Old Testament, ultimately, only makes complete sense in the light of the incarnation. The mosaics on the nave, depicting the events of the history of Israel, all conduce us here to the concrete reality of the incarnation."

This was only half the story, however, so I went on. "The relics of the *birth* of Christ are conserved under the altar. Around the altar itself, down through the centuries, the faithful have gathered here to commemorate the *death* of Christ. It is the very same mystery. Jesus emptied himself of his divinity to take on human flesh and be in communion with us. Then he endured his passion and death to unite himself to us in our state of separation from the Father. The entire decoration and layout of this building is designed to lead us through the history of salvation, a step by step disclosure in which the Lord reveals himself to us progressively, until we arrive here – at the crib and altar

– to the reality of the self-sacrificial incarnation and immolation of God."

The protestant wife raised her hand. "Actually, we were discussing this the other day," she said, "the centrality of sacrifice, I mean. Doesn't one of the psalms say, 'I do not ask for sacrifice or oblation, but an open ear'? I wonder if all this emphasis on sacrifice is really helpful?"

As she said this, she was looking over at Father Pat, as if seeking his approval. I looked over at Father Pat as well, hoping for a word of affirmation. He didn't have to make any deep theological pronouncement. If he had simply said, "Sacrifice is at the heart of the Catholic understanding of the Incarnation and the Eucharist," I would have been more than happy. Instead, Father Pat returned her gaze and said, "Yes, maybe we do talk about sacrifice and penitence too often. I think it can be helpful sometimes to describe redemption in other terms."

Once again, I was literally left with my mouth open. Was Father Pat really going to leave things there? The psalm the protestant wife had quoted was only objecting to sacrifices made in the wrong fashion. For example, we can imagine a wealthy man making a big public sacrifice of the best animals from his herd, while he himself lives a life of moral corruption. Not only does the psalm *not* condemn sacrifice *per se*, but it in fact holds up for us a different model of the practice, that of sacrificing one's own *will* in openness to the will of God.

It seemed futile, though, to begin that sort of debate right here and now. The next group of tourists was already standing at the top of the aisle, waiting to occupy our space in front of the altar, and their guide was looking pointedly in my direction. Trying with difficulty to suppress my feelings of indignation towards Father Pat, I led the group to the back of the basilica.

The next day, Saturday, August 6th, was going to be an easy day for me. We would make the forty-five minute drive out of Rome into the Alban Hills to visit the town of Castelgandolfo. The palace here was used by the papacy as a summer residence from the 1600s onwards. We would have Mass in the parish church to celebrate the feast of the Transfiguration, followed by free time and a return to Rome. The afternoon would be dedicated to shopping, while later there would be dinner with music and a night tour of the city.

1978 was the year of three popes. On August 6th that year, Pope Paul VI died at the residence in Castelgandolfo. His successor, Pope John Paul I reigned for only thirty-three days, leading to the election of John Paul II, the first non-Italian pope for four hundred and fifty-five years. The death of Paul VI on the feast of the Transfiguration was taken by some commentators to be particularly appropriate. After – against all the odds – rallying the world bishops to consensus and bringing the Second Vatican Council to a successful conclusion, Paul VI endured a very difficult end to his papacy. Wracked by ill-health, his spiritual suffering was even greater as he witnessed growing divisions in the Church and open dissent on matters such as the indissolubility of marriage and birth-control. That he died on the Transfiguration was interpreted by some to be an endorsement that the Lord's favour rested on him, that his sufferings were being transformed into light, just as happened with Christ.

Maybe it was just a coincidence, maybe Father Pat already had his homily for today written before the exchange in St Mary Major the previous day, but, in any case, the theme of his talk was sacrifice, even if he never actually mentioned the dreaded "s" word. When Jesus went up the mountain and began to shine like the sun, Father Pat said, he was giving his disciples a preview of what would happen *after* his passion and death. In the end, Christ will be transfigured by the cross. "Why is that?" Father Pat asked. He then gave the frequently used example of a mountain climber who endures the struggle and fatigue of scaling the mountain. Without the struggle, there is no joy from the achievement. A helicopter ride to the top of the mountain will not give the same satisfaction. In the struggle and difficulties of the challenge, we are stretched, improved, purified. We begin to shine after the cross. "Renunciation of self," he said, "is not an optional extra, but a necessary pathway to fullness of life." Then Father Pat said a significant phrase that reminded me of Fra Angelico's work, even if the phrase did not include the word "sacrifice." "The cross is the plough with which the Lord tills the garden of our lives, causing it to flower."

Even if Father Pat had studiously avoided the word "sacrifice," his homily nevertheless threw light on the Catholic understanding of the Eucharist. Sin, egoism, pursuing our own volition – these are what disfigure us, ruining in us the image and likeness of God. Renunciation of our own will and obedience to the will of the Father restores in us the beauty of the image of God. Of course, we are unable by ourselves to make that renunciation, but Christ becomes one of us and makes the sacrifice in our stead. When we partake of the Eucharist, we participate in the self-immolation of Christ.

During Mass, I was sitting on the back pew because the sacristan, Maurizio, had asked me to keep the tourists out. The life of the courier alternates between being a shepherd from the front and a guard dog from the back. People could stand in the glass porch and admire the beautiful architecture of Bernini – this was one of the first churches entirely designed by him - but they were not to go wandering up the aisles. From my position at the rear, I had a good view of the proceedings. The protestant couple, predictably enough, were sitting bolt upright in the front pew, listening attentively to every word of Father Pat's homily. Many of the Catholic pilgrims, I couldn't help but notice, were slouched in a variety of distracted postures throughout the church.

By the time Mass was over, I felt more at ease. It had been a disquieting few days because the Catholic view of the Mass seemed to be dismissed too lightly. Now

Father Pat had spoken well and given us all food for thought. There was little to be gained by pursuing this debate. I could go back to giving the usual tours without feeling that Catholic teaching had to be defended at every turn.

The theme of sacrifice, however, just didn't seem to want to go away. Next day we were in the catacombs of St Callixtus. Here, the tours are often provided by professional guides, but sometimes they can be given by members of the Salesian community. This complex has been in the care of the Salesians of Don Bosco since the nineteen twenties. Our guide was an elderly Salesian priest from the United States, Father Richard. The descriptions he gave contained all of the history and archaeology that could be expected, but they were couched in religious terms. Seeing that the catacombs are basically a cemetery – albeit spiritually precious because they contain the tombs of martyrs, and culturally important because they contain the earliest Christian works of art – his main concern was to show how we are given the possibility of eternal life through the sacrifice of Christ, the Good Shepherd who lays down his life for his sheep.

Towards the beginning of the tour, we gathered in the underground crypt of the popes, the burial ground of nine of the early successors of St Peter and one of the most sacred cemeteries in all of Rome. Father Richard described to us how Pope Sixtus II was celebrating the Eucharist in this very place in 258 AD with a number of deacons when the Roman soldiers arrived. The pope and his deacons were beheaded. "It was a terrible thing to happen," Father Richard commented. "Yet, for a faithful Christian, what better way to die than to give your life for the faith in the midst of this very celebration, Christ's sacrificial giving of himself for us? We believe that the priest at the Mass takes on the very person of Christ when he offers the sacrificial gifts, but, of course, in normal circumstances the priest doesn't actually die. Here, Sixtus had already become Christ for the Church when he lifted the chalice of Christ's blood, and then he actually shed his own blood for the Church minutes later."

It was a humbling experience to listen to this frail Salesian priest. A few days previously, I was behaving as if the modern-day responsibility for continuing the counter-reformation depended on me, but it was becoming clear that I didn't really need to say anything at all.

The next day, we had a day trip to Assisi, the beautiful town in Umbria of St Francis and St Clare. Our tour began from the higher part of town with the basilica of St Clare. About eleven years younger than Francis, Clare was inspired to follow his way of life after hearing him preach in Assisi. She would eventually outlive him by many years and, following his death, became the touchstone for interpreting how the Franciscan way of following Jesus should be pursued. Many people had their own view of what characterised the special charism of Francis, but few people could doubt that Clare herself was a living exemplar of the spirit of the "little poor man" of Assisi.

Before entering, I recounted two standard stories from the life of Clare. While Francis was out of Assisi on one of his many pilgrimages, the town was surrounded by the hostile forces of the Holy Roman Emperor – which, as historians never tire of saying, was neither vaguely holy nor remotely Roman. Clare took it upon herself to defend the city in the only way she knew. The sacred host in which Christ is present was placed in a monstrance - the metal vessel with a glass centre that is used to display the Eucharist during periods of adoration - and she took it up as someone else might take up a weapon or a banner of war. Then, as some accounts have it, she exited the city walls and marched down the side of the hill of Assisi.

When the battle-hardened troops of the emperor saw a girl coming down the slope from the city holding nothing but the Eucharist, they were struck at first with astonishment and then with terror. To a man, they fled. Who could hope to defeat a girl such as this, with faith like hers, holding aloft what she was holding?

The second story concerned the stigmata of St Francis. In 1224, two years before he died, Francis received on his body the five wounds of the passion of Christ, the first person in history of which we have documented evidence of the presence of these wounds, and the evidence comes from Clare herself. The reality of the wounds is incredibly important. Already, during his own lifetime, people were wondering what to make of Francis. Was he a madman, a fool, or a living image of Christ? Even before he died, the order he had founded was already casting a critical eye on his renunciation of worldly things and his radical dependence on divine providence. Many, even among his friends, wondered if Francis had gone a little off the rails.

When a person is marked with the very wounds of the passion of Jesus, however, then all such voices cease. It is hard to deny that the stigmata were God's seal on the life of Francis. In the centuries that followed, the debate shifted from *whether* or not the Franciscan way was valid to the question of *how* that way should be organised for a community of followers.

Because of the stigmata, no-one could deny that Francis was a true disciple of Jesus. And because of Clare, no-one could doubt that the stigmata were real. As documented in the earliest biography of Francis, written while St Clare was still alive, the funeral cortege of the little poor man passed in front of San Damiano, the place where Francis had received his original mission from Christ many years earlier, and now the home of St Clare and her sisters. Clare came out to the cortege and witnessed the wounds of the stigmata. If, in her life, she would become the exemplar of the Franciscan way, in her verification of the stigmata she became the witness of the divine rightness of that way.

The protestant husband and wife were standing right up at the front of the group while I recounted these stories. I had avoided using the word "sacrifice" when describing the manner in which Francis had joined himself to the self-offering of Christ. No point in rubbing people up the wrong way. Anyway, as I was beginning to realize, when you visit these places connected to the saints, maybe it is better just to let the facts speak for themselves.

A few days later, the week in Rome was coming to an end. The flight was in the evening and we had a busy last day planned. It was August 10th, the feast of San Lorenzo - St Lawrence of Rome - an important figure in the history of the early Church. The day would begin with 7.45 am Mass in the crypt of St Peter's, followed by a tour of the basilica. In the late afternoon, we would visit the church of St Lawrence and then continue to the airport.

The church of St Lawrence Outside the Walls (whose name distinguishes it from other churches dedicated to the saint within the ancient walls) is so significant that it was placed by St Philip Neri on his Seven Churches pilgrimage around Rome. This penitential exercise is still carried out to this day, beginning from the tomb of St Philip in Chiesa Nuova near the Tiber in the early hours of the morning and covering the twenty-kilometre route to the seven churches on foot. St Lawrence's church appears on the pilgrimage because of the steadfast devotion of the Romans to this saint through the ages. As one of seven deacons in the early Church of Rome, he had the responsibility of distributing the resources of the community to those in need. During the persecution of Emperor Valerian in 258 AD, Lawrence was arrested. The emperor was aware that the deacon was responsible for the management of the material wealth of the Church, so he demanded that Lawrence bring that wealth to him. The deacon went out and gathered some of the poor of Rome and then returned to Valerian. "This is the wealth of the Church of Rome!" he said. The emperor, in his fury, had Lawrence undergo terrible tortures before his eventual martyrdom. The symbol of the saint in Christian iconography is the grill upon which he endured these torments.

At the church of St Lawrence, we gathered in the area underneath the high altar where the relics of Lawrence are conserved, along with some relics of St Stephen, who was also a deacon and the very first martyr of the Church at Jerusalem. Despite the big feast day, the church was quiet and we were able to have a very peaceful tour.

Afterwards, as the group wandered around the church for some free time. I sat at the back and recalled what had happened that morning in St Peter's. It had been an early wake-up call at the hotel with breakfast set for 6.30am. The walk across St Peter's square in the cool temperatures of morning had been a pleasure for most members of the group, who had been adjusting with difficulty to the hot and sticky conditions of daytime Rome. We encountered virtually no queue at the metal detectors. As we stepped into the enormous interior of St Peter's, one could sense the awe of the pilgrims in this majestic space. I asked the group to wait for a few moments at the statue of St Andrew under Michelangelo's breath-taking dome while Father Pat and I went into the sacristy.

According to our booking, we were scheduled to have Mass in the Irish chapel of St Columban in the Vatican grottoes below the floor of the basilica. The sacristan consulted his list upon our arrival and informed us that the previous group for the chapel had arrived late and would not be finished for some time. The best solution, he said, was for Father Pat to vest, join the group at the statue of St Andrew, and then we would be called down to the crypt to take whatever chapel became available first. I was not too pleased by this change and made sure to keep a very evident frown on my face so that the staff would be aware of my displeasure. The group, after all, had specifically requested the Irish chapel. As it would turn out, however, the altar that came available was the most important of all, the one directly in front of the tomb of St Peter. As we were shown into the pews in front of the most sacred spot in Rome, my frown quickly vanished.

The altar is set back from the tomb so that the faithful who file by continually during the day can pass as close as possible to the bones of St Peter. As Mass in this little chapel progresses, the faithful in the pews have as a backdrop the wall in which the earthly remains of Peter are conserved.

The group had a sleepy look about them as they sat in their pews. Before Mass began, I went to the microphone and said a few short words about the place we were in, pointing out the portion of wall containing the bones of St Peter. A few minutes later, Father Pat had begun the celebration and was giving us a brief summary of the life and martyrdom of St Lawrence. The readings for Mass were taken from the feast. We all stood for the Gospel and Father Pat read to us the passage from St John:

Very truly, I tell you, unless a grain of wheat falls into the earth and dies, it remains just a single grain; but if it dies, it bears much fruit. Those who love their life lose it, and those who hate their life in this world will keep it for eternal life. Whoever serves me must follow me, and where I am, there will my servant be also (John 12, 24-26).

The Mass went on. During the Eucharistic prayer, as the priest raised the host and chalice, according to the sacramental theology of the Church, he – Father Pat - became Christ. On this feast of St Lawrence the martyr, while the chalice was held up, with the wall containing Peter's bones as a backdrop, it was easy to have a sense of how the Christ event, which is an event of sacrificial love, permeates history and is made manifest in the life of the Church and her saints. History is being gathered into that event.

A few hours later, as the pilgrimage was coming to a close, it occurred to me that I had been off the mark in my way of responding to the protestant couple. Instead of talking directly about the Mass as a sacrifice, a better approach would have been to discuss the notion of sacrifice by itself. Their problem with sacrifice, surely, was that they saw it as a negative thing, something associated with potentially hollow rituals. What I should have done was discuss something that they in their married life already knew: to love another person, we must move out of our self-absorption; love is fundamentally sacrificial; to be open to another person or to God, we must forsake our appetites and our selfish interests. And if that is the mark of human love, then it is also the mark of divine love. In fact, sacrificial love is the very mode of being of God.

There is much in the historical behaviour of our Church, in my own historical behaviour, that is not worthy of the faith we profess, but the Catholic understanding of the Eucharist is so fitting that it can only have a divine origin. In contrast to the protestant wife's assertion, Christ's sacrifice is not something over and done with in the past. He has entered history and changed its course. Before his coming, disobedience to God reigned. Upon his incarnation, self-sacrificial submission to God's will is seeded into humanity and will bear final fruit at the end of time. He is like a medicine that has been administered to creation. The medicine is coursing through the veins of humanity, but it is an unusual medicine, only fully efficacious when the patient co-operates with it. How does the patient co-operate with it? With the same act of self-sacrifice that characterizes the medicinal act of the passion itself.

The celebration of the Eucharist is the source and summit of God's act of restoring the world to health. Christ's sacrificial offering is made present so that the faithful of every age can unite themselves to him with a sacrificial offering of their own. This is not a mere ritual.

This is the DNA of love. The Eucharist is the festival of sacrificial love in which God pours himself out for the world and we are given the opportunity of pouring ourselves out for him and others. In a profound sense, the Eucharist is the generator by which the Lord is driving salvation until the task is complete at the end of time. The Mass is the powerhouse of the world.

When we got back on the coach for the final journey to the airport, Father Pat asked if he could say a word on the microphone.

"Earlier in the week we were talking about the Cure d'Ars and the priesthood. We were also talking about how other Christian groups view the Eucharist. Some denominations emphasize that Christ is the only high priest that we need, so they don't have ministerial priests at all. You know, the Catholic view actually agrees with that in one essential way! At the Mass, the priest assumes the identity of Christ, for it is Christ himself who is the supreme priest making the offering."

The coach was already moving and Father Pat was trying to balance himself as he stood up facing those seated. "During the week, many of you prayed aloud at the Masses, many of which were petitions for family members in need. Do you remember?"

There was a chorus of assent from the coach. Father Pat went on, "Along with those petitions, you were really offering your own sufferings and worries. You were placing them all before the Lord, isn't that correct?" Again, there were sounds of agreement. "You might wonder what's the use of placing all those offerings in *my* hands? How could I possibly offer them in the right way to God?"

The priest gave a chuckle. "It's very clear than an offering made by *me* is going to fall impossibly short! But that is exactly the point! It is not about me. Christ is the one whose offering alone is perfect. He is the all-holy, all-pure, all-obedient priest who makes a worthy return to God. When I offered the host and the chalice on the altar, it was really Christ himself, and not me, who was taking your offerings and joining them with his own."

As we pulled in to the airport, the tension of the previous days had been forgotten. All that fretting about the need to defend the proper understanding of the Eucharist had evaporated. Now, without me saying anything, enough – and more - had been said and done.

At the check-in desk, we were told that the incoming flight from Dublin was delayed by two hours. There was little option but to check the group in anyway. I shook everyone's hand as, one by one, they deposited their luggage and made their way towards the departure gates. The protestant couple were the most gracious of all as they spoke of how much the trip had meant to them.

We had a group arriving on the incoming flight, but the delay meant that there were two hours of free time. I went downstairs to arrivals and seated myself on a bench far from the crowd, not in the mood for talking to the other couriers who were also there killing time. My abiding memory of the arrivals' hall in those busy years when we did back-to-back flights is regret for the parting of the group who were still upstairs. I had been doing everything for them this past week, even ordering their coffee. Were they really going to board a plane all by themselves without me? How dare they!

Not really knowing what to do, I took out a notebook and jotted down the sequence of happenings of the previous days, in the unlikely event the details would ever be needed to fill a book. Very rarely over the years have I written anything down, not because my memory is reliable – quite the contrary - but because these events get etched on the heart, not in the mind. You know exactly what I mean, dear reader, for you too have things etched indelibly on your heart. Oh, and by the way, if we ever meet again, I'd like to tell you all about the umbrella pine. Until then, I pray that these muddled memoirs of mine might be for you, by the grace of God, an instrument of blessing.

K.T. Our Lady Help of Christians, 24.5.2024

I SEE HIS BLOOD UPON THE ROSE
More Tales from an Irish Tour Guide in Rome

We are all aware of how polarised our culture has become, and how difficult it is to discuss religion or politics in a rational way. This book avoids polemics and uses narrative as a way of exploring the faith. It is composed of true stories that are entertaining and enlightening. Some of the tales recount blessings, or manifestations of the divine.

The book could be described as apologetics through narrative. It aims to bring people closer to God with the oldest form of entertainment in the world: the telling of a story – or, rather, a series of them. Humour is a central ingredient of this book, taking its inspiration from John Masefield's insight that laughter has its origin in heavenly joy:

Laugh and be merry: remember, in olden time.
God made Heaven and Earth for joy He took in a rhyme,
Made them, and filled them full
with the strong red wine of His mirth
The splendid joy of the stars: the joy of the earth.

We pray that you enjoy the read!

Other works by K. Troy:

In the Stars the Glory of His Eyes: Tales of an Irish Tour Guide in Rome (Ignatius, 2022)

On the Revolutions of the Internal Spheres: A New Theory of Matter and the Transmission of Light (AuthorHouse UK, 2018)

LAURETUM

Printed in Dunstable, United Kingdom